WHAT MOTIVATES ME

Put Your Passions to Work

Adrian Gostick & Chester Elton

New York Times Bestselling Authors of
The Carrot Principle and *All In*

Names of those identified in this book by only a first name have been changed.

The Culture Works Press
PO Box 742, Kamas, UT 84036, USA

First hardcover edition September 2014.

Manufactured in the United States of America.

Library of Congress Library Control Number: 2014907257

ISBN: 978-0-9960297-0-4

E-Book ISBN: 978-0-9960297-1-1

Publisher's Cataloging-in-Publication Data

Gostick, Adrian Robert.
  What motivates me : put your passions to work / Adrian Gostick and Chester Elton.
  Includes bibliographical references.
  ISBN: 978-0-9960297-0-4 (pbk.)
  1. Employees—Attitudes. 2. Work—Psychological aspects. 3. Organizational behavior. 4. Employee motivation. 5. Psychology, Industrial.   I. Elton, Chester. II. Title.
HF5549.5.M63 G67 2014
650.1—dc23
                              2014907257

Early Praise for *What Motivates Me*

"Our goal at Bridgestone Americas is to be a Premier Place to Work. The tools and insight Gostick and Elton unveil in this excellent new book provide a step-by-step process that can help anyone bring their best self to work. As a leader, I believe we should continually be seeking better ways to motivate our teams. As we do, we can develop a culture of continually higher performance throughout our organization, enhance feelings of trust, reduce turnover, and attract more qualified candidates."

Gary Garfield
CEO and President, Bridgestone Americas, Inc.

"Gostick and Elton's book isn't just some theory. This book is a real-world way to find more fulfillment at work. You don't have to quit and open up a fruit stand, you can absolutely succeed within your current organization with their ideas. If you feel stalled in your career, read this book!"

Kent Taylor
CEO and Chairman, Texas Roadhouse

"Gostick and Elton's infectious enthusiasm jumps right off the page, as if it's grabbing you by your shoulders and shaking you into action. *What Motivates Me* is a great guide for life, let alone a career path."

Michael Wallace
Anchor, WCBS 880 New York

"Once in a great while a business book comes along that everyone is talking about. Trust me, this is that book. Gostick and Elton open a window into what motivates us, and how making small changes to our work can drive big gains in our fulfillment and engagement. It will not only teach you about yourself and your drivers, but you'll learn a lot about your teammates too. A fascinating and practical book that you'll find yourself referring to for years to come."

Mark Servodidio

Managing Director, United Kingdom, Avis Budget Group

"*What Motivates Me* offers one of the best resources I've seen to teach anyone how to unlock their potential and create a roadmap to guide their career journey. This book transcends the workplace, providing a wonderful reference for those who want to fulfill their desire for continuous growth and personal development in any aspect of their lives."

David Kasiarz

Senior Vice President, Global Compensation and Benefits, American Express

"*What Motivates Me* is another example of Gostick and Elton as masters of motivation. Their message of finding your leader from within by harnessing your passion will inspire any reader to build a better life and career."

Lori Ann LaRocco

Bestselling Author, Opportunity Knocking

CONTENTS

"In every block of marble I see a statue as plain as though it stood before me ... I have only to hew away the rough walls that imprison [it]."

—*Michelangelo*

Chapter 1

Discovering Your Personal Motivators

The Sculptor Who Could See Through Rock

E veryone was a critic in Florence in 1504.

After young Michelangelo unveiled his latest statue— of Biblical hero David—local artists complained that there were flaws: the right hand was a touch too big, the neck a little long, the left shin oversized, and something about the left buttock was not quite right.

Piero Soderini, head of the powerful Florentine Republic, informed Michelangelo that David's nose was too large. The irascible artist nodded and climbed back up his ladder with marble dust hidden in his hand. He then appeared to chisel on the offending proboscis, but in reality was simply letting the dust fall to the ground. Soderini examined the unchanged nose and announced it was much improved and far more life-like.

Despite the objections of the naysayers, twenty-nine-year-old Michelangelo knew he had created a masterpiece. Indeed, five hundred years later the statue remains one of the most recognizable pieces of art in the world. And yet the artist didn't credit his great achievement to his understanding of anatomy, rare for a renaissance artist, or even his skill with a chisel. No, Michelangelo believed his unique genius was in seeing possibility where others only saw a secondhand, mishandled piece of rock.

He said, "In every block of marble I see a statue as plain as though it stood before me ... I have only to hew away the rough walls that imprison [it]."

There is a lesson in this story for many in the working world. If we want to be happily engaged in our work and performing at our fullest potential, we've got to look inside ourselves, to understand what truly motivates us. We can't rely on what others think we should be doing, or be enslaved by preordained notions of chasing money or prestige or power. All of us host a unique blend of motivators, core drivers that should guide us in sculpting the work life that's right for us.

Far too many people are casting about in confusion for what would make them more successful and happier at work. Far too many able, intelligent people know they're not as productive or motivated as they could be from day to day, while some are actually demotivated—with aspects of their work that are in direct opposition to what drives them. That's not good for

2

individuals, and it's certainly not good for their managers or organizations either.

Turn the mirror upon yourself: most days at work, are you doing what truly motivates you? Or back up: Before now, have you taken the time to reflect on what fuels your fire on the job, what matters most to you? What are you doing, exactly, on those days when you are excited and energized in your work, when you have that proverbial skip in your step? Only when we identify those unique drivers can we begin to chip away what constrains us and unleash our full potential, our best ideas, and our productive power. Only then can we silence the critics around us and realize happiness is not about any pre-conceived notion of what should be meaningful, impressive, or logical to you. It's about aligning the work you do every day with what *motivates* you.

The Need for Meaning

It would be hard to overstate how important meaningful work is to human beings—work that provides a sense of fulfillment and empowerment. Those who have found deeper meaning in their careers find their days much more energizing and satisfying, and count their employment as one of their greatest sources of joy and pride. Sonya Lyubomirsky, professor of psychology at the University of California, has conducted numerous workplace studies showing that when people are more fulfilled on the job, they not only produce higher quality work and a greater output, but also generally earn higher incomes. Those most satisfied with their work are also much more likely to be happier with their lives overall. For her book *Happiness at Work*, researcher Jessica Pryce-Jones conducted a study of 3,000 workers in seventy-nine countries, finding that those who took greater satisfaction from their work were 150 percent more likely to have a happier life overall.

On the flipside, research by the Gallup organization found, not surprisingly, that people whose work is out of alignment were much more likely to be depressed, anxious, and have damaged relationships in their personal lives. And what about those out of work completely? Tom Rath of Gallup reported, "We found that there was nothing more detrimental to your well-being than being unemployed for more than a year. Our well-being actually recovers more rapidly from the death of a spouse than it does from a sustained period of unemployment."

If you find yourself unhappy or unfulfilled with aspects of your work, understand that you are by no means alone. Job satisfaction and employee engagement in the United States have been on a steep and steady decline for an entire generation. According to a survey conducted by business research association The Conference Board in the summer of 2012, more than half of all US workers were estimated to be unhappy in their jobs—an all-time low. On a global scale, research by Gallup in late 2013 showed 87 percent of the world's workers are either not engaged in their jobs or have become actively disengaged. This is a global crisis.

Of the thousands of people we've interviewed over the past two decades researching workplace trends, many feel about their work the way this man colorfully describes his job: "I haul my sorry carcass out of bed every morning and trudge off to my job, do work I won't get credit for, get yelled at by the boss for things that aren't my fault, try my hardest to keep everything afloat, then return home to repeat the process the next day."

But we've also found stories that gave us hope. There are individuals and teams among us who are deeply fulfilled by their work, who are passionate about what they do, and are energized when Monday comes. So what's their secret? In most cases, they have taken control of their careers.

For twenty years, we've worked with some of the world's most successful organizations in increasing employee engagement and team performance. Over the last decade alone we have conducted three research studies on workplace trends for our books, comprising more than 850,000 interviews. And what all that work has revealed is a key difference in those who are most energized on the job. What is it? Those people have aligned more of their work with their core motivations. As for those who are most unhappy, as you might expect, their jobs are out of whack with what they are passionate about.

That probably seems logical, doesn't it? Then here's the million-dollar question: why don't we all do something about it? The problem is, most people feel either helpless or overwhelmed. Many wait for an outside force like a manager to fix things. But even well-intended managers who want to motivate their teams have to sift through vastly different notions about what motivates workers: one author has a list of three things that really drive employees, another says no—it's this list of five other things, and so on. Unfortunately the fixes out there on motivation are much too simplistic and categorical to help many people. In our research, we have found that each individual is driven by a unique set, or blend, of internal and external drivers. Every person on this planet has a thumbprint-like makeup of what makes him or her most happy 9-to-5 (and in the rest of life); and those prints vary considerably.

The good news: when people's jobs give them the opportunity to do more of the kinds of things that satisfy their key motivations, they are happier and more engaged in their work. The sad news: most people don't have a clear understanding of what their strongest motivators are; and even those enlightened souls who do understand how they are motivated often don't know how to put those passions to use in their daily work.

There is a solution, and in most cases it doesn't require a major career or job transition. Though there is a prevalent notion that if you're unhappy with your work it will take a Herculean effort to change things, that you have to quit and find your "dream job," for the vast majority of people, that's just nonsense. Most don't need to take a risky leap; they just need to make small changes in their work lives. Many of the happiest people we've spoken with didn't find their bliss down a new path; they made course corrections on the path they were already on.

What follows in this book is a simple but empirically tested method to identify people's individual blend of core motivators, figure out what disconnects may exist between their passions and their current work situation, and then work with their managers to fix it. (FYI, this method of identifying core motivators is also helpful for students who are wrestling with what they want to do with their lives, even deciding what major to choose in college.)

The chapters that follow are primarily intended to offer guidance about the kinds of changes in responsibilities that might increase engagement in one's current role. In our consulting work, we have found that this diagnostic process can be remarkably empowering for teams of employees and their managers. On one level it helps people take charge of their careers and put their fingers on the specific things that are causing them dissatisfaction in their work, and it also gives them positive language to discuss with their bosses and fellow team members some relatively small changes in job responsibilities or work situations that could create huge boons in productivity and commitment—just the things their managers are looking for.

We call this type of modification "job sculpting." For employees, the benefit of this process is obvious. But for leaders, the payback can be powerful as well, as sculpting can help diagnose how each team member's specific tasks are (or are not) aligned with his or her motivations, and uncover subtle changes that can lead to increases in team morale, engagement, and results.

The truth is, very few managers know what's really motivating to their people or, even if they do, they're unsure how to apply that information to day-to-day work. The best leaders, however, have discovered that the surest way to help their employees lead happier and more successful work lives is: First, help them understand their motivations. And second, do some sculpting of the nature of their jobs or tasks to better match duties with passions.

But what if that kind of job sculpting isn't enough?

The process we will unfold in this book will also help some readers identify when a larger change is needed and the kind of change it might be. Perhaps it's time to transfer to another department, or it could be a full-blown transition to a new profession. After all, if an individual is completely miscast or miserable it's not good for them, their customers, or their managers. So in Chapter 6 we offer up some key considerations when pondering a change of this kind. These transitions are not for the faint of heart, so we always recommend the sculpting process first.

In our research, we found so many people who felt they were at a crossroads in their careers, confused about why they aren't as happy as they should be at work. Perhaps they had even been engaged at one point, but maybe their motivators had changed. Unlike our *personalities* that are largely formed when we are children, and *strengths* that often remain more constant through life, our motivations can change as we age. What motivates someone just graduating from high school or college could be quite different when she has a few kids at home, or when those kids have left and she is perhaps nearing a second act in her career. Our age and station in life and work are constantly changing, and with those experiences, so can our motivations. For instance, our research has shown a large number of people start out in life driven to make money and achieve a prestigious high-level position, but as goals are achieved or life situations change, so do their motivations. Some have children they want to spend more time with, others find themselves more determined to do work that contributes to a noble mission. In contrast, we also found individuals who started out devoted to a social cause or a helping profession in their early years, but who realized in the later stages of their careers they would be more driven by the challenges or remunerative rewards of a more traditional corporate role.

Seismic shifts like this can be tricky to recognize in ourselves. They take place over years through varying influences. We've found the simple diagnostic method we introduce in this book is a powerful way to achieve clarity about small course changes, and can help people commit to taking the necessary steps toward improving their situation wherever they find themselves.

In our study of thousands of teams and leaders, we can assure you that a profound quality of life can result from figuring out the right path to take in your work. Consider just one quick case in point.

Finding Your Own True Motivators

We'll tell a number of stories throughout the book of people we've studied who have found their own unique formula for success at work. One of our favorites is Jimmy Casas, an Iowa educator we met in 2013 after he'd just been named one of three finalists for the prestigious National High School Principal of the Year award, handed out every year by the National Association of Secondary School Principals.

It had been a long road to that award banquet.

As a college freshman, Casas was on the point of flunking out. The son of Mexican immigrants, he admits he had a chip on his shoulder about how society treated him as a Hispanic young man from a low-income family. "No one ever told me I was college material," he says. "People were surprised I even got in, so I didn't expect a lot of myself." He ended up dropping out after his first year of college and taking a job selling insurance.

Now sales, that was something he *was* good at. He was a natural. Quickly he outpaced insurance agents with decades of experience; and less than a year later, the company brass offered him a coveted spot as regional sales manager. The starting salary: $30,000 a year, plus sales commissions on top of that. This was 1987, when the national median household income was less than $24,000. He could easily earn twice that amount. Casas would be set, or so it seemed.

He rushed to tell his boss and mentor Ed the good news; but when he found him, Ed was slumped over, in tears. "The job I'd been offered was his! He was fifty and had no education. He asked, 'Who's going to hire me?'"

It was a wake-up call for Casas: "When I was Ed's age, they'd most likely treat me the same way."

He turned the job down and returned to college, but more importantly he looked at his life in front of him and asked why he'd been put on this earth. It wasn't to sell, he knew that much. He was good at it. He liked interacting with people. But it didn't really speak to his core. Casas was determined to find what he was passionate about. After just a few weeks, as happenstance would have it, he noticed a flyer posted to a telephone pole on campus. A local elementary school was desperate for a tutor to help three young immigrants learn English as a second language. At the time it seemed a way to hone his rusty Spanish. "I started volunteering one day a week. Then they asked me to come in two days a week; then it was three. Soon I was working at the school full time for no pay, but I absolutely loved it."

Casas had found his reason for being; he would work with minority kids from poor families, kids that reminded him of himself at that age. "I was that kid with a chip on his shoulder, thinking, 'You don't like Mexicans. You think I'm worthless.' I made excuses." While his job in sales was people-oriented, it hadn't aligned with a strong drive to help others improve their lives. And while the insurance job had been lucrative, and he didn't mind cashing the paychecks, he realized he wasn't really driven by money. The money was nice, but it wasn't why he got up every day.

Nearing graduation, Casas had more than his share of job offers. After all, he says, he was Hispanic in a teaching profession that employed mostly Caucasians. He was male in a career that attracts more women. And he loved to teach kids, and that passion shone through. Some of the finest school districts in the Midwest offered him spots, but he was headed to the inner city.

"I got my ass kicked at first," he admitted. "I didn't know how to deal with the apathy, the violence. I started questioning my motivations."

Slowly, very slowly, he began to realize he *could* make a difference. He couldn't change the entire school as he'd first imagined, but he could serve one student at a time. He spent his days, evenings, and weekends building relationships with kids one-on-one, many of whom didn't have a father or mother, many who felt hopeless.

"Every person has a story, and I started to listen to the stories that were out there. I learned I could help kids develop in areas they were passionate about. We live in a society that preaches to kids all the areas they need to improve in: you need to be better at this or that. But those aren't their passions. We are trying to convince them of things they don't care about. I got them thinking on their own, figuring out who they are."

Now, after twenty years as an educator and administrator, Jimmy Casas has inspired thousands of young people to do more than they ever thought possible—letting them know they have worth and are important. "My greatest motivation?" he says in answer to our query. "That's simple. It's making a difference."

The same personal qualities that made him such a natural salesman have contributed significantly to Casas being such an amazing educator, but they've been applied to something that is truly motivating to him.

We've found that for some, like Casas, the journey of discovery unfolds through a similar organic process of introspection, mixed with periods of painful trial and error and realization, finally capped by joyful moments of enlightenment. Those are the happy stories. Yet in so many instances, people know they aren't completely content at work, but they just can't seem to get clarity about what's really dissatisfying or what would get them more engaged.

The Myths of Motivation

Frankly, one reason it's so hard for many of us to self-diagnose is that human psychology is so complex. There's no WebMD to plug in our myriad worries and frustrations. A host of deep psychological factors—a fear of failure, depression, anxiety, aging, or even learning disorders—can influence individual motivation. The bottom line: motivation is complex, and yet the prevailing wisdom about the subject has been marked by an unfortunate set of misunderstandings and oversimplifications.

For many years the prevailing wisdom was that workers were most motivated by extrinsic rewards, primarily things like pay, bonuses, promotions, active supervision, and recognition. In recent years, this perspective has been challenged. As Daniel Pink wrote about in his book *Drive,* a good deal of study, in particular by psychologists such as Frederick Herzberg and Edward Deci, has shown that extrinsic motivation can actually have a negative influence on today's knowledge workers, and most productive people are almost exclusively *intrinsically* motivated. Workers flourish, Pink suggests, when they seek out jobs in which they have autonomy (they are given as much freedom as possible to carry out their tasks); mastery (they are encouraged to build their competence, leading to feelings of personal accomplishment); and purpose (they have clarity about how they are contributing to something bigger than themselves).

We agree that this view of overall human motivation may be accurate from a 30,000-foot-view, but we also know that the truth of *individual* motivation is actually much more complicated. And understanding how varied we all are is crucial to figuring out why one particular person might be unhappy or not as engaged as he could be at work, especially when compared with others on the same team who are all-in.

In our two decades of diving deep into the subjects of employee engagement, team performance, and corporate culture with clients from American Express to Procter & Gamble to AT&T, we've found that even people who have those three above-cited intrinsic motivators in abundance can still be unhappy in their jobs. For instance, we have been asked to work with a bevy of health care firms that have high turnover and strong disenchantment in staff and clinical areas. And, believe it or not, often *doctors* are those with the greatest discontent. Now, in what job could a person gain more autonomy, mastery, and purpose than diagnosing and curing patients? Physicians are asked to solve complicated problems every day; get to prolong human life (certainly an honorable purpose); and have more authority, respect, and autonomy than a sultan. So why are so many of them miserable? Their number one complaint by a country mile: their compensation.

It seems intrinsic motivation is not the whole story, and extrinsic motivation isn't entirely bad. If monetary rewards and other extrinsic factors were completely ineffectual, or worse, counterproductive, that certainly would let companies and bosses off the hook. But completely disregarding extrinsic motivation would be misguided. For one thing, many of the foundational, cited studies that argue for the negative effects of extrinsic rewards were performed on small test groups of college students in psychological laboratories, children in grade schools, or even animals in cages. These findings rightly challenge the sole emphasis on extrinsic factors—we should always question and push boundaries on so-called "accepted wisdom"; but the argument for putting all our emphasis on intrinsic motivation is *also* skewed.

One key failing is that many of the recent studies mistakenly suppose the primary extrinsic motivator that managers use is monetary rewards, largely ignoring the positive effects of praise, promotion, leadership attention, the admiration of peers, and so on. We personally have been told by hundreds of employees around the world some variation of what a young professional woman told us in 2014: "Two years ago my CEO sent me an awesome thank you note. When things get tough I pull that note out and read it. It still reenergizes me." A wealth of studies performed in real workplaces, rather than in the lab, have shown that recognition like this can be highly effective in creating a more engaged and productive workplace. Our own ten-year study of 200,000 people, for our book *The Carrot Principle*, showed levels of return on equity were three times higher in organizations that effectively recognized the excellent work of their employees.

The concept of intrinsic motivators has not caught on widely in the business world in building better teams— whether in factories, restaurants, hospitals, or high-tech computer mazes—for a few reasons. First, extrinsic rewards are quantifiable in a way that intrinsic motivators are not; they can fit into a spreadsheet, be measured, and be regularly evaluated to see if they are working. It's also easier to understand how to implement extrinsic ideas such as recognition, raises, promotions, and the like, certainly much easier than helping employees through so-called "soft" issues. These, of course, are not valid reasons to use extrinsic rewards in place of thoughtful management. The right reason to use them is that, when used in a smart way, extrinsic factors *can* work.

Intrinsic and extrinsic motivators are not diametrically opposed. They are not good and evil. To feel the most highly motivated, most of us in the working world must have some of both.

To move forward, we have to discard the vague notions of motivation and get to a more granular, individualized level in assessing what motivates each of us. After all, we really are all different.

Steven Reiss is a Yale-educated PhD who completed his clinical psychological internship at Harvard Medical School. He conducted extensive studies of what motivates people and argues that we are individuals to a much greater extent than many experts admit. He said, "Individuals differ enormously in what makes them happy—for some, competition, winning, and wealth are the greatest sources of happiness, but for others feeling competent and socializing may be more satisfying. You can't say some motivators, like money, are inherently inferior."

Take This Job and Love It

Whether you are looking to reignite your passion in your current job, just starting out in the work world, or still in school trying to decide which major or career best fits your passions and values, you'll find that success is not about chasing the latest hot job trend in the news—"Oh, if only I were a computer programmer or physical therapist, all my troubles would be over." It's not about doing what anyone else thinks is right for you, nor is it necessarily about seeking a job that pays well if money is not what floats your boat. It's about aligning more of your work with what motivates you.

Please note that the process we present in this book is an entirely new method for discovering how to optimize personal motivation, not a test to determine color type or to help you know if you are an INFP according to the Myers-Briggs Type Indicator. Those are certainly interesting and useful classifications that can help anyone learn more about their personality and those they work with, but in many cases they do not put people on a path toward major life and work decisions.

Our goals in the pages that follow are to help anyone who reads this book answer two age-old questions: "What is it that motivates me?" And then, with that information in hand, "What can I do about it?"

Whether you work in a large corporation or small business; if you're an entrepreneur, teacher, student, athlete, or artist; a manager trying to figure out how to get your team working together more smoothly; or a CEO looking to make corrective changes within your organization's culture, taking the time to go through the process we present will be not only eye-opening but can truly be empowering—helping you understand and work with your own primary motivators to craft a realistic plan for optimizing your education, work, and personal goals that will satisfy and engage you. If you are a leader, it will help you take your team through this process, too. In most cases, the end result will have you modifying your current role, focusing a little more on responsibilities and tasks that involve your passions. In a few cases it may reinforce what you already know: that you are miscast and need to choose a new path forward in life. Either way, this book will help you make the important life choices you face.

We recently presented these ideas to a group of brilliant, yet cynical scientists at an environmental engineering firm in the Midwest. Halfway through a hard-fought day of winning these scientists over to the idea of helping find and develop their individual motivators, a gentleman raised his hand.

"You know," he said, "this is a bigger deal than we think it is."

It was something we'll never forget, making us all laugh and everyone think. Indeed, this really is bigger than most of us might imagine. The motivations that drive us are the hinges upon which our lives swing, and it is only when we understand what makes each of us passionate about our work that we can begin to bring about a boom in our personal productivity, our collective success, and most importantly, in our happiness and fulfillment.

Our hope for all of us is that one day, many years from now, we will look back on our time on this little blue planet and be able to say we lived true to what motivated us.

Chapter 2

The Motivators Assessment

First the Motivators, Then the Identities

Just because people are successful doesn't mean they are fulfilled. We learned that firsthand.

To back up, this book began with our consulting work with organizations all around the world. With the clarity of outsiders, again and again we could see that so many people's work assignments just weren't engaging them in the right ways, but it was hard for these individuals or their managers to see that or, if they did recognize it, to have a way to address it. As workplace researchers, we were aware of the literature on motivation, we lectured and consulted on motivation, but all the theories didn't really hit home until we had our own personal "aha" moment. It triggered our interest in driving down to a finer, more individualized understanding of the subject.

For many years we wrote our books and did our consulting for a fine large corporation. We were paid well, the work was interesting, we had ample autonomy, traveled the world, and our team had a strong belief in the "why" of what we did. We felt that our noble cause was to teach managers how to better engage their employees. If the two of us had been tested on our levels of the traditional gamut of intrinsic motivation—interesting work, challenge, responsibility, autonomy, mastery, purpose, and the like—we would have scored through the roof.

And yet we had lost our motivation.

One day we sat together and looked up at a blank sheet of paper on the wall. We had a notion: in order to understand why we had not been content in that comfortable but unfulfilling environment—and to be more successful going forward—we had to identify what really drove us. So there we sat, wondering exactly what our drivers were, and what precisely had been the root cause of our discontent. We wrote at the top of that pad of large easel paper the phrase that would shape our lives from that point onward: "What motivates me?"

With a Sharpie in hand, we began to list everything that we cared about personally and professionally, which ranged from creativity to integrity, owning our work to having a voice, achieving big things to giving back to others, from doing work that makes a difference to being respected, and having our contributions cheered for. In all, we compiled a list of more than fifteen motivators at that sitting—some intrinsic and others extrinsic.

We then decided to prioritize them, each for himself, working on his own. Then we revealed to each other what we'd chosen.

It was surprising and reassuring as business partners to see how much we had in common—and revealing to see where we differed.

Top on the list for both of us was that we wanted a much greater ability to "make a difference" with our clients. Rather than bouncing from city to city, client to client, we wanted to go deep and really make an impact on the organizations and the leaders, managers, and employees who worked for them, to make lasting changes. In addition, "ownership" appeared on both our lists. We had a strong desire to control our own destiny. We also both prioritized family. We wanted to give equal time and attention to our loved ones and our work. But we also differed in a few key ways: one of us had a more powerful need to be "recognized and rooted for," while the other felt more of a need to be "creative."

This exercise helped us realize that these key drivers simply hadn't been satisfied, no matter how interesting our work was or how much mastery or autonomy or purpose we gained. So as we built our business going forward, we structured our work to meet our true motivating needs. And as we added people to the team, we began to go through a more refined process of identifying each person's motivators, which helped us understand our new partners' drivers, goals, and values, and align their work accordingly. We also made this talent-screening process part of the standard onboarding procedure we encouraged for our consulting clients.

The success we saw from helping people align their jobs more closely with their motivators—in terms of both their happiness and productivity—encouraged us to dig deeper. We took about every personality- and strengths-based test imaginable. Since we live on opposite sides of the country from each other, our results were emailed back and forth and dissected.

By the time we were done with this assessment taking, we had categorized tests into two large categories. Into the first bucket we placed some popular assessments—MBTI, DISC, and StrengthsFinder for instance—which we found quite useful in giving us insights into who we were or what we were good at. Still, as effective as these assessments were, what they did not answer was our fundamental question: "What drives me?" There was a puzzle piece missing.

Into the second category of assessments we placed those that unfortunately produced disappointing findings for us, as we heard they consistently did for others. Numerous people told us these other assessments were too generic: "Like a horoscope," or "Too vague to be helpful," while some tests were so specific and at the same time off-target to illicit, "That doesn't seem like me at all."

One man got us laughing when he remarked on one test's results: "My greatest weakness was supposed to be empathy. I told my wife that and she said, 'That's not true; you are very empathetic.' So I told her what was supposed to be my greatest strength. It was listening. She just about lost it. She yelled, 'You're a terrible listener!' So now, years later, whenever we have a fight and my wife accuses me of not listening, I remind her of the test and say, 'No Honey, that's actually my greatest strength.' It's pretty funny ... at least I think it is."

After this process, we knew we needed to create a robust diagnostic tool that would help both individuals and teams not only accurately identify their strongest motivators but also think through and provide a way to have meaningful discussions to align their work better with those specific passions.

First, the Motivators

To pursue this concept in a scientific manner, we started by embarking on a statistical data mining operation, sifting through the findings of three huge studies conducted for our previous books, encompassing surveys of more than 850,000 people over the past decade. We were looking for answers to three questions:

1. What helps people feel engaged, enabled, and energized in their daily work?
2. What factors increase or decrease levels of job satisfaction and motivation?
3. What is it that makes people want to quit a job?

From that data mining, we identified quite a large group of potential workplace motivators. We then took those findings to San Diego to meet with Dr. Travis Bradberry and Dr. Jean Greaves, authors of *Emotional Intelligence 2.0* and cofounders of the intelligence assessment company TalentSmart. These eminent psychologists and their remarkable team of behavioral scientists took the list of motivators we had culled from our research and tested a group of 761 working adults from around the world to determine which of these motivators were the most common and significant. Their work also revealed a couple of motivators that our data crunching had overlooked.

This vetting process produced numerous intriguing insights into the psyches of working individuals; most fascinating was the final set of twenty-three workplace motivators that survived the testing. They are:

Autonomy	**Friendship**	**Problem Solving**
Challenge	**Fun**	**Purpose**
Creativity	**Impact**	**Recognition**
Developing Others	**Learning**	**Service**
Empathy	**Money**	**Social Responsibility**
Excelling	**Ownership**	**Teamwork**
Excitement	**Pressure**	**Variety**
Family	**Prestige**	

Yes, each person on this planet is as unique as a snowflake, but the data showed that we all do share this group of fundamental drivers. The nuances in a person's specific nature shows up not only in which of these specific motivators are most important to him or her, but also in the particular order of priority that individual regards them—from one to twenty-three.

Think of this prioritization as akin to the way DNA shapes each person. Every one of the billions of DNA strands on this planet contains the same basic building blocks, but what sets each person apart as a distinct human being is the sequencing of his or her genes. Those who grew up in the same household, those with the same educational degree, or those in the same profession will have different priorities in life.

As we've shared this core insight in our consulting work, it has resonated. Last year we visited a large medical center suffering from shockingly high turnover in its nursing ranks. Valuable CNAs, LPNs, and RNs were walking out the door almost as fast as the organization could hire them. As we spoke with the senior-most leader about this subject, he reached an epiphany: "The more I'm thinking about this issue the more I believe we've missed the mark with our nurses. What motivates a labor-and-delivery nurse is vastly different from what motivates an emergency room nurse or an oncology nurse. But we've been treating them all the same—they have all been 'nurses' to us. We need to start understanding what really motivates someone joining a particular team, or even someone who's been here for a long time. We need to put people in the right roles, for sure, but we also need to give each nurse specific assignments they'll find motivating."

Well said.

Next, the Five Identities

As we worked with this data we noted that certain of the twenty-three motivators seemed naturally to be linked closely to others—for instance, it seemed *creativity* and *learning* would be first cousins; likewise that *challenge* would be aligned somewhat with *pressure*. You can probably guess about similar clusters that would emerge from the list. We thought that if we could identify groupings of the motivators, those concepts that truly do align with one another, we might point to a set of general types of individuals, those people who have deeper connections with certain sets of motivators. We knew people might be able to see themselves in these archetypes, and they might also see others they work with. We were excited to be able to offer portraits of these archetypal motivational types for individuals to share with their coworkers, managers, and mentors; compare and contrast themselves to; and not to mention—learn from.

The notion of personality types is well established in psychology, the distinction between introverts and extroverts is just one example. We're accustomed to thinking of ourselves, and others, in these ways—whether we call someone a "type A" personality, an "alpha male," a "right-brained" thinker, or so on.

We did our best at sorting the motivators into clusters that made sense to us, but we realized our work was just a guess. So we tasked our team of scientists to go back to the data and assess whether our groupings were statistically valid. They conducted what's called a "factor analysis," a tried-and-true method in psychometrics to reduce a large number of variables to a more fundamental list of "types" that have commonalities.

It was fascinating to see five clusters of commonly related motivators emerge from that analysis, indicating that people who score high in certain motivators will inevitably score higher with related motivators in the archetype. The data supported our hypothesis that there would be groupings, but produced some corrections in our guesses. For instance, one grouping emerged that included motivators all related to being rewarded. We hadn't seen that coming. In other words, if a person's recognition motivation was very high, the statistical probability was high that the other reward drivers, money and prestige, would also be nearer the top of his or her list of motivators.

Another grouping we had not expected was a clumping that showed a statistically strong correlation between motivators relating to being empathetic to others, spending quality time with family, and having fun. Makes a lot of sense now, but we just hadn't guessed that those particular three motivators would be so closely aligned.

On the flipside, we had imagined we'd see a grouping that

would portray a type of detail-oriented person who is motivated by accuracy, truth, procedures, and the like. After all, don't we all know highly analytical people? We found those characteristics may form a personality type, but they are not motivators. Excelling, solving problems, being challenged—those can be strong motivators to the left-brained among us—but people weren't getting out of bed in the morning to be accurate. The motivators relating to those ideas had to be discarded as invalid; the data just did not back them up.

So, after all the analysis, we termed the five clusters of motivators the **Identities**. They are:

The Achievers: Those who thrive on tight deadlines, tackle ambitious goals, and love a good challenge and solving a problem. Often type A personalities, Achievers usually like to be in charge of others, or at least in control of their own destiny.

The Builders: Those purpose-driven individuals who are hardwired to develop others and serve those around them. They cultivate loyal friendships and thrive in strong team environments. The Builders typically believe it's important to speak out on significant issues.

The Caregivers: Those caring souls who are often more tuned in to others' emotions. They are more motivated when they have regular fun at work, and believe balancing time at work and time with their families is important.

The Reward-Driven: Those who are typically more *extrinsically* motivated, driven to win prizes—whether money or applause or the admiration of others. Many of the Reward-Driven believe that the cocktail-party question, "What do you do?" is extremely important.

The Thinkers: Those who are often more creative, who love to learn, enjoy a varied routine, and like to feel an adrenaline rush now and then. Most Thinkers get frustrated with red tape and bureaucracy, and want their work to make an impact on the world around them.

Here's a table that summarizes where the motivators appear in each identity:

Achievers	Builders	Caregivers	Reward-Driven	Thinkers
Challenge	Developing Others	Empathy	Money	Autonomy
Excelling	Friendship	Family	Prestige	Creativity
Ownership	Purpose	Fun	Recognition	Excitement
Pressure	Service			Impact
Problem Solving	Social Responsibility			Learning
	Teamwork			Variety

Note: While the factor analysis identified some identities with six motivators and some with three, through empirical weighting we are able to statistically balance the results on an individual's Motivator Profile.

It's important to stress that, as with any psychological type, almost no one is a perfect Achiever or Builder or so on—just as no one is a one-hundred-percent introvert. Rather, envision each identity as having a spectrum from low to high. We all have each of these five identities in us to some degree, and we all fall in various places along the spectrum of each, making us a unique blending of types. Maybe one person is a strong Achiever, but perhaps her Builder score is almost as high. She might also be moderately driven by Caregiver motivators but only slightly driven by her Reward-Driven and Thinker motivators. A fellow she works right next to might be most inspired by Reward-Driven motivators, with Achiever then Thinker identities not very far behind. His Builder and Caregiver motivators, however, score quite low. His best friend might have findings that fall in the opposite direction—Caregiver #1, then Builder, Thinker, Achiever, Reward-Driven.

So how is this information useful in diagnosing what changes we should make in our work? Let's use an example of a professional woman who takes the assessment and discovers her number one identity is Thinker. Indeed, she also looks through her prioritized list of motivators and finds many Thinker motivators, such as creativity, autonomy, variety, impact, and learning, are near the top of her list of twenty-three. That certainly feels right to her. It also seems appropriate that near the bottom of her list are motivators such as pressure, teamwork, and money. Those do not get her jazzed, she agrees.

It would make sense, then, that she would be happiest in work that allows her to exercise that creativity with a great deal of autonomy, work that provides variety and allows her to seek unique paths to completion rather than some predetermined mandate. It might seem natural, then, to find she works as a creative director at an advertising agency. Case closed, right? After all, wouldn't that job allow her to exercise her creativity every day, in a place that gives her a fair amount of autonomy and variety crafting pitches and developing campaigns? You'd think so, but the woman we are referring to is real. And she spoke to us because she was becoming increasingly discontent with her work.

It seemed the job was high pressure, which was demotivating to her, and she did her work almost exclusively for one big technology client, which gave her little variety or the learning opportunities she craved. She was loyal to the agency, and wanted to stay and thrive there, but the pressure to produce on her client's demanding schedule was frustrating, and she was, in her words, feeling "straight-jacketed." She looked at her list of motivators and realized it was time to sculpt her job. After a few open, back-and-forth discussions with the company's senior executive, they identified a need that was unfulfilled in the firm. She was able to form a major deal group, which pitches to win new clients. Today it's her job to do just enough to win a deal, and then she turns that new client over to one of the fulltime creative teams. In a given year she'll now work on dozens of pitches, meeting with potential clients to learn about their product strengths, their competitors, their consumers, and then delivering a creative pitch that shows how the agency's strategy aligns with the customer's specific goals. She jokes that she's become a hired gun. And you know what? She loves it.

Here's another example: Take the case of a man we met who had been a lawyer at a prestigious corporate firm in New York. Since childhood he had thought of himself in terms of a classic Achiever. It is one big reason he was so drawn to the legal profession. He wanted to win cases, sway juries, solve complicated legal problems. And indeed, he had been very successful at the law, and was on track to become a partner at the firm. It was a senior role where he'd begin earning a yearly salary well over $1 million. That's like winning the lottery, right? The problem was, he was miserable and close to a breakdown. He hated the constant demand to win new clients and the money-focused definition of success in the firm. He had very little of the Reward-Driven in him.

At the end of his rope, he had left the firm and taken a job as an assistant district attorney for a fraction of his previous salary. The result? Today he considers himself much more successful. Why? Because he's helping fight crime and keeping the streets safe? Sure. But more importantly we'd argue he's happy—on a deep and sustainable level—because he's satisfying the motivators within two of his strongest identities: Achiever and Builder. His prosecution work is extremely challenging and high-pressure; it involves a great deal of problem solving and ownership of complex cases, but it also satisfies the need to *build* in him. He's doing something he considers socially responsible, he's called on to be a team player every day, and he's able to teach those junior to him the ins and outs of building solid cases.

The work he was doing at the big firm fulfilled his Achiever motivations, but clashed strongly with his Builder ones. He was miscast. The work in that large law firm was better suited for a person with a strong combination of Achiever and Reward-Driven motivators.

In order to help everyone make diagnoses and sculpt changes in their work, we have taken our process to the next level in developing a simple online assessment that allows people to start by identifying their top motivators and identities.

The Motivators Assessment

It took our team of behavioral scientists more than a year to build, test, and validate The Motivators Assessment. Our first priority during development was that it pass the "face validity" test, which is the scientific way of saying that each person's results must *feel* right to him or her. Next, we moved to the "construct validity" test, in other words calculating scientifically if the assessment measures what it is intended to, in a reliable manner. We were pleased to find that it is as reliable as, or more so than, very popular personality and strengths assessments that have been taken by millions of people. In other words, we can say with a great degree of confidence that this assessment is an accurate measure of a person's motivations at work.

We then moved to the beta testing phases, introducing the assessment into organizations around the globe. By the time *What Motivates Me* hit bookshelves, it had been field tested with people in major corporations, midsize firms, small mom-and-pops, nonprofits, and schools. Workers, leaders, and CEOs have now taken it in industries that have run the gamut from high-tech to manufacturing to banking to health care to charities.

While the assessment is in fact a highly accurate way of measuring a person's core drivers, it has actually been most gratifying to pour through the written feedback and read comments to the effect of: "Yep, this *feels* like me."

That meant we were *halfway* home.

We then had to develop a set of exercises to help individuals and teams take the information about their motivators and identities and diagnose where shortfalls exist in their current work, and then come up with ways to sculpt the job they're in.

Taking The Assessment

It's now time to take The Motivators Assessment, which will take about twenty minutes.

It's important to note that this is a process to determine your motivators at *work*, so please answer with your career in mind and not your personal life.

Also remember how important it is to be honest. A typical question on the assessment will ask you if you are more motivated by, say, taking care of others versus taking care of yourself. No one will ever see your individual answers, so don't respond based on how you wished you felt, or how you *want* others to perceive you, but how you really feel in this moment about your desires in your career. If you do indeed think more about taking care of yourself than others, then answer on that side of the scale. Trust us, no one has ever received an assessment that says he's a heartless jerk. What you will get, if you are authentic and forthright, will be an assessment that shows what truly gets you jazzed in your career.

The Motivators Assessment will reveal your motivators in order, from one to twenty-three, as well as your identities ranked from one to five. Any motivator in your top seven is considered a core driver (the most important); those in the next seven are moderate drivers (significant at times, but not dominant in your thinking). The remaining motivators are in what we consider the neutral zone—they are not why you get up everyday and go to work. Remember these are all still very positive ideas, and you may look at one of these lower scoring items, let's say it's Money, and think, "But money *is* important to me!" What the results are showing is that compensation may be a satisfier or a vehicle to achieve more important motivators, but it's not a huge motivator for you, in and of itself.

As for the identities, priority order is even more important here. The rankings are based on the composite score of each of the motivators in that grouping. The top three identities will be of most interest to you, especially the highest-ranked identity. Chances are you'll identify yourself to others as a "Thinker" or "Achiever" (or whatever your top identity is) numerous times in the future.

With your results in hand, you can flip to the descriptions of the motivators and identities that fit you in the next chapter, as well as the more detailed descriptions of your identities in the Identity Reference Guide in the back of the book—helping you better understand your drivers and find ways in which your current work might be sculpted somewhat to better fulfill your needs. You might also share (and compare) your results with trusted advisors such as family, friends, coworkers, managers, mentors, and coaches. These discussions can often reveal insights that prove helpful as we consider first steps in making incremental changes in our work to live in closer alignment to our motivations.

For teams, it's also a terrific exercise to sit down together to understand what the test has revealed about your colleagues and your boss, where there might be opportunities for increased understanding, or why there might be sources of friction between members of the group. That's a starting point from which you can brainstorm what you might be able to do to make those relationships better and improve your individual and team's overall performance.

Your assessment results can help you begin to grasp what truly gives you greater joy in your career (which will most likely impact the rest of your life, as well).

~

With that said, we would recommend digging into the remaining chapters in some detail, focusing not just on the motivators and identities that apply most to you. Start by taking a few minutes to read through *all* the descriptions in Chapter 3. We've found that the process of considering the other motivators and identities will help you honestly address any flawed notions you've been harboring about what drives you. As one test-taker said, "I would have bet I'd score highest on Reward-Driven or Achiever, but the test found I was a Builder first and then a Caregiver. And as I think about it, I'm in my forties now, and leaving a positive legacy at work and my family are a lot more important to me than making more money and climbing higher up the ladder. The test knew me better than I did."

Another value of reading through all the descriptions of the motivators and identities is to help you become aware of sources of misunderstanding or conflict with people you work with, perhaps your colleagues or even your boss. As we describe Caregivers or the Reward-Driven or Thinkers, most people will inevitably consider how they do, or do not, fit that description, but they'll also think about those they work with. This can be a huge help for teammates or managers in understanding what makes their fellow workers tick, and how to better motivate them. (Or, you might be like the woman who reviewed one identity and told us, "That was good to read. I remembered now why I hate those people." Not *really* our intent.)

Following a quick read of those descriptions, proceed to Chapter 4 and go through the series of exercises to diagnose what may be underlying any dissatisfaction with your current work, and to help determine what changes you might make with your manager to feel more engaged on the job. Then, in Chapter 5, we tell the stories of a number of people we've interviewed who were able to make the job sculpting changes we describe—from the story of a man who had to decide which identity to focus most on to reengage himself, to that of a woman who learned to apply her Purpose motivation on the right target. Our hope is that reading these stories will provide both inspiration and practical guidance about how readers might go about their own job sculpting.

How to access The Motivators Assessment online:

A. Open the envelope containing your unique passcode found in the back of this book.

B. Access the assessment using the URL provided in the envelope.

C. Enter your unique passcode and begin taking the assessment.

D. After completing the online assessment, you can explore your profile online, and you can download it to review later or share with others. You can revisit your online profile at any time.

Chapter 3

23 Motivators and 5 Identities

Who Are You?

W hat follows are brief descriptions of the twenty-three motivators discovered in our research. As you read through these ideas, you'll most likely notice that a majority could be motivating to you in some degree, with only a few being truly demotivating. For most people, these are mostly positive concepts. But the priority order for each person is vitally important.

23 MOTIVATORS

Autonomy: This motivator leads people to want to be their own boss (inside or outside a corporate setting) and have a degree of freedom in their work. Those for whom autonomy is high on the list tend to prefer working alone to working on a team; nine times out of ten they'd opt to work by themselves because they feel they just get more done that way. For the autonomous who work in corporations, red tape and rules can drive them crazy.

Challenge: This motivator leads people to thrive when tackling difficult issues and overcoming obstacles or roadblocks. When things get really hard, those motivated by challenge feel they're at their best. They will usually keep going no matter what they face, and they revel taking on the perplexing, difficult, or even seemingly impossible.

Creativity: People driven to be creative want to be able to take time to explore, experiment, and discover new things. They enjoy facing the unknown and want to make things work in their own distinctive way, not by following prescribed models.

Developing Others: This motivator leads people to enjoy bringing out the best in those around them and helping others reach their full potential. That may mean mentoring, coaching, managing, or just guiding those who are closest to them. Sometimes they challenge people with stretch goals, other times they offer constructive criticism.

Empathy: People for whom this is a strong motivator relish getting to understand others and seeing things from their perspective—all so they can help those people through their problems or offer them a level of comfort. The empathetic listen to others and get in tune with their emotions so they can relate to them on a deeper level. It's highly rewarding when others tell the empathetic that they really "get" things.

Excelling: This motivator leads people to crave the feeling of successfully completing a task, especially when the bar is set high. They want to feel they're doing the highest quality work and are meeting or exceeding expectations. They want to get things done on time, and will do pretty much whatever it takes to do so; in fact, they probably can't remember the last time they missed a deadline. They sometimes admit they feel guilty if they aren't giving their all. They enjoy having ambitious goals and having a plan to reach them.

Excitement: Those strongly driven by this motivator want some sense of adventure and at least a little risk in their work. No one ever accused them of being boring or shirking opportunities to put themselves out there, and they get frustrated quickly by stale routines.

Family: People motivated by family want their loved ones to be proud of them and to know they'll always be there for them. They try to make family a high priority, which means balancing home and work time. Their greatest goal is to leave a legacy of love.

Friendship: Those strongly driven by the desire for quality friendships put great emphasis on developing close relationships both in their personal life and at work. Their network of connections is important to them, and they feel good knowing people rely on them to help out and keep confidences. Being trusted is highly rewarding, and it's important for them to feel this is mutual and that they can trust their colleagues.

Fun: This motivator leads people to seek to lighten things up at work and make others smile. They enjoy the humor of others, might share a wisecrack now and then, but almost always bring a sense of levity, lightheartedness, and optimism to the workplace. They tend to believe that we learn more and do more when we are enjoying those around us, and so they make an effort to set everyone at ease.

Impact: Those who are highly impact-driven want to know they are doing work that is important. They often feel a sense of destiny, that they are supposed to do something that will create positive change in the world, and they are usually willing to lead out and can become frustrated if they don't see the positive outcome of their efforts.

Learning: Those for whom this is a major driver thrive on trying new things and growing. For some, the pursuit of knowledge is its own goal, while for others the emphasis is on making themselves better at what they do. They understand they might appear a little nerdy at times, but the stimulation of making new discoveries and seeking out new information outweighs any hesitation to be seen as a bit eggheaded.

Money: For those strongly driven to earn a good deal of money, it's too simple to say they're just materialistic or greedy. For these people, how much they earn is often a way to keep score with the world and a confirmation of their personal value and their contributions. For some, they see compensation as a source of validation, safety, and a responsibility to fulfill their potential; for others, money may be a source of freedom and empowerment.

Ownership: This motivator leads people to want to be the person in charge, not only having the ability to control their own destiny, but also to directly influence the behavior of others. It gives them great satisfaction when people ask for their buy-in, and they have little problem making a final decision. They also tend to feel a great sense of personal accountability—which means they own up to their mistakes as well as successes.

Pressure: Those highly motivated by pressure tend to believe that stressful situations bring out the best in them; that they do some of their best work when deadlines are looming or they are asked to multitask. Some might admit that they do require a push now and then from supervisors to get started—that kind of external pressure helps them focus, and they get satisfaction from the adrenaline rush of having to put the pedal to the metal.

Prestige: Those for whom prestige is important highly value the respect of those in their inner circle but also the larger community around them. Job titles are important, as is the type of office, vehicle, or other perks they have. Their reputation means a good deal, as well. They would usually prefer to work for an organization that is considered among the best rather than one that's up-and-coming, and they don't mind at all when people ask the common cocktail-party question, "What do you do?" In fact, it can be more annoying if people don't ask it.

Problem Solving: When this is a leading motivator, people tend to get a great deal of satisfaction from finding solutions, especially in a crisis, and from resolving conflicts. They also enjoy helping others to come up with ways to solve their own problems—not just listening and being supportive, but digging in to come up with a realistic plan. They relish the mental exercise of looking at challenges from multiple angles; and trite as it may sound, they really do see problems as opportunities.

Purpose: Those driven strongly by purpose long to be a part of something bigger than themselves; they like being an integral part of a group or organization they admire; and they want to get behind a cause they believe in. Not only do they long for deeper meaning in their work, but they also want to be aligned with a strong vision and mission, and to feel that they are significantly contributing to it.

Recognition: Those strongly motivated by receiving acknowledgment for their good work highly value the respect and admiration of those around them. Philosophically, they think it's important that people's efforts are cheered for, they tend to be strong believers in meritocracy, and they enjoy proving their value. These people think it's important that others know about their victories, and the lack of such demonstrated appreciation seems to them a sign of disrespect, something that's fundamentally unfair.

Service: Those driven to serve tend to believe it's a moral obligation to help those around them. That means they put the spotlight on others' needs, and helping others takes precedence over helping oneself. Don't expect them to blow their own horn, and they often don't respond very well to suggestions that they should focus more on their own goals, such as getting a promotion or winning an award. They take great satisfaction from being willing to sacrifice of themselves, giving their time and talents to others.

Social Responsibility: Those driven by this motivator feel that it's important to speak out on issues that are vital to the world, whether political, social, economic, or rights-related. They are strongly guided by a moral compass, and often an ethical or political school of thought. They tend to believe that it's a person's responsibility to influence others to understand important social problems, and they can be greatly satisfied when they can see that they've had an effect in moving the needle of that awareness.

Teamwork: Those who are especially driven by working in teams believe that we tend to do our best work when we pool our talents, and they enjoy being a central bonding agent and figuring out how people can complement one another. They typically enjoy the sense that they're collaborating, and dislike it when anyone on a team tries to take too much credit or grab the spotlight. A key driver of their performance is that they don't want to let their teammates down, and they tend to feel very strongly that it's important to keep promises, respect others' ideas, and be dependable.

Variety: For those highly motivated by variety, routines are deadly; in fact, they can drive them batty. They like to change responsibilities frequently to keep things interesting. Trying new work tasks, being given new assignments, or working on a cross-functional team can give them a terrific charge.

5 IDENTITIES

To recap, in our research we found five clusters of motivators that we call identities. It's important to stress that we're not saying that any given individual is purely one of these following types, just as almost no one could be described as purely an idealist (with no realist tendencies at all) or a one-hundred-percent introvert. These are archetypes and each of us will inevitably tend to have stronger associations with some of these types over the others.

What follows is a general overview of each of the identities (there is an entire section in the back of this book that goes into much more detail on each of the five).

The Achievers

Chances are we all know our share of Achievers. These go-getters often do well under pressure, enjoy rising to a challenge, and love to solve problems. They are known for setting plenty of goals to strive for, and in the pursuit of a goal can appear hell-bent to not let anything get in their way.

Achievers are valuable to any organization, primarily because so many are "attainment-oriented," which means they are motivated to finish tasks on time and to high standards. Achievers are usually action-oriented and determined, high-energy people who are disciplined and focused.

Common characteristics of Achievers include:

- ☐ They love a good challenge.
- ☐ They are driven to excel.
- ☐ They thrive under pressure.
- ☐ Completing tasks is crucial to them.
- ☐ They feel guilty if they aren't giving their all.
- ☐ They are highly accountable.
- ☐ They like to be in control.
- ☐ They have a strong belief in their own talents.
- ☐ They set ambitious goals for themselves.

The Builders

Builders tend to be ideal-oriented with a strong desire to be part of something bigger than themselves, to align with a greater purpose. They are often the glue that keeps a team working together, and believe it's important to serve others and develop those around them—which is why many in this identity make good leaders.

Builders often tend to measure success not by their paychecks, but by the difference they are making on the world around them.

Common characteristics of Builders include:

- ☐ They want to help others grow.
- ☐ They've long felt a sense of destiny to help others.
- ☐ They want to be surrounded by a passionate team.
- ☐ They believe everyone is a leader.
- ☐ They are loyal friends.
- ☐ Doing good is more important than making money.
- ☐ They connect well with others—especially those with the same beliefs.

The Caregivers

Caregivers are often people-people—those who prefer working with clients and bonding with teammates to working independently, those who think it's important to be light-hearted and fun at work. They also tend to have rich lives outside of the office, spending plenty of time with family.

This group of individuals can be great with customers, but is also important in building team morale as Caregivers may enhance collaboration and appreciation among team members.

Common characteristics of Caregivers include:

- ☐ They are good at empathizing with those around them.
- ☐ They are natural communicators and good listeners.
- ☐ They are dependable.
- ☐ They respect people no matter their level.
- ☐ They try hard to balance work and home.
- ☐ They are genuine.
- ☐ They are positive and lighthearted.
- ☐ They typically don't want to be in charge.

The Reward-Driven

Whether it is vying for money, marbles, gold stars, or simple bragging rights, those who are strongly Reward-Driven tend to be highly competitive and have been since childhood. Their determined natures can help them accomplish great things for their organizations.

Some in this identity are most motivated by monetary rewards, while for some the prestige of their job is paramount, and still others want to be regularly recognized for their great work. We're all driven to some extent by these types of extrinsic rewards; it's just that for this type, they are much more important.

Common characteristics of Reward-Driven include:

- ☐ They are doers.
- ☐ They like regular indications of recognition.
- ☐ Their identities are strongly tied to their work success.
- ☐ They believe they should get a piece of what they create.
- ☐ They are good stewards of their time.
- ☐ They do their best work when incentivized.
- ☐ They believe in meritocracy.

The Thinkers

Some people believe that being allowed to exercise their imagination at work is a key to their success. They tend to prefer autonomous work, want to be free to take risks, and like to follow their own interests now and then. These people are the Thinkers, those who tend to challenge the status quo, who crave opportunities to explore and discover and make a big impact, those who can grow bored and frustrated if their work becomes routine.

As a group, Thinkers are resourceful and artistic, and are happiest when they are constantly putting new stuff out into the world. As such, they can be the lifeblood of innovation in an organization.

Common characteristics of Thinkers include:

- ☐ They dislike bureaucracy.
- ☐ They want to know the "why."
- ☐ They value novelty and variety.
- ☐ They like to see the impact of their innovations.
- ☐ They think before they act.
- ☐ They draw on a wide range of experiences.
- ☐ They don't like being told how to do their work.

Chapter 4

Job Sculpting

Who Am I, Where Do I Want to Go,
How Will I Get There?

Why is it so hard for so many people to figure out what's causing them dissatisfaction at work? In this chapter, we'll explore many of the most common reasons, and also provide individuals and their managers with a set of exercises to pinpoint exactly the challenges that may be at play.

First, we find it helps to recall why we got into what we do in the first place. Many people took a career path because the profession was hot when they were in school and it seemed to offer good job prospects. Others were encouraged to go into a line of work by their parents, a teacher, or counselor—perhaps it seemed a good fit—or maybe mom and dad wanted their child to follow in their footsteps (or were adamant they *not* do so). For some, the stability, or prestige, or pay may have been alluring in their work. After all, there are strong cultural conventions in most societies suggesting that we should all value these qualities in jobs.

And yet, while most people may have started their careers excited about what they were doing, passions and drives can change. What motivates us can evolve over a lifetime; the trouble is, our work responsibilities might not have.

Looking back, chances are we got into our current work because we were good at it. It was a strength. There is a prevailing notion that we should do work that optimizes the use of our talents, the things we have a natural aptitude for, and that makes a great deal of sense on the surface. A lot has been written in recent years about the importance of identifying and playing to our strengths to succeed on the job. Our schooling certainly tends to support this notion—pushing us into tracts that best use our natural abilities and away from ones we don't do well in. Most of us came to the conclusion through the course of our schooling that we're just not a math person, or that we have little talent for expressing our views in writing or making a cogent argument via public debate, while other work came so naturally we gravitated to it.

Developing one's talents is absolutely important, we can't stress that enough. The strengths movement has certainly helped many people become more successful in their jobs. But the fact is, our greatest strengths may not align that well with what we're motivated by. Many people find themselves going into a line of work more because they're good at the fundamental skills it requires than because they are really drawn to the nature of the work itself.

It seems commonsensical that we would be most interested in doing the things we're good at, but motivators and strengths are different, and motivators typically precede strengths. Strengths are what we are good at; motivators are what drive us, and often the most rewarding success comes from learning to be good at something we weren't that proficient in at the start. On the flipside, sometimes playing to our strengths can make us miserable.

Here's a family example to hopefully clarify that point a little: Adrian's son Anthony was a soccer goalkeeper in high school. He was strong and quick and fearless between the posts, earning the starting spot as a sophomore on the varsity team. And yet in his junior year he confessed, "I really don't like playing goal. There's a lot of standing around, and when the play comes your way it's a ton of pressure. If you let in a goal you're the scapegoat, even if the defense let the guy go by like a bunch of matadors."

No matter how many shots he stopped, his disposition made him much more bothered by the ones that went in. He had been put in goal early in life because of his talent—or *strength*—for it. At every age along the way he'd been the best in the school at stopping the ball. But was being a keeper motivating to him? Not at all. He looked at the guys playing out on the field and longed for their nonstop action, the opportunity to move the ball up field and score, and even their carefree attitudes and absence of pressure.

How often in people's working lives do they get pigeonholed because of strengths?

Perhaps Amanda has a strength for keeping on top of the details, so she is inevitably given behind-the-scenes responsibilities on all her projects—even though she would love to get just a little time working with clients. She wishes she could push herself to do more, learn, and grow, but "details" are what someone has decided she is "good" at. Or maybe Terrell works as a computer programmer because he innately "gets" technology. But programming is a solitary existence, and he would love to get to brainstorm and develop now and then with his other teammates; that's when he really thrives.

Or let's think about a college student: Perhaps Kate has always been good at math, so her parents encouraged her to study engineering. A year into her studies she finds the subject a slog. Instead, she is absolutely captivated by a class she took on women's studies. She discovers she's excited about the idea of being involved in a socially responsible movement and fighting for the rights of others. Mom and Dad are definitely not onboard with this income-limiting career shift, so she persists for another few semesters calculating the stress levels of steel girders under wind loads until she finally admits she isn't being true to herself. She drops out after lost years of effort.

The point: it's possible to be held hostage by focusing on our strengths alone.

Tennis great Andre Agassi says as soon as he could hold a racket, his father began grooming him to become the number one player in the world. Agassi was forced to hit for hours with a ball machine his dad had souped-up and nicknamed "The Dragon." His dad would stand on the sideline yelling, "Hit harder!" Agassi said he quickly learned to "hate tennis." But his father gave him no choice; he was determined to spawn a champion out of this young man who was undoubtedly talented.

When he was ten, Agassi lost a match for the first time to Jeff Tarango. He was devastated. Agassi hated the feeling of losing so much that from that day on he devoted himself to perfectionism despite his growing hatred of the sport.

Now, why did he resent tennis? Partly because he came to believe that playing tennis was his only option for an occupation. It was his greatest strength, his talent. As anyone who saw him play can attest, he *was* very good at it.

Agassi compares himself to the countless other people in the world who chose a career path because they showed a penchant for it at an early age or because they thought it would pay well or offer job security. How many people find themselves in an occupation because they happen to be good at it, but are not as satisfied or engaged as they could be?

Make no mistake; we do not advocate a world filled with

people who do only what they love with no consideration of realistic opportunities to succeed. The economy cannot possibly sustain any more professional beer tasters, movie stunt men, or cruise ship crooners. Nor do we think that everyone everywhere can be whatever they want to be professionally with no consideration of talent. No matter how hard the two of us try we'll never play professional hockey or dance in the Bolshoi. Things we are passionate about, but not very good at, are what we call *hobbies*.

But in this working world we do find that many people are unhappy in their jobs because they got into it—not out of a true motivation—but because they anticipated they would be good at it, or they were *told* they would. And thus many people find themselves slightly off plumb in their careers. Perhaps they do like parts of their work, and much about it does fit with their motivators, but—and this is a big but—some key components are missing or are at odds with what motivates them. This can lead to feelings of confliction, and understanding what changes need to be made can be perplexing and frustrating. That's why the majority of workers make very few changes throughout their careers.

We need to understand that most people do not need to make a big leap into the unknown and start a new career; in fact, the majority of individuals can make small changes to get back on track.

Take the example offered by Jane Hutcheson, then vice president of learning and development for TD Bank Financial Group. She had a group of professionals whose job it was to work with internal business lines to determine what they needed from her learning and development department. Of one employee she explained, he'd been at the bank for thirty years and doing his current job for five. But over time he had developed a passion for public speaking, and his job didn't involve anything like that. "He and I have built that into his job in a way that his colleagues doing the same job don't have." That includes going to colleges to deliver presentations on career planning—one way the bank has enhanced its image as an employer of choice with a new generation of students.

She added, "It's important to him, in terms of getting a sense of satisfaction and feeling good at what he does, that the job has elements of what he loves to do." If we had to guess, we'd say her employee was a Caregiver, he sought a little fun and socialization in his job, and he probably had strong Builder and Thinker tendencies as well—seeking Variety, Excitement, Learning, Purpose, and Service. He did his nine-to-five job quite well, and would continue to do so because a smart manager found a way to sculpt in just one new activity that met so many of his needs. It was a small adjustment that kept him engaged in all aspects of his work, and all because he sat down and told his manager what motivated him. That's how it all starts.

The problem is: when we're in the thick of the day-to-day grind of our jobs, it's unlikely we'll step back to assess like this to understand how well our work aligns with what we would really like to be doing. And maybe some of us are thinking that we don't have a manager like Jane Hutcheson. It's probably fair to say that most of us are running as fast as we can to just stay on top of our work, and no one has ever taught us to think about aligning our tasks with our motivators. And thus, disconnects are never identified and addressed.

Instead, most of us tend to fall into traps. We either blame ourselves, saying we're just not good enough at the work to really excel. Or we blame our boss, colleagues, or company, even the job itself.

Now, as the next step in this chapter, we want you to go through a series of exercises to help assess your current work situation—comparing the work you do day-to-day with what you now have discovered about your key motivators and identities. The goal is to identify where your work *is* currently satisfying and engaging and where it is *not*. And then, if it's not, to understand, *why* isn't it?

We've found these quick exercises are extremely helpful in gaining perspective to identify the disconnects that exist between people's work and their motivators. We'll start by having you Discover: "Who am I?" Then, we ask you to Evaluate: "Where do I want to go?" And finally we lead you to Sculpt: "How will I get there?" This is where your manager comes in, to help you make some changes. Building an empowering dialogue with your manager around what is motivating can elevate goal-setting discussions to another level.

Overall, you'll find the exercises will help you remember why you got into the particular type of work you do in the first place, will push you to think deeply about what you do and don't like about the work you are currently doing, and will ask you to consider how you can best align your specific tasks with your strongest motivators.

We'll start by looking backwards.

What Motivates Me Job Sculpting Worksheets

What follows is a series of four exercises that will require some introspection, all with the intention of helping you answer the following critical questions:

- **Who am I?** – *Discover what's important to you.*
- **Where do I want to go?** – *Evaluate your current role and responsibilities against your motivators and identities.*
- **How will I get there?** – *Sculpt your work to align with what drives you.*

Many people never achieve true happiness and success in their jobs because they don't understand what truly motivates them. In searching for a "dream job," many people feel they have to make a dramatic leap into the unknown. That's usually not the case; in fact, we found the vast majority of people are able to sculpt their current roles so they can do more of what they love to do and a little less of what they find demotivating.

Let's start this process of discovery by taking a look into the past, your past.

DISCOVER: WHO AM I?

Exercise 1: Engaged, Enabled, and Energized

A. **Best Work Experience** – Think about a time in your life when you were most engaged, enabled, and energized at work. It should be a time when you really cared about your colleagues and the organization; when you gave extra effort without being asked; when you felt supported, well trained, and empowered to succeed; when you believed your work was valued and really made a difference; and when you had the energy to keep going and succeed.

Job Title:

Organization:

B. **Best Work Specifics** – In the space provided <u>write</u> the details about the job you were doing at that most motivating time in your life. Why was it your best work experience? What specific assignments and responsibilities did you have? What tasks and activities were you engaged in? Most importantly, why did that particular job make you so excited about coming to work every day? Be as specific and introspective as you can as you write this narrative. You might even include why you left that job if you are no longer there.

Assignments/Responsibilities/Tasks:

C. What's Important to You at Work? – Take a minute
   and read through what you've written in B and <u>circle</u>
   or <u>underline</u> those key concepts that jump out at you
   as the most motivating. What did you learn about
   yourself from your responses? Any new insights into
   what's important to you at work?

Now, <u>prioritize</u> the items you just circled and list them in order
of importance to you—from MOST to LEAST. In the right hand
column, identify which of the 23 motivators best fits each item.

Most Important

	Assignments/Responsibilities/Tasks	Corresponding Motivator
	Least Important	

D. What's Missing? – Finally, review the list above. Is
   there anything important that's missing from your
   current work? If so, place an ✗ in the box to the left. If
   the item is present in your current role, place a ✔.

Note: *If you are currently hunting for a job, complete these exercises with
your last job in mind.*

SAMPLE

Note: After each worksheet you will see responses to the exercise completed by a real person, used with his permission. He works in the oil and gas industry. We will maintain his privacy by calling him "Ben."

Ben's Exercise 1: Engaged, Enabled, and Energized

Best Work Experience

Job Title: | Project Manager

Organization: | "ACME" Oil & Gas

Best Work Specifics
Assignments/Responsibilities/Tasks:

Key responsibilities included working with a team to optimize the planning and execution of a major capital project. This end was achieved through structured team workshops and one-on-one coaching. I worked hand-in-hand with the team through the entire project. My leaders engaged me by setting clear expectations then giving me autonomy to operate and deliver meaningful and quantifiable results. I was excited by the work because there was such a tangible prize, not only in the achievement itself but the possibility of formal recognition within my company.

What's Important to You at Work?

Most Important

	Assignments/Responsibilities/Tasks	Corresponding Motivator
✓	Autonomy	Autonomy
✓	Achievement	Excelling
✓	Quantifiable Results	Impact
✗	Formal Recognition	Recognition
✗	Tangible Prize	Recognition
✓	Clear Expectations	Excelling
	Least Important	

EVALUATE:
WHERE DO I WANT TO GO?

Exercise 2: Current State

A. **Current Responsibilities** – Now, let's return to the present to review your current roles at work. Start by listing all the major day-to-day responsibilities in your work in the left hand column in the graph below. List at least seven tasks in general terms (for instance: sales support, project management, patient care, etc.) in priority order—MOST to LEAST important.

B. **Your Identities** – At the top, list your top three identities from your Motivators Assessment Profile. Then, compare each identity against each responsibility by circling or underlining Y for Yes if the current responsibility *does* significantly fulfill or N for No if it does *not* fulfill that identity. For example, if sales support (a *responsibility*) fulfills your need as a Caregiver (an *identity* of yours), then circle or underline Y.

C. **Total Your Ys & Ns** – Now, add up your Yeses and Nos vertically and then horizontally.

D. **Identities View** – Review your results vertically. If the Nos outweigh the Yeses for two or more of your identities, a more comprehensive job sculpting or transition approach may be required to bring your current role into better alignment with who you are at your core.

E. Responsibilities View – Review your results horizontally. If the Nos outweigh the Yeses by responsibility, especially those near the top, it could be time for introspection and job sculpting on specific responsibilities to make them more engaging (we'll help with that in the next exercise).

Your Current Responsibilities Most Important	#1 Identity	#2 Identity	#3 Identity	TOTALS
	Y N	Y N	Y N	
	Y N	Y N	Y N	
	Y N	Y N	Y N	
	Y N	Y N	Y N	
	Y N	Y N	Y N	
	Y N	Y N	Y N	
	Y N	Y N	Y N	
	Y N	Y N	Y N	

Least Important

TOTALS

SAMPLE

Ben's Exercise 2: Current State

Your Current Responsibilities Most Important	#1 Identity Reward-Driven	#2 Identity Thinker	#3 Identity Achiever	TOTALS
Project Management	Ⓨ N	Ⓨ N	Ⓨ N	3Y
Providing Feedback	Y Ⓝ	Ⓨ N	Y Ⓝ	2N
Coaching	Y Ⓝ	Ⓨ N	Y Ⓝ	2N
Meeting Facilitation	Y Ⓝ	Ⓨ N	Y Ⓝ	2N
Results Reporting	Ⓨ N	Ⓨ N	Ⓨ N	3Y
Data Analysis	Ⓨ N	Ⓨ N	Ⓨ N	3Y
Administrative Tasks	Y Ⓝ	Y Ⓝ	Y Ⓝ	3N
Least Important **TOTALS**	4N	6Y	4N	

Summary Analysis: Ben knew he enjoyed parts of his work. As you can see, project management (his most important responsibility) meets the needs of his three top identities. However, he also knew he wasn't completely fulfilled, but before this exercise hadn't been able to put his finger on why. As he looked across the rest of the rows horizontally, he realized many of his major tasks were not completely satisfying his identities, and he realized some slight modification of those tasks could help. As he looked down the columns he realized his Reward-Driven and Achiever identities were also not as fulfilled as they could be (there were more Nos than Yeses). He decided he needed to consider a longer-term job sculpting process with his manager—one that will make him more engaged and much more likely to stay with his organization over the long haul. Great idea!

SCULPT:
HOW WILL I GET THERE?

Exercise 3: Ideal State

A. **Sharpen the Chisel** – Before you begin to sculpt, you must evaluate your list of current responsibilities from the previous exercise to determine where you might begin (of course, this will involve working with your manager).

Ask yourself these three questions:

- **What Can I Add?** Are there one or two specific tasks that could be added to your list of current responsibilities that would help fulfill your dominant identities and motivators? Here it's a good idea to review your answers to "What's Missing?" (Question D from Exercise 1: Engaged, Enabled, and Energized). Also consider work done by other team members around you: are there unclaimed or emerging opportunities you could take on?

- **What Can I Alter?** Are there current responsibilities that might be altered somewhat to become more fulfilling to one of your top identities?

- **What Can I Transfer?** Are there current responsibilities that you might be able to do less of or even remove entirely that aren't fulfilling, especially items that don't align with your highest ranking identities and motivators or those that are least important to your job? Are there members of your team who might be interested in swapping responsibilities to freshen the team and open up opportunities to try new tasks?

B. **Sculpt Like a Boss** – Based on the three questions above, on the next pages pull forward only those responsibilities you believe you can realistically Add, Alter, or Transfer. As you approach the following pages, consider how each responsibility links to your top identities and motivators and sculpt using the following factors to significantly increase your chances of success:

- **People** – Think of who you can enlist to help you in this process, whether managers, mentors, coworkers, coaches, family members, friends, teachers, etc. Are there any people in your work environment you believe won't be supportive of this process? What are some ways you might begin to win them over?

- **Roadblocks & Strategies** – What roadblocks will you encounter and what strategies will ensure greater success? Using the job sculpting strategies in the Identity Reference Guide in the back of the book can also help you recognize tactics that will help you successfully apply your identities in your quest to do more of what you love and less of what you shouldn't.

Add

New Responsibility You Would Like to **Add:**

Identity or Motivators Impacted:

People You Should Involve:

Roadblocks You Anticipate:

Strategies to Ensure Success:

First Steps You Must Take:

Add

New Responsibility You Would Like to **Add:**

Identity or Motivators Impacted:

People You Should Involve:

Roadblocks You Anticipate:

Strategies to Ensure Success:

First Steps You Must Take:

SAMPLE

Ben's ADD Example

New Responsibility You Would Like to **Add**:

Regional marketing

Identity or Motivators Impacted:

Identity = Thinker & Reward-Driven

Motivators = Creativity, Recognition & Impact

People You Should Involve:

John, Michael, Sarah, Jose

Roadblocks You Anticipate:

No major roadblocks expected if I get buy-in early.

Strategies to Ensure Success:

Hold prep discussions with Sarah and Jose to gain buy-in and input. Dig deep on data to make it relevant to the industry and to submit to my company's Best-of-the-Best award submission.

First Steps You Must Take:

Prep materials for APPEA conference to meet reps from Escra. Generate a high-quality submission for the Best-of-the-Best award. This will ultimately provide both internal recognition and relevant marketing material to drive sales.

Alter

Current Responsibility You Would Like to **Alter:**

Identity or Motivators Impacted:

People You Should Involve:

Roadblocks You Anticipate:

Strategies to Ensure Success:

First Steps You Must Take:

Alter

Current Responsibility You Would Like to **Alter:**

Identity or Motivators Impacted:

People You Should Involve:

Roadblocks You Anticipate:

Strategies to Ensure Success:

First Steps You Must Take:

SAMPLE

Ben's ALTER Example

Current Responsibility You Would Like to **Alter**:

> Coaching (formal) - Make it more of a key
> performance indicator (KPI). Make it measureable.

Identity or Motivators Impacted:

> Motivators = Impact & Recognition

People You Should Involve:

> P.A., S.T., S.Z., B.L.

Roadblocks You Anticipate:

> 1) Leaders making time and seeing the value in the
> process.
> 2) Keeping myself motivated.

Strategies to Ensure Success:

Writing up contracts and committing to make this a
visible KPI.

First Steps You Must Take:

Develop coaching contracts with P.A., S.T., S.Z., B.L.
Then track each session with a one-pager.

Transfer

Current Responsibility You Would Like to **Transfer:**

Identity or Motivators Impacted:

People You Should Involve:

Roadblocks You Anticipate:

Strategies to Ensure Success:

First Steps You Must Take:

Transfer

Current Responsibility You Would Like to **Transfer:**

Identity or Motivators Impacted:

People You Should Involve:

Roadblocks You Anticipate:

Strategies to Ensure Success:

First Steps You Must Take:

SAMPLE

Ben's TRANSFER Example

Current Responsibility You Would Like to **Transfer**:

> Meeting facilitation

Identity or Motivators Impacted:

> Motivators = Teamwork and Autonomy

People You Should Involve:

> N/A

Roadblocks You Anticipate:

> There's no one else to turn this over to on the team.

Strategies to Ensure Success:

Change my thinking. View it as a critical input for my desired project results.

First Steps You Must Take:

Not really feasible to transfer this now. Learn to deal with it and make it my own (autonomy).

Exercise 4: Ask the Big Questions

Now, let's put this all together.

A. **Personal Elevator Pitch** – From the exercises you've just completed, imagine you have just thirty seconds to describe your ideal job to your current manager, a mentor, or to a future employer if you are a student or unemployed. Describe, from your understanding of your motivators and identities, the kind of work that drives you and what you would be passionate at. Be as specific as possible. Explain how that work would fulfill you and make you more productive for the organization you work for.

B. Finding Fulfillment Outside of Work – Finally, if after all of this process you believe you won't be successful at sculpting your current job, you'll need to identify how to fulfill your identities and motivators through other avenues. Some very viable solutions (even for those fulfilled in their current job) include volunteer service outside of their organization, serving on a cross-functional team at work, helping out in other areas of the organization, etc. Brainstorm how you might use your passions outside of your nine-to-five role and responsibilities to better live in alignment with and fulfill your motivators in your life:

SAMPLE

Ben's Exercise 4: Ask the Big Questions

A. Personal Elevator Pitch:

In my ideal work environment, I would be given ample space to operate, thereby fulfilling my need for autonomy—my strongest individual motivator. I would not be micromanaged. Performance expectations would be understood with clear, simple indicators in place. I would enjoy and feel fulfilled by my work, if not every day then certainly over the long term. I would think of creative ways to involve my hobbies and passions in my work, which would keep me, and others around me, more engaged. Rewards and recognition would have clear links to performance expectations.

B. Finding Fulfillment Outside of Work:

One of my strongest motivating concepts is creativity. I feel the greatest sense of achievement when I create something out of nothing, e.g., writing music, authoring a paper or a story, developing a new tool for the workplace. Maybe this is the year I finally write that short story, or get back into writing music, or become more serious about photography.

Part of being Reward-Driven is that I'm all about seeing quantifiable results from my actions. I recently introduced new ways to quantify and share results with a volunteer organization where I hold a leadership position. No one had ever done that before so they liked it, and it also helped me enjoy the role more than I otherwise would. I must continue to look for opportunities to do this.

Chapter 5

Finding the Right Blend

Stories of Sculpting

It's not out of the question at this point to be thinking that even with a good understanding of what is and isn't motivating in your current work, you will still face challenges to make lasting changes. You might wonder if your boss will be supportive, or perhaps you worry that you don't have the skills necessary to make the shifts you want.

In this chapter we'll tell you the stories of a number of people who successfully made the changes that were right for them. They range from relatively minor tweaks to their current jobs, all the way to major changes in their life direction while still in college. We hope they inspire you to know that a bright future really is possible, and that (thankfully) in most cases it usually involves fairly simple tweaks. As you read through the following stories, think about the changes you might make.

❧

He asked us to keep his name confidential because he didn't want to go through the hassle of getting approval from his company, but "Ryan" is responsible for billions of dollars in risk and cash management for one of the world's largest companies. As a treasurer, he has a job that is as responsible, analytical, and left-brained as they come. And yet he is also one of the most servant-oriented managers we've ever met.

To back up, Ryan started his career highly achievement-driven, working as an auditor at a Big Four firm. It was, he says, "like getting an MBA in finance from Harvard." With a chance to work in all the aspects of bookkeeping, he found himself drawn to treasury. "It's a place to really make a difference," he said. "Eventually I got the opportunity to be treasurer of a small business unit here. I did everything and worked my way up."

In addition to the chance to excel, solve problems, and be challenged daily in treasury, Ryan soon realized he also loved developing people—not only those who worked for him, but also others in the company.

"I suppose it came from my dad. He was a production manager. He managed 330 people. I remember going to his factory on Sundays and watching his assembly line. He managed people from all different backgrounds and languages. Watching him deal with adversity was amazing. He'd have someone come up and say, 'I got something in my eye, and

I need to go to the nurse.' He took care of them, but it was a teaching moment. Pretty soon they were promising to wear their glasses. They were being told off and were smiling about it."

At some point on his journey, Ryan realized he wanted to develop his Builder motivators even more than those on his Achiever side. His Builder side may not have been dominant, but he wanted it to be; we'd call that his aspirational identity. As such, he started thinking about his work team as a second family. "Watching them succeed began to be my success. As I saw them get bigger jobs, then I was successful. I loved to see them think up projects on their own, finish things together as a team, get recognized. I think you have to be wired this way to have a passion to develop others."

Now, as we mentioned, Ryan does have an incredibly complex job that requires his full attention. The company he works for does business in many countries around the world and with that comes risk. As a treasurer, Ryan and his team help protect the company from volatility in those markets. The team also manages liquidity. For instance, they ensure there's enough cash to fund operating needs on a daily basis in each country, and that the company can bring that cash home when needed. They also evaluate and fund the large mergers and acquisitions the company undertakes.

It was interesting to listen to Ryan explain his role to us. He used the word "we" a lot.

"That's a habit. I was the captain of my soccer teams in high school and university. We all learned to cheer our team on and help bring the strengths out of each person. Even though I played defense, I would show the forwards what their best moves were against me. If you help people understand their strengths you gain their trust. Running a team is like being a captain on the soccer field. We get people to buy into the system here, but also the goals of the organization. Leaders fail because they think they are smarter than everyone else. You've got to listen."

Now, as if developing others who work for him wasn't enough, between 6:30 and 7:00 in the evening Ryan does what he calls his "mentoring job." His company is extremely diverse, and headquarters is packed with brilliant people from dozens of countries. Sometimes leaders fail to acknowledge the challenges that come with such diversity. For instance, many of these smart people don't think in English, since it's their second language, and that translation process can slow their communication skills. Lately he has begun mentoring people from the Pacific Rim.

"This started with an Asian woman who wanted me to be her mentor; she wasn't progressing in her career like she wanted. The first exercise I gave her was to walk around our building and take notes on people she thought were successful. She returned with a list of things they did: they were good dressers, good communicators, had good posture, were confident, things like that. Half of those were easy fixes. I sent her to a good store for some nice suits; and she went to my wife's stylist. She practiced standing straight when she walked into a room.

"Then we worked on her communication skills. In her role she didn't have the chance to pitch a lot of ideas, but the more practice she got the better she was going to get and the more confident she'd be. So every other week she has returned and presented an idea to me. I've noticed a complete change."

The gift for Ryan is that some of the company's best people knock on his door when he has a job posting. "I think of myself as a teacher first, and a treasurer second. I told HR the other day I'm overpaid for what I do. It's not about the money for me, it's about grooming people and watching them grow, and making them successful."

In Ryan's case, a passion to build and develop others trumped achieving, it trumped the almighty buck, and all that was needed was for him to recognize his desire to develop people's skills and make it part of his regular schedule. Ryan still achieves, he still is a treasurer, but he's given his Builder side some attention and he's much happier and more fulfilled— and his company now has a terrific people-manager to boot.

While much sculpting we see is like that—subtle—there are times that individuals end up assuming new or additional duties.

Former director of the MBA Career Development Program at Harvard Business School, James Waldroop tells an interesting story. He was visiting with a Canadian company where he met a talented senior executive, the chief information officer, who told him she was planning on leaving the organization soon. The woman's strongest motivator was in doing creative work. In fact, she had just finished leading a project to update the company's entire information system and had done a masterful job. However, now her role had evolved to maintaining and operating the IT system, where a strong analytic penchant was needed. Little creativity was required in this maintenance work, and she had quickly grown uninspired.

The professor took her to have a talk with the company president. After some back and forth, he worked out a deal that would allow her to take on an additional role overseeing the company's marketing efforts, despite the fact that she had no experience in that area. The president knew she was imaginative and smart, and guessed she had a good chance of learning the role and succeeding. She did.

"She didn't quit," says Waldroop. "They gave her a little more money, but certainly not enough to compensate for the fact that she now had two jobs. But she was delighted. After all, none of us are single-dimensional automatons, we all like opportunities to expand our skill sets. And the president was thrilled because she was staying."

~

As we grow up we begin to develop a notion of the kind of work we should do. Sometimes we're inspired by a parent or mentor who does that job, other times we simply have an aptitude for science or math or writing or mechanics and find ourselves pushed in those directions. For instance, a voracious reader might guess she'd be a good book editor, a talented artist in school could lean toward graphic design, someone who loves to debate might become a lawyer. For some fortunate souls these preconceived notions are dead on, and they get to do what they love from day one. For others, however, it can take years to come to the realization that the work they've selected is not fulfilling them as they'd hoped.

For those who are in school or just starting out in the working world, we recommend they consider not just what they are good at but also what motivates them before selecting a direction in life.

Blake Mallen, for instance, almost took the road *more* traveled.

He says there was something missing at his college graduation. His friends were there, Mom and Dad, even aunts and uncles once removed. Everything, from outside appearances, was quite normal. That is, except for one thing: Mallen was not taking the path everyone expected. He was not going to law school.

It's funny how things don't always go the way we plan.

Mallen had graduated at the top of his high school class in Newbury Park, a small suburban town forty-five minutes up the freeway from Los Angeles. He'd been student body president of that über-competitive high school; and had collected more ribbons and plaques in his first eighteen years than most people do in their lifetimes. He'd then finished college in just three years and was supposed to jump right into law school. "Because that was what I thought I was supposed to do. In my family if you are successful, you become a doctor or a lawyer—and I don't like blood."

Mallen is, by every stretch of the definition, a born Achiever—he loves competing, raising the bar, winning. "My mom was a principal; my dad was a cop. I was raised to do the right thing, and for me that meant excelling."

Mallen paused and then chuckled, "I still have all my certificates of perfect attendance from elementary school."

For some, Blake Mallen's story might sound familiar. As children, Achievers like Mallen receive more than their share of accolades. They do well under pressure. They are often competitive. Many graduate with honors and apply to highly ranked collegiate programs—to become lawyers, doctors, titans of industry, Hollywood producers, rocket scientists. And why wouldn't they? It's an achievement to simply pursue these careers. But are Achievers attracted to these fields because they're competitive or because they are actually interested in curing diseases or leading people or building space telescopes?

Blake Mallen was following his planned path partly because it's not easy to distract an Achiever from a goal—even if it's not the right one for him. Indeed, everything seemed on track. He had earned honors during his undergraduate studies at the University of California, San Diego, carrying a packed class schedule. That is until a vague chat message arrived on his computer one evening while he was huddled over an assignment. "Wanna make some money?" read the message from an old high school acquaintance who was attending a neighboring college.

Like any college student, Mallen was hard up for cash. He agreed to attend something the messenger referred to vaguely as a "meeting."

"I was little naive, and more than a little anxious," says Mallen. "I had no idea why I was going to meet these people. So I invited a bunch of my friends. If I'd agreed to do something weird, at least I didn't want to be alone."

As you might have guessed, Blake and his friends found themselves at a recruiting event for a multilevel marketing company. Typically these meetings explain why the company's products are better than those in stores, and there's a pitch to become a distributor or promoter for the company. The "opportunity" presented is that each person will not only sell products, but build a team of people to distribute and promote the products as well. The promise is when a person builds a team, he or she makes a commission from the team's sales, and then from the team's team's sales. That was the promise, anyway.

"I ran into a lot of ingrained biases about multilevel marketing very fast from parents and friends, but I didn't have any," Mallen says. "The people I met were genuinely excited about what they were doing and the energy was intoxicating. I felt this internal battle—this was definitely not my plan. It wasn't prestigious like being a lawyer. But I figured, 'Hey, I'm not a lawyer yet. I'm just a college student. And maybe I can learn something that would give me an edge later on.' It started out as my plan B."

Like everything else he does, Blake Mallen doesn't just try. Before he graduated from UC San Diego, Mallen was the youngest top-producing distributer in the organization—earning more money some months than many of his professors. He found building teams, motivating a group of promoters, and breaking records in the multilevel world came naturally to him. It was so motivating being on top that he couldn't imagine starting over at the bottom of the ladder in the legal world as a junior associate.

Instead he wanted to build his own business.

He broke the news to his parents at his college graduation. "They were not jazzed at all about my new career venture. They made me agree that if it didn't pan out in a year, I'd go to law school."

Fast-forward fourteen years: Blake Mallen is cofounder and chief marketing officer of ViSalus, one of the fastest growing direct marketing companies, earning more than $600 million in annual revenue. His company is best known for its weight loss and fitness platform—The Body by Vi 90-Day Challenge—which made Mallen a millionaire by age twenty-five, multimillionaire by twenty-seven, and decamillionaire by thirty.

"At a recent company event I was on stage telling my story to a sea of people," says Mallen. "They were our promoters and were decked out in our colors, wearing our logo, and cheering wildly. We had just announced that ViSalus had broken the $1 billion mark in total sales. People were ecstatic, and I was still thinking to myself, this wasn't in my plan. Never while I was striving for extra credit in school, or collecting my pink certificates for perfect attendance, did I ever say, 'When I grow up, I'm going to be a direct marketer.'

"But I found this work is really, really motivating to me. I get to take ideas and make them a reality. I get to inspire others to challenge the status quo and change their health and financial situations. I get to compete and win with a great team. And being passionate about what I do is what gets me out of bed every day with a big grin."

Now understand we don't present this story to suggest that college students like Mallen should all run out and sign up with multilevel marketing firms anymore than we're suggesting they all drop out of college to work full-time on that smartphone app they've been dreaming of. This is simply one man's story of finding his unique path—of blending his core motivators in a career that he finds stimulating, rewarding, and exciting for him.

As you know by now, our research clearly shows that just because a person's strongest motivators may drive them to achieve, for instance, the most successful people find balance with their other motivations. Consider Mallen. Although clearly driven to excel, and motivated to compete and surpass expectations in an industry that faces many daunting image and operational challenges, achievement alone isn't his only driver at play. He was willing to give up the prestige offered by the law because he has a big heart. He's a Builder who wants to make an impact on those around him—an identity that he believes gives him balance and greater perspective in his life.

"There's an obesity epidemic in our country," he tells us. "I find nothing more rewarding than to hear stories of people who transformed their own lives—their health and their confidence. These people give our company the credit, but they did it themselves. They did all the work. I didn't spoon-feed them healthy food. I didn't wake up every morning with them to jog. They did it. They lost the weight."

If you read those words again from Mallen it will become obvious that he came to understand his purpose-driven side, and he blended a drive to achieve with a healthy need to build something meaningful.

As we see, the journey of discovery is personal for everyone.

The bottom line for Blake Mallen: he believes deeply that he would not have been as fulfilled or successful in life if he hadn't answered that text message and tried a detour on his path up the mountain of achievement. As he summarizes, "When you stop doing what you think you are supposed to do, and start doing what you were meant to do, that's when the script ends and life really begins."

But what if destiny doesn't send a late night electronic message? Most of the time that doesn't happen. Nonetheless, Mallen's story has great relevance for not only college students, but also all who are thinking through the sort of sculpting they need to make in their work. Some of the people we've interviewed, those who are the most happy with their careers, initiated sculpting that appeared on the surface to involve abandoning what had seemed to define them growing up.

Consider, for instance, Jennifer Whitehouse, who was just about to become a nun.

~

A graduate student in theology at the University of Notre Dame, Whitehouse's studies were drawing her closer and closer to the biggest decision of her life: whether or not to become a novice in the Roman Catholic Church. But, she says, God had other plans. She would instead find her true calling—as an accountant.

Yes, we are serious here.

Today Whitehouse is the accounting manager at a fifty-person law firm in New Orleans, and she absolutely loves her work.

"I always thought I was called to serve. At the same time,

going through high school my analytical scores were off the charts. The counselors said they thought I'd be good at accounting, they told me God needs good bookkeepers, too. I studied theology *and* accounting as an undergraduate. I was still resisting."

Whitehouse finally had a moment of truth. "In life you don't always know which direction you're supposed to go, but it's very clear—if you listen—which way you *shouldn't* go." This is a wonderful insight: when you understand what motivates you it not only will lead you to making good career choices, but will help you avoid making bad ones.

A few days after arriving on the Notre Dame campus there was a get-together where the old graduate students mingled with the new students. In moving around the room, shaking hands, Jennifer ended up in front of a more senior student named Michael Whitehouse. "It was one of the most deeply religious moments of my life," she tells us. There was no doubt about it: Jennifer knew she would marry this guy. And happily Michael felt the same. At that moment, the course of her life changed forever—from a future of sacred vows of celibacy to one of a wife, mother, and employee.

But why accounting?

"I had to admit I was forcing myself through the reading and writing of my religious studies. It wasn't my passion. Accounting is my ministry; it's what I'm called to do in this life. I suppose because of my background, I believe in the truth.

Accounting is black and white. The truth may hurt sometimes, but the numbers are the numbers. People know I will tell it like it is, they know what they can expect from me."

Whitehouse has always been a Caregiver, endowed with a great ability to empathize. She's also an Achiever who loves to solve problems. But more than anything she's a strong Builder who is highly purposeful. She thought her purpose in life would be inside her church. It wasn't. She became happiest when she turned her focus toward accounting. Though she does readily agree that her religious training helped cultivate the warmer, more merciful side of her Caregiver nature. It's an identity that makes her unique and has helped make her successful in her job.

She adds, "We are human and we make mistakes. I'm detail-oriented, so the lawyers and paralegals all know billing time is due to me by noon today. But I have three emails from people who are on vacation or have family emergencies. They know I expect them to hit their deadlines, but we all have to exhibit understanding. We have to forgive each other. We learn from our mistakes and move on."

Forgiveness and mercy are not terms typically bandied about in business, especially by bookkeepers. Nor is the other idea Whitehouse says she's learned during her life journey: Love. She has come to understand that people in business need to find ways to demonstrate love to one other—a skill Whitehouse has developed but many with highly logical minds never seem to grasp, nor have any desire to practice.

"I think if we do something to make sure there's more love in the world by the end of the day, then we've done what God desires of us. Part of that love for me is helping others find their calling, whatever it is. You could be a stay-at-home parent, a teacher, a garbage man, or whatever. God doesn't want us to worry about how we get ahead ourselves, but how we can help others move forward."

With the insight and self-knowledge that she has, Whitehouse sought to find a place to work where the firm's leaders are passionate about their culture and their people, a place that realizes employees have lives outside of work. She said, "The leaders here want you to be fully present while you are at work, but they also want you to go home and be fully present with your family. Last week one of the partners sent me home because my son had been to the dentist and had to be anesthetized. He was with his father and the procedure took very little time so they were both home already. Still, the partner said I should be there with my son. I told him, 'But I have payroll!'"

The partner expressed his concern for Whitehouse and her family, and she expressed her concern about the rest of people in the firm and *their* families. "We finished payroll, and I went home early," she says. "There's an old saying that I think about often: *Preach often and if necessary use words.* The partner was a great example that day. I'm blessed to be part of a caring culture like that."

For some analytical types reading this, Jennifer White-house's pull toward the meticulous, precise world of accounting may ring true, while the development of her softer identity of Caregiving may seem incongruent or even uncomfortable. And that is one of the intentions of this book—to make readers feel a little discomfort and help everyone realize how their identities and motivators can create friction within them that should be joyfully embraced. Often, it's only by pushing through some confusing and conflicting impulses that a person begins to understand herself more deeply and frees herself to make the sculpting moves that are right for her, no matter what others might think about them.

Sometimes this process involves finding the delicate balance of our motivations, as was true for the treasurer Ryan; other times it requires consciously choosing to meet the urgings of a dominant identity that we haven't given enough attention to, as with Whitehouse.

To help you continue to think through the changes that are best for you, in the Identity Reference Guide in the back of the book we introduce sixty simple steps that you might take to boost your satisfaction with your work, organized by each of the identities. If you've determined that you're a strong Achiever, for example, we offer strategies that will help you increase the level of challenge you feel at work, enhance your ownership of projects, and hone the degree of problem-solving you undertake. Or, if you've discovered that you have a good deal of Builder in you that you hadn't fully appreciated, we'll suggest ways you can enhance your value at work by developing others, adding a greater sense of purpose and social responsibility to your work, and building a stronger team around you.

We hope implementing some of those strategies will do the trick, allowing you to sculpt your current job so that you feel much more engaged and energized. If these ideas don't work—and we sincerely encourage you to try at least a few before giving up—we now move on to the more challenging task of embarking on a more substantial career transition.

Chapter 6

Embarking on a Hero's Journey

From the Known, to the Unknown,
to the Known but Better

With all we've said about job sculpting, we must admit that sometimes it's in everyone's best interest for those who find themselves miscast or miserable to make more substantial changes to their work environment, changes that may seem radical. After all, there are enough disaffected zombies in the working world already.

While some people gain the clarity to make such a move quickly—seeing clearly the path they should follow—most major career transitions can be difficult and take years of effort. Honestly, many moves involve a cut in income with resulting reductions in things like vacations, social activities, and even living space to bring costs down. There can also be sacrifices of time for retraining or schooling, and there are almost always stresses along the way—including the loss of some aspects of your work that you do enjoy, such as time with colleagues. Many people who set out to make a transition decide to go into business for themselves or work as freelancers, and each of those choices involves distinctive challenges, too.

A career transition should not be undertaken lightly or without serious reflection and a good deal of research on the new endeavor. It will also require planning for the changes in lifestyle and income the transition may likely involve.

On the positive side, some of those who successfully make the leap do report greater engagement and satisfaction on the other side. Here are two quick examples of people who felt they had to make such a big transition:

Marci Alboher was lying on a beach in Brazil when she began her own process of reinvention. Alboher was taking her first vacation in two years when her cellphone rang. Her boss asked if she'd cut her trip short to take care of a crisis in the office. She said no. "I realized my corporate work just didn't matter to me anymore. After I hung up, I vowed to figure out a way to leave that job."

Her reinvention wasn't easy. It took two years to wean herself from the corporate world's steady paychecks and re-emerge as a journalist. She took classes, went to conferences, networked with writers and editors, and humbly learned from mentors ten years her junior. Even today, more than a decade into her new career, she earns only two-thirds of what she was making in her corporate job, but she says the trade-offs are worth it for her. She writes for publications that include the *New York Times*, and has written a career advice book for midlife professionals called *The Encore Career Handbook.*

Like Alboher, Arthur Brooks had to go through an arduous process of figuring out what to do with his life, which was difficult largely because he was so good at what he did. His job offered prestige and drew on his strong natural talent for music. Brooks played French horn for the City Orchestra of Barcelona until he was in his late twenties. But despite achieving success in a career that can be very challenging to find good work in, he said he was at best only "somewhat satisfied" with his work. He called his father back in Seattle and told him he was quitting music to go back to school. This is part of their conversation:

Dad: That's irresponsible.
Brooks: But I'm not happy.
Dad: What makes you so special?

Unfortunately, that's the mindset of too many: work is to be endured. But Brooks realized he wasn't doing anyone any favors by staying in a job that didn't engage him. He turned in his notice, went back to school, and has spent what he calls a "blissful decade" as a university professor and now runs a Washington think tank.

So, how long will a career transition take? According to research from the MetLife Foundation and Encore.org, the average big career transition takes about eighteen months, during which many people don't earn an income and must draw on their savings. Some spend even more of their financial reserves going back to school. In addition, it's common to take a pay cut if people move to a job more focused on mission than money.

We believe it's helpful for people who want to make such a big transition in their lives to think of the process in terms of the hero's journey. In Joseph Campbell's *Hero with a Thousand Faces*, the eminent mythologist describes the path of most mythological heroes as a formula with stages each hero must pass through. It's a formula that has been used in books and plays from the dawn of time and is still used in films and novels today from *Star Wars* to *The Hunger Games* to *The Hobbit*.

In this process, the hero-to-be typically receives a call to adventure by an external event or messenger, which the hero accepts reluctantly. The hero must cross the threshold from the everyday world into a world of adventure. At the outset of the hero's journey (and along the way when necessary), the hero may accept aid or counsel from a mentor—a wise wizard or fairy godmother for instance (or think Obi-Wan Kenobi or Mr. Miyagi here). The hero must face a series of challenges and temptations—from violent encounters with monsters to forces of nature—until eventually the hero reaches the climax of a final battle.

Only after successfully beating the odds can the hero return to the everyday world of daylight. Now, in the story, often an elixir has been used to defeat the enemy: it can be an object, but more often it is knowledge or courage that the hero has acquired during the adventure. That elixir is now put to use in the everyday world. Often it has a restorative or healing function, but it also serves to define the hero's role in society. Which means the hero comes back from this adventure not only stronger, but with the power to bestow boons on humankind.

Now let's use this hero's journey to think about career transitions.

For those driven to make such a change, the call tends not to come from an external messenger—though that can happen—but more often from within themselves. They find themselves becoming more and more discontent and restless, and unfortunately this can involve feelings of great frustration, irritation within themselves and with their work, which can manifest in resentment toward their boss, colleagues, customers, and even family members. Sometimes people facing these trials can even fall into depression. We encountered stories in our research of individuals who had horrible cases of the "Sunday dreads," who were having trouble sleeping, and who could barely drag themselves out of bed on Monday morning. Whether things get this bad, or people realize the need to change before the situation has become so dire, most journeys are driven by feelings of discontent and are kick-started by a moment of truth. The phases of the hero's journey at work can be described this way:

The Need for Change:
Dissatisfaction has come to override whatever pleasure and engagement they had in their work; they know they're not doing their best any more, which contributes to their unhappiness; and they are becoming increasingly frustrated, which may manifest in emotional turmoil and frustration with others around them.

The Call:
Most can tell us the exact moment they decided they had to make a career change. They then began to ask important clarifying questions such as, "What do I love to do?" or "What do I have to offer?" From there, they begin to form a clear picture of who they are, where they want to go, and how they will get there.

The Leap:
The journey truly begins when they cross the threshold and accept that things are going to get uncomfortable. They agree to move from a known to an unknown world.

The Mentors:
Pretty soon, they realize they can't do this alone and reach out to wise helpers as they try to find new roles that are more motiving, or significantly re-sculpt their current roles through a series of meetings with mentors or managers.

The Tests:
Inevitably there come roadblocks, challenges, and temptations to lure them to return to their old ways. Outside forces and internal doubts will conspire to bring them down, but the dedicated make it through these tests stronger. As Campbell writes, "The cave you fear to enter holds the treasure you seek."

The Lessons:
They not only learn lessons along the way but also find themselves involved in a process of development and growth. This can be a relatively long stretch of research and re-education as they learn how to best use their motivations to bring the greatest satisfaction and purpose to their work lives.

The Transformation:
One day, our heroes realize they are actually doing something that feels new and different but comfortable. They have successfully blended their motivators and identities and found a role that engages them and gives them greater satisfaction.

The New Beginning:
Reborn into a known but better world, the heroes find themselves daily doing something more motivating. They have developed ways to use their new knowledge and courage to create lasting change not only for themselves but often for those around them, too.

Naturally, making a life transition like this can impact anyone's mental well-being, so a sensible approach to career transition management is important. While most of the literature on making such a career change focuses on areas like job choice and re-education, the most successful people who make job transitions find that keeping a confident, realistic, and optimistic attitude can be one of the most important tools in bringing about positive change.

Professor Herminia Ibarra of INSEAD has done extensive research on effective career transitions. She argues that it's wisest to take small steps to determine the environments, tasks, and roles that best suit an individual. She suggests a three-part process of career change: experimenting with new professional activities to determine whether or not they really are fulfilling; connecting with new social networks in the new field; and working and reworking the story we tell ourselves and others about who we are.

Randall Hansen, PhD, a self-described "career doctor," offers some solid, practical advice about making a career transition. Here are just a few of his Dos and Don'ts:

- **Don't** rush into a new career field because you are dissatisfied or disillusioned with your current job, boss, company, or career field; **do** try sculpting first.

- **Do** have a well-developed plan for making your career change. **Don't** rush into a big change until you have thought it out and have developed a strategy.

- **Don't** worry if you feel insecure about making a change; these feelings are normal.

- **Do** expect to put in a great deal of time and effort in making the switch from one career to another, but **don't** allow yourself to get discouraged at the pace of your progress.

- **Do** leverage some of your current skills and experiences in your new career, but **don't** necessarily limit yourself to similar careers or jobs when making a change.

- **Do** consider that you may need to get additional training or education to be competitive in your new field, but **don't** jump headfirst into an educational program … start slowly with one class or seminar.

- **Do** take advantage of *all* your current network of contacts, conduct informational interviews with key people, and join professional organizations in your new career field.

- **Do** take advantage of career and alumni offices from your previous schools as well as your current school if you are going back for additional education or training.

- **Do** gain experience in your new career while you are still working in your current job. Volunteer or find a part-time job in the field, building experience, confidence, and contacts.

- **Don't** go it alone; **do** find a mentor. You need to have someone who can help motivate you and keep you focused on your goals when you get discouraged.

- Above all, **do** be flexible. You're starting your career anew, which means you may have to make concessions about job titles, salary, relocation, etc.

Chapter 7

Making a Good Living, Making a Good Life

Leaving the World Better Than We Found It

When it comes down to it, what we all do for a living and how much we earn aren't nearly as important as whether we find joy and value in what we do. And, we would add a concluding thought: If we can use our talents to positively affect the world around us, we are more than likely going to be happier.

In Charles Dickens's *A Christmas Carol*, Ebenezer Scrooge transforms from a ruthless moneylender to a caring and charitable businessman and philanthropist. In the triumphant final act of the book, his happiness has grown exponentially and we witness the impact of his actions on the community at large.

In terms we will all remember from our school days, we might say old Scrooge went from a D-level life to an A-level life, literally overnight.

Now, imagine if each act of each of our business lives was graded. Lynn G. Robbins, cofounder of the Franklin Quest Company (now FranklinCovey), suggests a model where business people are assigned A through F grade levels based on their motives and actions. We have modified his list here:

A Level

At this level, a person's primary motivation is to make a difference in the world, with a secondary motivation of earning a living. Now, when we say, "make a difference," we don't mean all A-level people work for charities. No, these people can be found not only in nonprofits but also in for-profit businesses from health care to manufacturing, retail to high-tech. What sets the A-level professionals apart is their concern for others wherever they work. These people define their roles in terms of their customers' or employees' or coworkers' needs, not their own. While level B and C professionals describe their businesses in terms of their products and services—the how and what—A-levels focus on the "why" of their work.

B Level

At the B level, an individual's primary motivator becomes making money. While these are still good people who want to provide decent products and services, the fact is making a difference for customers or employees has taken a backseat to making a profit. Says Robbins, if an A-level company goes public, concern for the stockholder and the bottom line all too often can force the company to the B level and sometimes lower.

C Level

At this level, it's not just money but the *love* of money that becomes a person's dominant motivator. C-level business people usually offer the minimal quality to be competitive and survive, and they will look for the cheapest way to produce their goods or deliver their services. C-levels often become indifferent to their customers, employees, and business partners, and their personal integrity may be compromised as they begin to engage in dishonest practices such as deceptive advertising or vague pricing strategies.

D Level

D-level business people have stooped to acting unethically, driven by unadulterated greed. The secondary result is that their clients are often harmed. It won't be hard here for us all to envision more than a few corporate giants that went out of business after their unethical business practices were exposed.

F Level

At the lowest level are those involved in organized crime, Ponzi schemes, Internet scams, and so forth. The work of the F level not only harms their customers, but society in general.

The grade levels, their drivers, and results are captured in this graphic:

Level	Primary Driver	Secondary Driver or Result
A	Making a Difference	Making a Living
B	Making a Living	Making a Difference
C	Love of Money	Indifferent to Customers
D	Greed – Acting Unethically	Harming Customers
F	Greed – Acting Illegally	Harming Society

In every profession we can find people at every level. We can all probably think of an A shopkeeper we know, and perhaps some D shop owners. How about A lawyers and D lawyers? Certainly there have been A politicians—think George Washington and Nelson Mandela—and D politicians.

Long-term, those in the A level are not only happier but also more successful. Yes, we admit there are C- or D-level business people who break the rules and appear to be prospering, but appearances can be deceiving and fleeting. Who do you think the majority of customers will naturally gravitate to over time? Who do you think most employees, bosses, and partners will want to work with long-term?

We once heard Warren Buffet give a lecture at the Harvard Business School. When Buffet, one of the world's richest men, was asked what he looked for in new employees or potential business partners, he said, "Integrity, intelligence, and a high degree of energy. But," he added, "if you don't have the first, the other two don't matter."

In *A Christmas Carol*, you'll recall that the ghost of Jacob Marley materializes in front of Scrooge, bound by the chains he forged through a life of self-centeredness and avarice. Scrooge countered that Marley had always been a good man of business. "Business!" cried Marley. "Mankind was my business. The common welfare was my business … The dealings of my trade were but a drop of water in the comprehensive ocean of my business!"

We could not have found more apt thoughts.

As we pursue our careers, our wish is that we all commit to deepening our understanding of our key motivators and start the journey toward putting our passions to work for not only our personal good, but also for the good of those around us—our customers, coworkers, employees, families, and communities.

Wherever your work takes you, may you be happy and successful, and may you strive to make the world a better place.

Indeed, let us make a good living, and let us all make a good life.

BOOK SUMMARY

What is the link between motivation and business results?

87 percent of the world's workers are either not fully engaged in their jobs or are actively disengaged. This is a global crisis that is not good for individuals, and it's certainly not good for managers or organizations.

When people are more motivated on the job they produce higher quality work and greater output, according to research from the University of California. They are also much more likely to be engaged, enabled, and energized, and to stay with their organizations longer, which reduces turnover.

As an individual, why is it important to know what motivates me?

Those who have found deeper meaning in their careers find their days much more energizing and satisfying, and count their employment as one of their greatest sources of joy and pride. Those most motivated at work also generally earn higher incomes and are 150 percent more likely to be happier with their lives overall.

Is this a personality test?

What Motivates Me offers an entirely new method for discovering how to understand our individual motivation and put our passions to work. This is not a test to determine personality type or strengths. The goals are to help everyone answer these questions: "What motivates me?" And then, "What can I do about it?" The book then offers a step-by-step process to craft a realistic plan for optimizing education, work, and personal goals that can provide more satisfying and meaningful work.

So what does motivate me?

Every human being is motivated by twenty-three fundamental workplace drivers. Our specific natures emerge as we understand which of these motivators are most important to us and also the order of priority. Every person differs enormously in what makes them happiest at work—for one challenge, excitement, and money may be paramount, but for another it may be working with a great team toward a purpose she believes in. The twenty-three motivators are:

Autonomy	Friendship	Problem Solving
Challenge	Fun	Purpose
Creativity	Impact	Recognition
Developing Others	Learning	Service
Empathy	Money	Social Responsibility
Excelling	Ownership	Teamwork
Excitement	Pressure	Variety
Family	Prestige	

Five clusters of commonly related motivators also appeared in the analysis. These archetypes were called identities, and are useful in helping teammates understand more about those they work with, as well as helping each of us begin to work on strategies to enhance our value as well as avoid blind spots in our work. The identities are Achievers, Builders, Caregivers, Reward-Driven, and Thinkers.

If I discover I'm passionate about something, what do I do about it? What if I can't change my role or my company?

In most cases finding greater happiness at work doesn't require a major career or job transition. The diagnostic process in this book is called "job sculpting," which helps people take charge of their careers and put their fingers on the specific things that are causing them dissatisfaction in their work. It also gives people positive language to discuss with their managers changes in job responsibilities that could create boons in productivity and commitment. The process works whether a person is mid- or later-career, just starting out in the working world, or even in college trying to determine a major.

If I'm a manager, why is it important to know what motivates my team members?

One of the best and simplest ways for leaders to help their team members be more successful and accomplish more is to have them understand their motivations and do just a little sculpting of the nature of their jobs or tasks to better match duties with passions. This can uncover subtle changes that can lead to big increases in morale, engagement, and results.

"If you don't know what your
passion is, realize that one
reason for your existence on
earth is to find it."

—*Oprah Winfrey*

TOOLKIT:
IDENTITY REFERENCE GUIDE

Identity Reference Guide

Characteristics; Where They Thrive;
60 Job Sculpting Strategies

What follows is a self-reference guide to understand and act on each of the five key identities. Included in each of the sections is a general overview of the identity, its common characteristics, and where the people within the identity tend to thrive in work situations. We hope readers will not only see themselves in a few of these profiles, but spot people they work with, as well. We've found the descriptions can be extremely helpful in understanding personalities you may be having difficulties with on the job, and determining ways you might work better with them. But most gratifying for us as researchers is to have people see themselves in these archetypes, then step back from the day-to-day of their work and spot underlying sources of conflict and dissatisfaction, and choose to work with their managers to make a few needed changes.

Most helpful, we believe, in each identity section is a list of job sculpting strategies organized into two parts. First come those ideas that might help you enhance your value to your organization and accomplish more in your career. Second are those concepts that will help you recognize common blind spots for the identity, address conflict points that can occur in working with others, and even identify some trade-offs you might have to make in your work life. For managers, many of these strategies can also be used to better lead and motivate the people in their care.

The strategies are culled from our experience working inside successful organizations for two decades and have been added to by our team of behavioral scientists. Please note that these ideas are not intended to be a feel-good, self-help guide, but are intended to push everyone to a heightened level of self-awareness and out of their comfort zones. Behind the concepts are a set of foundational beliefs about why the things most people try often fall flat, and what stands in the way of reaching dreams—often self-imposed doubts and fears. By working on just a few of these practical ideas, we've seen people begin to feel a greater sense of optimism and resiliency, which are fuel for movement in a positive direction.

We hope you find this Identity Reference Guide useful and filled with insights and illustrations that will help you understand more about yourself, but more importantly, assist you in diagnosing what might be making you less engaged than you could be in your work—and how you might go about fixing it.

THE ACHIEVERS

Challenge
Excelling
Ownership
Pressure
Problem Solving

WHO ARE THE ACHIEVERS?

The motivators clustered into this identity are:

- Challenge
- Excelling
- Ownership
- Pressure
- Problem Solving

Chances are we all know our share of Achievers. These go-getters often do well under pressure, enjoy rising to a challenge, and love to solve problems. Picture retired NBA commissioner David Stern as an example, a man who, according to some we've spoken with, was most energized when forced to resolve a thorny challenge that would leave most of us curled up in the fetal position—perhaps a public relations challenge involving a player.

One strong commonality among Achievers is that they set themselves lots of goals to strive for; it seems some times they live to hit their goals. And in the pursuit of a goal, Achievers can appear hell-bent not to let anything or anyone get in their way.

Achievers are valuable to any organization, primarily because so many are "attainment-oriented," which means they are motivated to finish tasks on time and to high standards, especially if there's what we call intrinsic-value or utility-value allocated to those assignments. In other words, Achievers usually must feel there's a sense of importance to attaining the sought-after results, importance that's imposed by the collective corporate culture, by themselves, or by an overall sense that the task is useful.

Researchers from Coventry University in England found people who do *not* show achievement tendencies tend to more often work within comfort zones, relying on others to set deadlines and standards, and can habitually need to catch up on missed work; while Achievers on the other hand are more apt to set higher standards for themselves and those around them and are constantly on the look out for new and better ways to improve their performance. That's all good stuff.

Microsoft founder Bill Gates is an example of someone who was driven to achieve from a young age, even valuing achievement over the praise and prestige of the world. After all, he did drop out of Harvard two semesters shy of receiving his degree. When he told his parents about his decision, they were supportive. Why? They knew their son: he had been achievement-oriented from the time he was a pimply teen who formed the Lakeside Programmers Group, a team of kids barely old enough to drive who were writing computer code for some of the largest businesses in the Pacific Northwest. Mom and Dad knew their son's goal was to start his own company, and they agreed his idea was time-sensitive and that he had the drive to excel at it.

This is not to say that all Achievers feel the need to buck the corporate system and start their own enterprises, or that they care nothing for prestige or the stamp of approval of others. We are simply stressing that goal attainment and getting things done are overridingly important to most in this identity, and usually it's within a structured organization. Achievers are action-oriented and determined, customarily they are pressure- and challenge-driven, and often they want to be in control. They also tend to be high-energy people who are disciplined and focused.

The Characteristics

- **They love a good challenge.** Achievers typically crave the feeling of accomplishment that comes from solving a problem—whether at work or elsewhere in their lives. They accept that problems will arise in the pursuit of their goals, and they tend not to be especially frustrated as they work through them, keeping their eyes on the prize. In fact, they tend to see problems as opportunities, welcoming the challenges that break up the doldrums and give them a rush.
- **They are driven to excel.** Being in the top group of performers when compared with peers is important to those in this identity, as well as surpassing their own past performances. They thrive when expectations are raised regularly.
- **They thrive under pressure.** Rather than avoiding high-pressure goals and situations, they usually look for them. They are not people who "choke" when things get intense; instead, they often do better and rise to the challenge.

- **Completing tasks is crucial.** Achievers want to get a lot of things done every day, and they tend to love to cross things off their lists.
- **They feel guilty if they aren't giving their all.** If they aren't going the extra mile, Achievers typically don't feel right about things. They don't thrive during periods in which they can coast at work.
- **They are accountable.** Those in this identity often feel a heightened sense of personal ownership for their decisions and actions—which means they own up to their mistakes as well as their successes. They'd much rather step up and take the hit for a failure than let someone take the blame for them.
- **They want to be in control.** Achievers usually want to be the one calling the shots. They more often like to take responsibility for setting the course, preferring to lead rather than follow.
- **They believe in their own talents.** Achievers usually are confident about their abilities, and they tend not to need much coaching or handholding. They don't typically need to have others tell them what they are good at.
- **They set ambitious goals.** Whether they write them down or not, Achievers regularly set short- and long-term goals for themselves and have a plan to reach them.
- **They take deadlines seriously.** Many Achievers can't remember the last time they missed a deadline.

THE ACHIEVERS

Much more than a suggestion, deadlines are almost a sacred promise to these Achievers. They will move heaven and earth to get things done on time.

- **They are willing to take a few risks.** Risk-taking may not be a primary trait of Achievers—that's more of a pure Thinker characteristic—but most are not averse to "pushing the envelope" if they're convinced it will produce results. However, they will tend to carefully assess potential rewards before they leap.

- **They don't wallow.** Like anyone, Achievers are prone to become negative when things aren't going well, and may vent about how lousy a situation is. But a distinguishing feature is that they usually won't drop anchor in that negative place and allow the emotion to feed on itself for very long. Instead, most will recognize that whatever caused the pain (a business or personal problem or failure) is something to learn from and they move on.

Where Achievers Thrive

Those driven by Achievement are happiest and most successful working in organizations or on teams that are meritocracies—environments that value individuals based on their performances and contributions more than tenure or title. Workplaces where people are all treated the same, regardless of performance, can be frustrating to Achievers.

In the best roles for those in this identity, results matter more than effort, interpersonal relationships, or political games. That's not to say being kind and respectful to others, as well as being savvy about office politics, won't be important in Achievers' careers, it's just that when tangible outcomes are the most important arbiter of success they will tend to thrive.

Achievers who are unhappy with their work should think about ways in which they may be held back from the sources of satisfaction we've listed in the characteristics above, and also about ways in which their strong need to achieve may be causing clashes with colleagues or their boss. A few sources of friction to note: Achievers can sometimes get on colleagues' nerves as their desire to be in charge can lead them to assert control where they don't really have the authority. Some Achievers can also have a tendency to bite off more than they can chew, not quite seeing the dividing line between stretch-but-not-break goals and the simply undoable, which few bosses are enamored of. And their natural confidence can be perceived as arrogance. They must be careful about these pitfalls.

Achievers tend to be happiest working with colleagues who either are also Achievers or Reward-Driven, or those Caregivers, Builders, or Thinkers who don't misinterpret their drive and competitive spirit. Their best bosses will find ways to keep the Achievers chalking up successes.

To consider an Achiever, take the case of Joy, a designer we met in Arizona, who loved her job of drafting luxury kitchen and bath remodels for high-end homes. She took extra time to get to know her clients' likes and dislikes, painstakingly walked through their properties with them, and found great satisfaction when her designs were chosen over others—which they often were. But she was feeling increasingly disengaged on the job and couldn't figure out why. She took The Motivator's Assessment and discovered that she was a close fit with the Achiever identity. This helped her see that her job was allowing her to do the problem-solving she so loved, while the competition to win clients gave her a healthy amount of challenge and pressure, not to mention satisfied her need to excel. But she realized her very strong desire for "ownership" was not being fulfilled.

No matter how much effort she invested, how many deals she won, or how her reputation grew, she was not in control of her own destiny at work. She was an hourly employee. She approached her employer about sculpting her job to meet her need to "own." She even had a specific plan, asking if she could take on additional responsibilities and perhaps even a supervisory role. The company brass was unwilling to budge. She was firmly told that only family members were managers in that firm, and that's the way it would always be.

She considered starting her own kitchen and bath design company, but when a competing remodeling firm heard Joy was unhappy, it didn't take long for the savvy general manager to make this exceptional woman an offer—one that added supervision of two other designers and a bonus tied to her team's win percentage. She still does kitchen and bath designs herself, but today she influences three designers' pens, not just one. She didn't need to become a small business owner; she found satisfaction within the walls of an established business—but one that was a lot smarter about considering her motivators. And by the way, the firm Joy joined is growing like gangbusters.

THE ACHIEVERS

THE ACHIEVERS

SCULPTING STRATEGIES FOR THE ACHIEVERS
How to Enhance Your Value and Accomplish More

Make every assignment a challenge. A unique ability cultivated by some talented Achievers we've studied is to look at each big project not only as getting things done but also as an opportunity to expand their skill set. That means they do more than the minimum required: researching industry trends relating to their assignments; talking with colleagues inside and outside the organization for best practices; and taking the time to dream up innovative ideas that might help their projects. When evaluating those ideas, they'll look in terms of the potential value that could be generated for the organization—the return on the investment of time or resources—then cull the list down to one or two that have the most potential to help them personally excel as well as have a meaningful organizational impact. The bottom line: the amount and quality of work an Achiever contributes to the organization will most likely be valued; but even if it's not, take our word for it—Achievers intrinsically feel better about themselves when they give their all.

Keep score. Many highly fulfilled Achievers realized at some point in their careers that part of pushing themselves included measuring and reporting on a regular basis. It didn't really matter whether they worked in a fast-paced environment or one that was *laissez-faire*, they knew they needed to keep score and hold themselves accountable for hitting goals. That meant establishing performance benchmarks, and not being afraid to share those goals and their progress with teammates and, gulp, even the boss. The best benchmarks are ones that make people stretch but are not unrealistic (keeping them from getting discouraged), they are goals that can be measured without the need to wait for a third-party to give numbers: I will keep my daily development meetings to no more than fifteen minutes, or I will shave thirty minutes from my personal production time by September 1. When Achievers focus on measuring their own progress, they will always know where they stand. But remember, we get what we measure—so we recommend individuals take the time to ensure they are measuring and reporting on the right things—those that are valued by the organization or clients. A good way to ensure measurements are on target is to keep in mind the acronym: SMARTER. Goals should be specific, measurable, attainable, relevant, and timely; but also regularly evaluated and revised as needed. SMARTER goals need all seven qualities to be effective. And to be sure they are moving forward, we recommend Achievers keep a log of achievements that's updated as often as daily.

Recall early ambitions. One idea we suggest to frustrated Achievers is to take a few minutes to recall their first day at work in their current positions, then ask themselves these two questions: What did I hope to accomplish by working here? What goals did I have professionally for this job? We then recommend they write down those remembered ambitions and assess if they have changed at all or if they've been reached or abandoned. If they are still viable goals but haven't been attained, it's time to set a course to go after the highest priority items. It's never too late to achieve those early aspirations.

Keep nonessential tasks moving. Since many Achievers are driven to reach lofty goals, it can be easy for them to let non-urgent or development activities slip week-to-week. Time coach Elizabeth Grace Saunders suggests achievement-oriented individuals plan "acceptable minimums" into their calendars for fringe activities. In other words, decide on the minimum amount of time that should be spent on nonessential goals or projects each week. For example, perhaps an Achiever is charged with a website redesign but it's become a low priority.

Also let's say she wants to continue developing her skill set and expanding her expertise despite a crazy-busy schedule. She might plan to spend at least two hours a week on the website project and one hour a week reading about trends in her industry, and she'll make these blocks of time recurring events on her calendar. Ideally these blocks will fall early in the day and early in the week so they won't fall off. "Although an hour or two may seem like too short a time to make real progress, it's amazing at how much can get done when time is invested consistently in these areas," says Saunders.

Do some influence expanding. Once upon a time companies could move high achievers from job to job to keep them challenged and groom them for larger responsibilities. That's not nearly as viable an option today due to downsizing, cost cutting, and the need for job specialization; and in small firms those opportunities never existed and probably never will. Organizations that are growing, developing new products, opening additional markets, or acquiring other business may offer Achievers more opportunities to be involved in cool new projects and ventures. But even if an organization is less dynamic and more mature, there are still ways for Achievers to flourish. They can volunteer to head up a project that's over their head, one where they know they'll have to grow, solve complex problems, and meet tough deadlines to have any hope of success. Or they can seek out chances to serve on multidisciplinary teams, task forces, or committees. For instance, an assignment to a team evaluating customer service improvements could help improve their research, presentation, and leadership abilities. Another option for Achievers looking for a challenge is to volunteer for assignments outside the organization. "On loan" executives or volunteer board members can support a charity, gaining valuable experience not available in their work environment, while also helping strengthen their company's relationship with the community. We find Achievers are usually the most motivated when they are expanding their sphere of influence, so they should identify where their skills need improvement and then seek out every training and educational opportunity offered by their organizations—or opportunities they can find on their own. The most successful, happy Achievers do more and accomplish more throughout their careers, and that means along the way they recognize the need to fill skill gaps and constantly enrich their abilities to reach lofty goals. As a starting point, we recommend they set up meetings with people they admire, either within their company or outside, to learn how those people invested in learning their trade. We also suggest they visit with human resources and their corporate training departments to find opportunities they may have missed at work. And finally, they shouldn't forget the free options. For instance, we met many who asked mentors or bosses to tutor them every week in specific skills—such as budgeting or cold calling.

Get a good coach. Even high-achieving sports superstars like Tiger Woods or Gabby Douglas need coaches. Every great Achiever needs to be pushed to find what he or she is truly capable of, which means Achievers need someone to instruct, guide, and push them. Achievers should choose a mentor, whether it's their boss, a senior colleague on their team, or someone else in the organization or even someone outside work, like a family member. They need to ensure that there's trust in the relationship, the mentor has sufficient time to invest, and there's good chemistry. Then, week by week, the Achiever should ask the coach to help her understand what success looks like, honestly assessing strengths and weaknesses, and assisting in defining the next steps in the person's career progression. The pace at which Achievers work is often supersonic, so it's important they and their coach get their aim right, and then adjust as needed.

How to Address Blind Spots and Potential Conflicts

Learn to achieve with respect. Achievement-oriented people who are most successful long-term develop a heightened sense of respect. David DiSalvo explains in *Forbes*, "The intersection between drive and respect is an important one, because we all know people who are highly driven but think nothing of running others over along the way." So while many Achievers are habitually tenacious, not allowing challenges to stop them because they've trained their thinking to immediately seek out other ways of reaching a goal, DiSalvo says respectful Achievers always keep the well-being of others in mind. If one of those alternate routes will harm someone, then that route isn't an option, period. In line with this, it is also critical that Achievers show respect to others by learning to express their plans clearly and well in advance of an undertaking—getting buy-in and help. After all, some Achievers can have a tendency to go into Tasmanian-devil mode all by themselves and be hard to steer or stop once they get rolling.

Balance with softer skills. Endeavoring to achieve is not by its nature unhealthy behavior; but it can become so when a need to achieve and control one's environment drown out a person's other dominant identities. That's called perfectionism; and there is no such thing as healthy perfectionism. Now it's relatively easy to peg the perfectionists: they strive unhealthily with most activities in life, pushing themselves to excel because they won't allow any other outcome. They are the people who are hard to feel comfortable around because they seek almost constant approbation, and yet never seem satisfied with the reinforcement they receive. Achievers must carefully avoid crossing over the line between a healthy striving for excellence and clinical perfectionism. Clinical psychologist David D. Burns from the University of Pennsylvania has examined business executives, lawyers, high-level athletes, and other Achievers. He concludes that perfectionistic strivings tend to actually hamper success, and that the most successful people stop short of perfectionism because, in part, self-punishment is an ineffective learning tool. Of course, we are not suggesting all Achievers are doomed to a miserable existence. Hardly. Pursuing goals with fearless abandon can be highly rewarding. Chances are we all know high Achievers who maintain healthy stress levels and have rich social and family lives if—it's a big if—they balance their need to achieve with their softer side.

THE ACHIEVERS

Slow down and polish skills. During the early phases of an Achiever's time in a new job he is most likely growing rapidly, challenged by interesting new assignments, turning heads with his determined nature, and as a result highly satisfied and engaged at work. But if the job doesn't change much after a year or two, his engagement can start to wane, along with his satisfaction. The too-frequent consequence is the Achiever starts looking for another job. Many high Achievers practice unnecessary job rotation between companies. And the hard truth is this: prospective employers looking at a candidate who has been in numerous positions in various organizations, no matter how attractive their CV or resume is, will worry that their team will be just another pit stop. Most Achievers need to slow down and take the time to polish their skills, gain experience, and go beyond a superficial understanding of the work they do to gain a deeper knowledge and expertise of their craft. The reasons to change jobs should always be long-term career focused—helping learn a valuable new skill set, substantially increasing responsibilities, or the chance to tackle a big new challenge. Switching jobs is an important life decision, so we recommend the decision be made carefully. Long before bolting, Achievers should look at some of the strategies we've outlined earlier in the "How to Enhance Your Value and Accomplish

More" section and see if they can make their current roles more rewarding.

Realize others won't be perfect. Some Achievers admit to us that they can be demanding with teammates and tend to have a low tolerance for mistakes. Some also fall into a habit of valuing people based primarily on their perceived utilitarian criteria, such as whether or not those individuals accomplish something that *they* believe to be of worth. The point is: unless it's going to cost a life or a lot of money, Achievers with these tendencies probably need to learn to loosen up a bit, give in now and then, and accept that people around them bring varying levels of skills. It will reduce their stress levels and build a stronger team if they stop expecting others to be perfect.

Learn patience regarding career development. Most Achievers we have spoken with acknowledge they need to foster greater patience regarding their career development. It's not unusual for highly driven individuals to get frustrated when raises and advancements don't come on their timetables. Remember that increased responsibility looks just about as good as a promotion in today's economic climate. Achievers will do well to polish up their resumes and internal credibility with increasingly challenging assignments and some notable and cool accomplishments. Achievers—like everyone else—will do well to stop and smell the roses, to live in the moment. They will be happier if they appreciate how far they've come and celebrate their successes—and quit fixating so much on the next step up the ladder. Our advice: take a deep breath and enjoy the journey.

THE BUILDERS

Developing Others
Friendship
Purpose
Service
Social Responsibility
Teamwork

WHO ARE THE BUILDERS?

The motivators that form this identity are:

- Developing Others
- Friendship
- Purpose
- Service
- Social Responsibility
- Teamwork

Builders tend to be ideal-oriented and have a strong desire to be part of something bigger them themselves—aligning with a greater vision. The inspiring math teacher portrayed by Edward James Olmos in *Stand and Deliver* is exemplary of this archetype.

Over the years we've had the opportunity to observe many Builders, and they can be extremely valuable members of any work team. They often serve as the glue that keeps a team running; they focus on serving and developing others, and are usually driven by furthering the larger purpose of the group versus their own agenda. Most Builders tend to measure success not by their paychecks, but by the impact they are having on the world around them. They are also often committed to leaders of causes and devote themselves to noble missions.

Doing work that has a valuable purpose is a strong desire of many people. A poll conducted by Rutgers University for Net Impact showed that a majority of North American workers say that having a job that aligns with values they believe in is more important to them than having a prestigious career, wealth, or a powerful position—even more important than having children! As for college students polled, 45 percent say they would take a job that paid significantly less if it were with "an organization whose values are like my own." For Builders, this desire is central to their motivation and their sense of self.

Those in this identity tend to make good leaders because, contrary to the popular notion that high-impact managers tend to have huge intellects, egos verging on narcissism, and demanding personalities, studies show that workers achieve much more for leaders who are concerned with their employees' development and well-being. The best leaders articulate a clear purpose, and show authentic interest in their people and their goals; and that's a classic Builder for you.

THE BUILDERS

The Characteristics

- **They want to see others grow.** Builders tend to consider it their personal responsibility to do whatever is in their power to nurture the professional development of their employees and coworkers. They might demonstrate that through: offering ongoing training; taking a personal interest in both the life and work issues of those on their team; avidly promoting ideas and suggestions of colleagues and direct reports; or encouraging everyone's involvement in decision-making and brainstorming. Some of the best Builder leaders we've observed have career conversations with their employees monthly or even as often as weekly, helping ensure their people are getting the right assignments, training, and coaching they need to succeed and grow.

- **They believe everyone is a leader.** Herb Kelleher, former CEO of Southwest Airlines, was a clear Builder. He believed that flight attendants were the most important leaders in the company because they had the biggest impact on the customer experience. Like Kelleher, Builders tend to believe workers at all levels have something important to contribute to the mission of the organization.

- **They've felt a sense of destiny.** Many in this identity say they have believed since they were young that they were supposed to do something important with their

THE BUILDERS

lives, mostly in helping lift others; call it a personal mission if you will. Perhaps they didn't set out to be the next Mother Teresa, but they wanted to do something that positively affects the lives of those around them.

- **They want to be surrounded by a passionate team.** It's a hope of most Builders to be aligned with other mission-driven people, and as such, they feel that they and their colleagues collectively can do great things. One of their biggest fears is to be put in a group of clock-punchers—those who seem to have had their passion sucked dry. A bigger fear is to become one of those people themselves.

- **They are loyal friends.** Builders typically enjoy building deep relationships—whether with their customers and coworkers, or friends outside of work—and they customarily feel a strong sense of responsibility to those they care about.

- **Doing good is more important than making bank.** Don't get us wrong, money is still important to many in this identity; they've got to pay the rent, don't they? But for most, wealth doesn't mean as much as working with a team they trust, directed toward a purpose they believe in. So when they do go asking for a little more money, leaders should understand Builders wouldn't ask unless they really needed it. Money means subsistence to most in this identity, not status.

- **They have good people skills.** Builders typically have a heightened ability to get along well with others, especially those who share similar beliefs. This doesn't mean they are necessarily pushovers; they can be outspoken and assertive, but they usually try hard to make relationships positive and often take the position of "wingmen" who inspire and back-up others.

Where Builders Thrive

Builders are characteristically happiest and most successful working in organizations where they see and can contribute to a clear greater purpose. This doesn't mean they need to work in social services, teaching, or the nonprofit sector, though some are drawn to this terrain. No, Builders can bring a greatly energizing sense of meaning to work in corporate settings, too.

Managing people often brings out the best in Builders, and can provide them with a sense of purpose many crave. In our experience with a wide range of companies in numerous industries, many of the most admired supervisors, managers, and executives are often in this identity.

Builders tend to thrive in cultures where team members are encouraged to contribute to the mission, and where everyone is considered important to the success of the enterprise. On the flipside, Builders will be increasingly unhappy if they're in a job or culture where the bottom line seems to be the overwhelming focus, or where people are not encouraged to help each other out with projects and problems, or where workers are actually meant to compete with one another. Putting in time in such an environment can become drudgery or, more likely, a stress if they are not careful.

One fascinating Builder we met is Nancy Aldritt.

After college, Aldritt was about to put in an application to serve in the Peace Corps, a step toward a long-anticipated career in economic development in the third world. To save up for this career, rich in intrinsic rewards but humble in pay, she took a temporary position at a bank supporting an officer in the trust department.

That was fourteen years ago.

Today, Aldritt is vice president and senior trust and fiduciary specialist with Wells Fargo Private Bank in Walnut Creek, California.

While she says banking at first was a stepping-stone to what she thought would be more meaningful work, she was touched by how the trust group helped families through difficult transitions such as the loss of a spouse or parent, or the onset of age-related dementia. She grew to think of the job as a sacred trust to protect and grow families' assets.

And that meant she was flirting with a new idea: a career in trust as a fiduciary. Her biggest worry? That she'd be selling out.

"I thought I had to be compensated on the lines of a social worker to do meaningful work. But after a lot of discussions with people who have more wisdom than I do, the idea crystalized over the months that in trust and fiduciary work I'd be helping families create a legacy that will live on well after they are gone," she says.

Aldritt also satisfies her Builder motivations by doing volunteer work in her community. She's active with at-risk youth groups and has volunteered with a nonprofit that supports women-owned start-up businesses. "I didn't need to go to South America or Africa," she tells us. "When we fully live what we are doing every day and do it with a gracious heart, that's when we touch lives around us."

Aldritt is a terrific example of how smart Builders can find work anywhere that fulfills their drive to serve, but can also find a great sense of fulfillment working with purpose-driven commitments outside the office.

THE BUILDERS

SCULPTING STRATEGIES FOR THE BUILDERS
How to Enhance Your Value and Accomplish More

Think confidently; start small. In order to make a difference in the world, Builders must first have the confidence that they *can* actually make a difference—wherever they are, whatever they do for a living. The fact is we all have unique, God-given abilities and talents that others around us don't, and making a difference starts in earnest when a Builder has the confidence to believe he or she has something important to offer the world: perhaps an ability to connect with others, maybe an aptitude to organize or lead or fix things or train. Now while many within this identity tell us they'd love to be involved in a big sweeping cause, most of the happiest Builders have to come to learn that they can have the greatest influence by affecting just a few people in a deeper way (recall the story of inner-city teacher Jimmy Casas from Chapter 1). We recommend Builders start small by putting their full energies into serving those in their close circle at work and by sincerely impacting the clients they serve. Even if Builders don't feel they are part of an organization with a particularly inspiring purpose, they can absolutely still make their work more meaningful.

THE BUILDERS

It starts when they ask themselves a series of deceptively simple questions: Who needs my help right now, and how exactly can I support them in reaching their goals? Do I have knowledge that someone new to the team could benefit from? Could something I've learned about the way things work here help my customers navigate their way to success? Is there any how-to knowledge I can pass along to someone else on the team?

Consider the *why*. Introspective Builders—those who already know what they love to do and why they love it—should consider themselves fortunate. But there are many with Builder tendencies who not only struggle to find meaning in their work, but even have a hard time explaining what is really driving them to serve or develop others. Why are they wired the way they are? Here's what we ask when helping Builders probe into their treasured hopes for their work lives: "Why does serving people or developing others matter to you?" We might have to lead them a bit with: "Is it to help others, be part of something bigger than yourself, for fame and fortune, because a great leader inspired you, to fulfill a need sparked in childhood, or another reason?" Then we follow up with a ton of why and what questions: "Okay, but why did that leader inspire you?" or "If you could fast forward a few years to make your job really rewarding, what do you think would be rewarding about it?" The better Builders understand their driving motives, the better able they are to define a clearer path in life.

Help build a strong team culture. Unless Builders are part of senior management, they probably don't have the sweeping power to influence an entire organizational culture directly for the better. But most people can improve their immediate team environment, and everyone can enhance their own sense of purpose at work. Anything done to improve a work environment for themselves or others will have a positive effect for Builders. Some of the happiest in this identity helped create a sense of community on their teams and worked to connect everyone with bigger goals. What does this look like? Builders we've interviewed have put together ways for teammates—even those on the fringes—to get together inside and outside normal work settings like group lunches, after-work activities, even events like a once-a-month bowling outing. Builders can be the catalysts to ensure bonding activities happen.

Inspire the uninspired. Builders who are in leadership roles often complain of frustrations that the people who work with or for them don't share their level of passion for their projects or company or clients. As you might imagine,

THE BUILDERS

we believe a vital first step to improving the engagement of others happens when a leader gets to know what motivates each individual on their team and then helps them align their work with their motivators. Another way is to care about people on a personal level, sitting down at their desk or work site and asking about their hobbies, family, background—basically caring about what they care about. Another important way Builder leaders we've studied inspire others is by pitching in with the least-favorite tasks of their coworkers or employees, rolling up their sleeves and helping when things get tough. They can aim their efforts to get others to connect more to the organization on a deeper level—understanding the why of their work—so they'll want to see the enterprise succeed, too. And finally, one of the most powerful ways to inspire engagement is by trusting people to do great things, or put another way: empowering them. The best Builders encourage others not by giving directions and micromanaging but by leading versus doing— believing that the people around them will figure out the right things to do at the right time. It may not be according to what the leaders were expecting, but it may be something terrific they hadn't thought of before.

Have a plan. It might sound obvious to start here, but the most successful Builders accomplish big things because they write down good, clear, and inspiring plans—and that's rare. It's amazing how real results start happening only after people put a road map down on paper. Customer satisfaction goals, new products launched, clients to be served; all result from a clear plan that people can follow.

Write a rally cry. A fun idea for those wanting to make a greater difference at work is to help their teams develop a clear and inspiring rally cry—the team's reason for being, the high-level, overarching idea about why it exists. Inevitably when we interview teams about "*why* they do what they do" we get as many different answers as there are people on the team. The best rally cries we've heard—those that are the most motivating—have little to do with shareholders or bosses, but are instead focused on how the team makes their part of the world a better place. For instance, at Zappos, the online shoe retailer, the rally cry is: "Powered by Service." Another great example: Employees of a very productive benefits department told us they weren't there to ensure forms were filled out properly or claims processed, but so that employees who got sick had someone to care about them and make sure they got better. Now, that's a cause that any benefits professional could get behind. Every person on every team should be able to explain in passionate language why they drag themselves out of bed every day and go to work—and how their specific team

THE BUILDERS

and their individual effort contribute to the success of the larger organization.

Network with other Builders. When speaking with individuals with other strong identities, we often recommend they broaden their perspectives and counsel with people different than them. Not so much with the Builders. We actually recommend they find a group of like-minded friends who they can meet with now and then, people who believe in them and their big dreams, people who inspire them and have similar big ideas. Builders need to have a support system that will make it easier to stay on track and chase their dreams. After all, it can be possible for people with grand ideals, like the Builders, to get discouraged by the challenges and apathy they may face day-to-day. The last thing they need around them are individuals who are pessimistic or hopeless. That's why we recommend they put together a group of fellow Builders who can regularly brainstorm, dream, and support each other. Of course, we tell them not to expect support without giving it, which means actively helping and encouraging those around them to chase their dreams, too. P.S. This also means Builders should stop being friends with any *internal* negativity. The word "decide" comes from the Latin *decidere*, which means, "to cut off." So, we advise them, decide to be positive and cut out the negative self-talk.

Pinpoint specific passions. To connect a Builder's talents to fulfill a greater purpose in the world, we recommend they take the time to pinpoint the specific issues they care most about, which groups of people they have the most compassion for, what changes in society or business they most wish to see. Only when they have identified the root causes that get them passionate, can they begin to research the changes to their current work tasks that might bring the greatest fulfillment. We usually see Builders most motivated and proud of their work when they are able to champion a few issues they innately care about in their day-to-day tasks.

Develop hard soft-skills. The best Builders who are leaders of people are highly committed to the growth and development of those in their care, which is actually a hard, not a soft skill. This means leaders must take the *real, practical* steps that will lead to development in their employees. As just one example, we've seen Builder leaders who are very good at putting their people in positions to shine in front of management and influential customer groups. Other great leaders we've observed regularly meet with their people to understand their career development goals and needs, assign them tangible tasks that will push them to learn new skills, and give them cross-training and educational opportunities

THE BUILDERS

to grow—even if that means these employees might leave the nest one day. When one senior leader once questioned the importance of developing his people, worrying that these individuals would just fly the coop after they were trained and given opportunities to grow, a fellow manager quipped, "What if we *don't* develop them and they stay?" While some Builders are good at the soft side of encouraging—cheerleading and being supportive—they must also learn to do the hard work of helping their people shine and grow. This is what sets transformational leaders apart from the transactional.

Market positively. While a few of the Achievers and Reward-Driven may be, ahem, perhaps a wee bit guilty of exaggerating their positive traits and accomplishments, Builders can sometimes have the opposite problem. Due perhaps to their chemistry, many people in this identity seem to give such an honest, unbiased, and sometimes underwhelming assessment of their skills or accomplishments that they can receive average or even poor reviews from bosses at raise time or those bosses who are looking to promote someone. A way to improve their prospects is for Builders to think about themselves as a commodity for sale and answer the following questions: What problem do I overcome for my employer? What is my personal mission and what

THE BUILDERS

are my values? What are my strongest qualities? What makes me unique? What challenges have I faced and how specifically did I address them? To help market themselves better, we encourage Builders to take stock of their accomplishments on at least a weekly basis by writing them down—from the seemingly trivial to major achievements. Some Builders accomplish a lot more than they give themselves credit for. Their journal of rich achievements will serve as a resume builder and remind them to take little bows now and then since they are probably due. The increased sense of meaning they can gain might be significant. Finally, we recommend another set of introspective questions to bring perspective to their value: Who benefits right now from what I am doing? How are things better because of what I do day-to-day? How does what I do affect positively what the larger organization or team does? Who is more productive because of what I do? What clients or other employees benefit indirectly from my work? The more Builders focus on how their work affects others, the more they realize their true worth, but also the more they will recognize opportunities for growth. Focusing on the individuals they work with will usually get them talking in a strong and energetic manner.

THE BUILDERS

How to Address Blind Spots and Potential Conflicts

Exert tough love when needed. Like a parent-child relationship in which the parent bails the child out of trouble by fixing problems or doing the late homework, when Builders on the team step in to take care of issues that arise, some other employees can actually be tempted to sit back and put in less effort, produce poorer quality, serve fewer customers, or put less thought into resolving issues or conflicts themselves. We aren't suggesting wonderfully service- and team-oriented Builders shouldn't come to the rescue when needed, but if they find themselves doing it over and over again for the same people, it's time to exert tough love and say no—at the very least requiring those they are constantly helping to step up and come up with solutions to the problems themselves.

Avoid whiners. We all know who they are: there's typically a group of people who complain about everything at the office, they are the whiners. If the boss pulls out her wallet and starts handing out twenty-dollar bills, this group will later moan that they weren't fifties. While it may seem counterintuitive for seemingly high-minded Builders, they can find themselves in this petulant lot. Why, when they can be so naturally full of purpose and high ideals? Actually, it's because of that. Builders often

THE BUILDERS

have a lofty set of standards, and they expect others to live up to those principles. When leaders or coworkers disappoint, it can lead to disillusionment and discontent for those in this identity. But complaining with no solution is a toxic habit for Builders (it's not very healthy for the other identities either). Sometimes making a positive difference at work is simply a matter of how a person chooses to think. We tell Builders to look for ways to be authentically positive; for instance, publicly acknowledging a coworker's accomplishment on completing a project. And even if it doesn't help change the office environment, we remind them they can always do this at home: telling their significant others or kids why they are inspiring, always using specific language not vague platitudes.

Try to bring purpose before jumping ship. Some purpose-driven Builders, in seeking to reach a level of fulfillment in life, will leave their jobs or turn from secure pathways to "find" themselves. Over the years it seems we have advised a whole stadium-full of bright-eyed people such as this to not forget to keep the lights on at home. Before leaving for pastures that may or may not be greener, and giving up their known world in the process, we always recommend trying to bring purpose to a current role first. Builders should take a long look at their current jobs and ask if they can sculpt things where they are. Next, we push them to understand exactly what difference they could make or would want to make in their current roles. And better yet, we suggest that they bring others into the exploration and have regular conversations about their career goals with their manager, peers, family members, mentors, or other leaders whose opinions they value. For those unfortunates who still do not feel they are able to build at work, all is not lost. There's always the opportunity to put extra time and energy into a nonprofit or school that is making a difference and needs their drive and talents.

THE BUILDERS

THE CAREGIVERS

Empathy
Family
Fun

WHO ARE THE CAREGIVERS

The key motivators associated with this identity are:

- Empathy
- Family
- Fun

Caregivers are often people-people—those who prefer working with others and bonding to working independently, those who enjoy being light-hearted on the job. Some in this identity are the life of the party, while others admit to us that it's not unusual for them to miss a deadline or be late to a meeting because they've been caught up in a conversation.

Caregivers typically prefer group activities when getting things done at work. And they often wonder why everyone in the group can't get along and have each other's backs. Many Caregivers can sit anywhere in the cafeteria and strike up a conversation, and usually a handful of people tend to stop to chat with them at their desks during the course of the day. Caregivers also tend to have rich lives outside of the office, spending plenty of time with family.

This group of people can not only be great with customers but also important to building team morale, in part by helping keep things light and often by breaking the tension in a room. They can also enhance collaboration and appreciation among team members.

To picture a Caregiver, think about Oprah Winfrey. Why

was her talk show successful for so many years while hundreds of other daytime shows came and went? The main reason was the compassion and vulnerability of the host.

Winfrey wasn't particularly hilarious like Ellen DeGeneres—though she does like to have fun and displayed a quick wit. She wasn't known as a hard-nosed interviewer like Larry King. She didn't offer advice to keep people alive longer like Dr. Oz. Instead, what drew six million viewers a day was a genuineness and empathy that are rare. She seemed to sincerely enjoy getting to know her guests and learning about their worlds. Her discussions were always two-way—she let down her shield, opening up herself about past abuses and struggles. And she kept things informative and lighthearted at the same time, proving television didn't need to be focused on the negative to bring in viewers. The magic of her show was that Oprah Winfrey wasn't just doing her job; she was enjoying herself in every episode.

That's a Caregiver at work.

The Characteristics

- **They can relate.** Caregivers endeavor to empathize with others—whether coworkers, customers, patients, or employees. They tend to assume good intentions in others and to accept and appreciate each person's special talents. Even when they are forced to be critical of certain behaviors or the performance of others, they are still sensitive to and accepting of the person.

THE CAREGIVERS

- **They are natural communicators.** Many Caregivers have strong communication skills—not only can they be good conversationalists, but also active listeners. They tend to bring an engaging level of attentiveness to the people-side of their work, asking good questions and listening attentively to the answers. They also often read people well and are attentive to what others are saying, thinking, and feeling.

- **They are dependable.** Caregivers tend to feel a strong sense of duty to teammates and others in their lives, and work hard to keep commitments. They are also typically respectful of confidences. Others tend to see them as trustworthy and full of integrity, a self-image that is extremely important to many in this identity.

- **They respect others.** Caregivers will tend to treat the office assistant the same as the CEO, the school janitor the same as their daughter's principal. That means they are usually courteous and kind, and rarely butt in when someone is speaking. In fact, they like to encourage all colleagues to speak up (especially the quiet ones), and they rarely nitpick or belittle. If they do point out a flaw, they try to do so with sensitivity and are often doing so in a sincere attempt to help the person make an improvement.

- **They try to balance.** It's not uncommon to see pictures of kids, siblings, nieces and nephews, parents, or grandkids on the desks of Caregivers (or in their vehicles, smart phones, wallets, or purses if they don't have a desk). They tend to leave work on time to be with those they love; and in order to be able to do so, the most efficient will pack a twelve-hour day into eight hours.

- **They are genuine.** Most Caregivers show a sincere interest in those around them and are willing to be vulnerable in sharing their personal highs and lows in hopes that others will learn from them. They display more warmth, friendliness, and candidness than many people, which can help customers and coworkers open up to them. And, a hint: if you are selling to a Caregiver, they usually want to develop a deeper personal connection with you before they'll buy.

- **They are positive.** One reason so many people are drawn to Caregivers is that they tend to have positive dispositions. Even when faced with challenges, they try not to get uptight or take their tension out on others. And they are frequently the ones insisting that teammates be celebrated when the big challenges are overcome or project milestones reached.

- **They are lighthearted.** Caregivers generally seem to be enjoying themselves at work, and often seize on opportunities to cheer others up. Many we interviewed displayed a delightful, playful, and often humorous

THE CAREGIVERS

approach to their interactions with clients and other employees.

- **They don't want to be in charge.** Not always, but in most cases Caregivers are not looking to be in control or in charge of work situations. This doesn't mean they can't make good managers; they can with the right training and mentorship. And even if they aren't managers, they are usually good to include in hiring decisions, as they are better than most at perceiving who will be good team players.

Where Caregivers Thrive

Caregivers are typically happiest and most successful working in environments that encourage people to care for each other and their customers, places that encourage some friendly and playful back-and-forth when dealing with coworkers or clients versus work environments that just push for numbers. Those with strong motivators in this identity also do best in jobs that allow them to balance work with family time. They thrive in places that support the notion that workers who are approachable, inquisitive, and positive with clients build loyalty and generate much more repeat business.

The typical desk-job can be a little frustrating for most Caregivers, as they would rather be out talking with people and generating buy-in than sitting alone hour after hour. They are also happiest in work environments that do not pit

THE CAREGIVERS

employees against each other, but in places where *esprit de corps* is fostered, where each person is valued for their particular set of skills and where collaboration is encouraged.

One of the most famous Caregivers we probably all have seen is the character George Bailey from *It's a Wonderful Life*. George took over his father's company, the Bailey Bros. Building & Loan, despite other ambitions for his life—all to keep the plotting Mr. Potter from taking over the only financial institution left that would make loans to the little guy. George was highly empathetic, especially to the working poor of his beloved town, and was devoted to his family—even to the point of taking personal responsibility when his absent-minded uncle lost a huge bank deposit.

George Bailey is an idealized Caregiver, of course, but we've met plenty of people who demonstrate similar qualities on a daily basis in their work in organizations around the world. As researchers, we believe every team does better when there's at least one Caregiver working among them.

THE CAREGIVERS

SCULPTING STRATEGIES FOR THE CAREGIVERS
How to Enhance Your Value and Accomplish More

Help others understand how to live up to expectations.
Many of the most successful Caregivers we've studied
have developed into wonderful storytellers, even though
for some it didn't come naturally. Now we don't mean
they're just spinning yarns about funny weekend barbe-
cue mishaps, but instead they've learned to highlight the
efforts of their team members by capturing and retelling
meaningful stories of personal achievement, innovation,
and customer service. Take the story told to us at a manufacturing company of an employee who was put on a
plane from the United States to Japan to deliver a product
worth a few hundred dollars because it was going to be late
for a big client and never-miss-delivery was the number
one priority in the firm. That's not a warm-and-fluffy
story; it's the kind that is told around the break room for
years after to make a point. Would there be any doubt
how important on-time delivery is to the teammates who
heard that? Would they go back to work determined to
get the order they were working on out on time? Most
likely. Good stories enable the listener to put vague be-

THE CAREGIVERS

haviors in a real context, and understand what has to be done to live up to expectations. Storytelling also helps Caregivers overcome the "us" versus "them" suspicions that can exist between team members and their bosses. Extensive studies show the most successful leaders are the ones with the highest scores for "caring," "affection," and/or "empathy," and good storytelling is filled with empathetic examples. These so-called soft practices are core leadership skills and are therefore a serious business tool. When we consult with teams, we encourage staff meetings not only be filled with talk about numbers and projects, but that someone on the team is tasked with sharing a quick, specific customer story that happened in the last few days—even if it's impromptu. It may be a small or routine challenge they faced, but it becomes instructive as the person talks about the customer's specific need, how the client felt at the beginning of the interaction, how the employee specifically helped that person, and the effect it had on the customer's day or business. When Caregivers themselves make a regular practice of sharing such specific, teaching anecdotes, they help everyone on the team understand that the customers they serve are flesh and blood individuals, and that means they'll be more likely to treat those clients with more caring and compassion. Great Caregiver leaders know an organization's customer experience will never exceed

THE CAREGIVERS

the experience they create for their employees. Service is a cycle that starts inside and moves outward.

Focus on tasks *and* people. Most Caregivers we've interviewed say they like working with people; they are easygoing, empathetic, and caring. And for that reason they can be important assets to any team. But some Caregivers admit they are not as good at structure and details as they are at the people-side of the business. To add the greatest value, we've interviewed Caregivers who said they had to learn to become task-oriented as well as people-oriented. That might mean they learned to put together spreadsheets to track project minutiae, had to block set times to work that wouldn't be interrupted, or became students of their business, its products, and its strategy. Task-oriented people tend to think about "things," while many Caregivers think about "feelings." People-oriented Caregivers "sense," while task-oriented individuals deal in "facts." We aren't suggesting Caregivers lose their vital emotional intelligence, but many of those in this identity who were lacking on the task side of the ledger have told us they got further in their careers by developing a few more practical skills, asking logical questions, and enhancing their business sense. The point is this: Caregiving skills can be valuable, and those who are able to communicate and build relationships are often seen by upper management as more confident, trustworthy, and better able to work with others. But if a Caregiver doesn't rack up accomplishments to go with their good communication abilities, some high-performing team members around them could begin to see them as loquacious time-wasters or even blusterers. Caregivers are most successful when they set regular performance goals for themselves and know how and when to simply get things done.

Ensure recognition is tailored and commensurate. Caregivers are often good at remembering to appreciate others, but a few we've observed have developed a bad habit of giving out one-size-fits-all praise and rewards. One Caregiver boss we met made sure everyone in her department was rewarded with a bag of M&Ms when they'd done something worthy of recognition. That was nice. But the trouble was it didn't matter if the worker had picked up the phones for an hour or saved a million-dollar client from bolting, everyone got the same bag of chocolates. When we asked if more commensurate recognition wouldn't be more meaningful in some cases, she got defensive and said, "When it's a really big deal, I put a bow on the bag." Oh, well, there you go. In contrast, the best Caregivers we've studied take the time to get to know the people in their care as individuals—whether they are teammates or employees—and find ways to reward them that are not only meaningful but tailored to what matters most to them and proportionate to their achievements. These great leaders create frequent, public celebrations of success with sincere words that don't just motivate that lone team member, but all in attendance. They create a climate where the entire team celebrates each other's successes and feels supported in their efforts to achieve. As such, they ensure that everyone on their team stop what they're doing and focus entirely on the message of recognizing success—even if customers are there.

Care by walking around. Our friends Jim Kouzes and Barry Posner put a new twist on an old concept when they talk about "caring by walking around." Caring leaders (or caring teammates for that matter) take time to notice what their teammates are doing, and not just what they're doing "right" or "wrong." More important is getting to know their team's attitudes, motivations, and strategies to accomplish big things. The most effective Caregivers strive to help their teammates understand how everything the team does should relate back to mission, goals, and standards of behavior. And armed with this understanding, they help each person on the team move closer, much faster, to what matters most. The time Caregivers spend with others in this way shows that they value their teammates as real people, and their teammates aren't just a means to an end. It also shows they have faith in their abilities to succeed. "The best leaders," Kouzes and Posner write, "have a special radar that picks up positive signals."

Solve more problems. The purpose of every profession is to solve some type of problem. People dial in to a credit card call center to get an errant charge removed, visit an emergency room to set a broken limb, go to a grocery store to alleviate empty shelves and looming hunger. Wages offered in any industry are generally proportional to the degree of difficulty and complexity of the problems that the people who work there must solve on a daily basis. The more problems an individual solves, and the larger the problems they address, the more valuable they are to their employer, the higher their salary, and the greater their importance in the company. That's why typically the quarterback makes more money than the lineman who protects him, the surgeon more than a general practitioner, and the manager more than an employee. In today's employment climate, harried leaders have little patience for those who don't solve problems. The most successful Caregivers not only are good with people issues, but also increase their value by being those who quietly and efficiently fix problems

$E=mc^2$

THE CAREGIVERS

and take ownership of thorny work issues. We all should develop an attitude about fulfilling assignments like Martin Luther King Jr. describes: "If it falls your lot to be a street sweeper, sweep streets like Michelangelo painted pictures, sweep streets like Beethoven composed music, sweep streets like Leontyne Price sings before the Metropolitan Opera. Sweep streets like Shakespeare wrote poetry."

Help identify other Caregivers. Finding truly empathetic souls with fun outlooks isn't easy, but fellow Caregivers are usually more in tune to finding like-minded souls and can be extremely helpful in hiring situations. Here are some questions to ask job candidates to find the Caregivers among the crowd:

1. How would you describe the team you work with now (or at your last job)? (Listen for positive comments rather than put-downs.)

2. How do you deal with tough personalities on your team? (Look for people who are honest about the challenges some teammates can be, and offer strategies about how to best deal with difficult personalities—all while maintaining an overall optimism about the good nature of people in general.)

3. How do you size up situations to determine if there might be a problem brewing on your team? Can you describe a time when you had to be flexible with those you work with? (Watch for empathy and an ability to tell stories to show they've learned valuable lessons about team dynamics.)

4. How would those who work with you describe you? For instance, are you optimistic or questioning, hopeful or realistic? And why would they say those things? (In these answers, the "why" is most important; we recommend pushing them to answer specifically why others would say they are cheerful, confident, etc.)

5. Explain a time you made an effort to improve the morale of your workplace. Why did you do it, and how did it go over? (Pay attention to the particular ways they've shown concern for their teammates, whether their actions were successful or not isn't as important as if they made an effort to think about those on their team.)

Make quicker decisions. When facing challenges at work, many of the more effectual Caregivers we spoke with said their career growth accelerated when they taught themselves to make faster decisions. That meant they committed to understanding the strategic

THE CAREGIVERS

objectives and mission of the company before problems arose. And then, when issues did arise, they fought the natural (empathetic) inclination some in this identity have to weigh every possible concern from every possible stakeholder's perspective. The main question to answer is this: of all the possible stakeholders to please or displease, which one is the most important and what would that group want us to do? Instead of trying to socialize a solution that everyone is happy with—and no one really is—some Caregivers told us they have one "anti-me" they turn to regularly, a person who will give it to them straight and offer a divergent but thoughtful point of view. By no means are we suggesting people under-think decisions, but the point is to avoid suffering from analysis paralysis.

Bring home the fun from work, and vice versa. A large part of being happy and balanced over the span of a career is learning to give your best self on the job and at home. While it might seem natural that Caregivers would take their fun personalities everywhere they go, some actually unpack the charm in one location but not the other. For instance, perhaps they are outgoing, witty, and personable on the job—their coworkers simply *must* seek them out each morning to hear the latest buzz, have a good laugh, and sample some of their contagious energy. In the workplace they are tolerant of mistakes and encourage improvement. But by the time they get home they've run out of steam. There they have little time for fun and games. Or, conversely, some are the life of the party at the weekend outing with the kids, but at work bring a brand of excruciating seriousness that drains the energy from any room they are in (not realizing that may be hampering their career growth). The happiest Caregivers we've met give their best at home: smiling daily at their family members, taking it easy on the kids when they bring the car home empty or ding the fender, coming up with creative family night activities each week, and so on. And they give their best at the office: making sure everyone lightens up in a warm, inviting atmosphere.

Set some rules. In a 350,000-person study for our book *The Orange Revolution*, we identified the characteristics of the world's best teams. One thing they almost all had in common was a set of simple rules they lived by. We called the three most common the Rule of 3: Wow, No Surprises, and Cheer. In other words, the most profitable, productive, breakthrough teams committed to being world class (Wow), communicated openly and honestly with each other (No Surprises), and rooted for each other and had each other's backs (Cheer).

And, we saw, it was often savvy Caregivers who pushed their teams to create people-focused rules like this to live by. Now, a team's own set of rules doesn't have to be the three we discovered, but they should speak in a meaningful way to the members, the team's unique challenges, and the organizational mission. And the rules should be collaboratively developed, a process Caregivers are naturals at leading.

Maintain a contagious attitude. Just as in everyday life, things can and do go wrong at work. Organizations want employees who are able to not only identify issues but also cheerfully go to work solving them. Some of the most successful Caregivers we've observed are counted on by coworkers and leaders because they maintain their naturally positive attitudes in the toughest times. After all, no one wants to be around an Eeyore. Pessimism and negativity in a crisis breed more of the same, but cheerful attitudes are also "contagious." Great Caregivers are cognizant about doing little positive things that people notice. They make eye contact and turn their faces and bodies toward people seeking their attention. They listen for true meaning during conversations, and don't just rehearse what they're going to say next. They ask probing questions and never allow a computer screen or text message to become more important than a customer's or coworker's thoughts and feelings. This fully-present policy applies to everyone. Caregivers send a powerful message when they put down their smart phones and interact with colleagues or their employees the way they want them to interact with customers.

THE CAREGIVERS

How to Address Blind Spots and Potential Conflicts

Learn to have tough conversations. Empathy and caring are terrific traits in anyone in a leadership position; in fact we would argue few qualities are more important. As such, Caregivers can make good managers. But when employees see their leaders as catering to employee quirks and demands in an extreme manner and not holding anyone accountable, they can become less likely to view that manager as someone to take seriously. Odd as it may sound, we find this lack of accountability problem rampant in many huge organizations we consult with. Leaders are just too nice (can anyone say Michael Scott?). To enhance accountability, Caregivers can have more tough conversations with employees if they focus on the customer—whether internal or external—and away from the person who is being held accountable. Thus, a conversation about a missed deadline isn't an indictment of a worker's character, but a genuine empathy for the customer and an honest discussion about how "we let them down." The truth is the vast majority of employees do want to be held accountable if goals are reachable and realistic. To inspire staff to heightened levels of performance, Caregivers must learn to balance their empathetic natures with clear goal-setting and fair-but-firm accountability. The best leaders, no matter what identity is dominant in them, never accept mediocrity. Here's an interesting and yet counterintuitive finding: when employees are asked to talk about a poor performer on their team, that lousy employee is rarely blamed for their own weaknesses. Who is blamed? The manager who allows mediocrity to continue. Caregivers must learn to make sure those around them hit deadlines, and have tough conversations if they don't.

Watch the small talk. Some interesting science: people who spend more of their days having deep discussions and less time engaging in small talk are happier, says Matthias Mehl, a psychology professor at the University of Arizona. This researcher has found that substantive conversations seem to hold a key to happiness. Why? Because human beings are driven to find and create meaning in their lives. "By engaging in meaningful conversations, we impose meaning on an otherwise pretty chaotic world," the professor says. In his studies, the happiest people—based on self-reports as well as assessments from people who knew the subjects—had twice as many substantive conversations and only one-third of the amount of small talk as those who were the most unhappy. Small talk made up only 10 percent of the happiest people's conversations, while it made up almost 30 percent of the *tête-à-têtes* of the unhappiest. This means that those Caregivers who are more talkative will actually make themselves happier by focusing their conversations more on substantive work issues and cutting back on fluffy chatter. As a step in the right direction, we recommend they try to have just one more thoughtful conversation each day about an important work issue, and also to walk away (nicely of course) from one bull session about nothing.

Limit social media. Few things can stall a people-person's career faster than spending an inordinate amount of time online posting comments on family or friends' social media pages when they should be working. We know, this may sound like officious advice for adults, but trust us; some in this identity fall prey to social media traps and end up missing important signals from bosses or coworkers. Human resource professionals have even told us that they search employees' computer histories for time-wasters when deciding those to lay off during downsizings. So if they don't absolutely need it for their jobs, we have had to advise more than a few Caregivers to turn off Facebook, Twitter, and Pinterest at work and save them for home. Yes, there are studies that suggest workers can be more productive when given regular breaks to browse the web, and time spent on social media can improve work-related knowledge and skills. No doubt. But many in this identity would do better to spend their time building face-to-face relationships with living, breathing clients or coworkers.

THE CAREGIVERS

THE REWARD-DRIVEN

Money
Prestige
Recognition

WHO ARE THE REWARD-DRIVEN?

The motivators associated with this identity are:

- Money
- Prestige
- Recognition

Whether it is vying for marbles, gold stars, money, or simple bragging rights, those who are strongly Reward-Driven tend to be highly competitive and have been since childhood. Their determined natures can help them accomplish great things for organizations.

Those in this identity tend to take the initiative and can be engines of productivity, which can also spur others around them to produce at a higher level. They can get a huge amount done, and are generally good at winning new clients and improving stalled processes. It's not rocket science to figure out what will propel the Reward-Driven to achieve more, in most cases you just have to ask them—they'll let you know what rewards they value.

Now, with all that said, their strong emphasis on rewards can lead some to see them as one-dimensional. Their competitiveness—which can cause them to trumpet their superior performances—can at times rile others. But it's important to understand that there is no rule that says people who are motivated by rewards can't also care about their jobs or coworkers and want to see them flourish, too. In fact, many of

THE REWARD-DRIVEN

the Reward-Driven tend to prefer their team members also to be driven (so they can glean big rewards together); and many in this identity do feel a true passion for their work, strongly believing in the goals of the organization or in the product or service they are selling.

Unfortunately certain coworkers and bosses see the Reward-Driven as overly ambitious, or even greedy or narcissistic because they make it so clear that they crave appreciation and rewards. That's a shame. Understand it's often not the reward itself that drives them but the perceived *value* or *meaning* of that reward. The money, recognition, or status they seek represents to them the *value* they bring to the world. How much they earn, how many awards they receive, or the prestige of their jobs gives them a clear sense of how others perceive their contributions. They're certainly not alone in this. We're all driven to some extent by extrinsic rewards. It's just that for this type, those types of rewards are much more important than for others.

The Characteristics

- **They are doers.** The Reward-Driven are action-oriented, typically not overly contemplative or philosophical types. They tend to want to be very busy, and will often seek out new opportunities to be recognized for their contributions.

THE REWARD-DRIVEN

- **They like regular indications of praise.** Those in this identity are most motivated when they receive regular, small touches of approval, rather than the typical management approach of waiting to give positive feedback only after a big achievement, or worse, only at review or raise time.
- **Their identities are strongly tied to their success.** Having a job that garners admiration from others is especially fulfilling to many in this identity, and they tend to seek promotion aggressively.
- **They believe they should get a piece of what they create.** Some in life are happy to have their work go almost anonymously into the betterment of the whole—a company or a cause. The Reward-Driven, however, are much more motivated when they know they'll earn at least a portion of the credit and maybe the profit from their work.
- **They are good stewards of their time.** Many of the Reward-Driven have become good at maximizing their effectiveness by getting a strong return on the investment of their time. They tend to object to their days being wasted, as in inefficient meetings, and when given a voice they can help quicken the pace of work throughout a team.
- **They like to be incentivized.** Those in this identity tend to be very good corporate players, learning

THE REWARD-DRIVEN

to optimize their performance on incentivized goals such as sales achieved, products launched, projects completed, or number of new clients won. The Reward-Driven will put their focus on what gets results and what gets rewarded, and they'll work hard to please customers or come through on deliverables if these will bring them the money, recognition, and prestige they're seeking.

- **They believe in meritocracy.** Some companies or managers stress that all employees make important (if not equal) contributions—from the person who answers the switchboard to the salesperson who lands million-dollar deals. This thinking drives the Reward-Driven crazy. They believe that not all ducks are swans, and that in fact, some people contribute a whole lot more than others—and therefore deserve commensurate rewards.

- **They believe accountability goes both ways.** Some in this identity have admitted to us that they would be perfectly willing to earn less money if their ideas or efforts aren't successful—in large part because they feel confident they will be—but wish their compensation was directly tied to their individual results so they could earn more. In short, some are willing to put more of their pay at risk for a potentially greater payout. They are generally

THE REWARD-DRIVEN

receptive to creative compensation discussions, including even forgoing traditional merit raises in exchange for shares, options, or profit sharing if they come through on goals set.

Where the Reward-Driven Thrive

Those in this identity are typically happiest and most successful working in environments that offer rewards in the form of monetary incentives and non-monetary recognition. The Reward-Driven generally thrive in work environments that ask a lot of their people, those that encourage them to be competitive with each other as well as outside forces. Some in this identity are most motivated by monetary rewards and are best suited for jobs where pay is tied to direct performance. For others, the prestige of their job is paramount, and they'll thrive in environments where promotions are regularly given, and where important-sounding job titles, large offices, and perks are rewarded to star performers.

Still others will be drawn most to organizations that regularly celebrate great work. One of our employees fit this bill. She confessed to us after we hired her that her primary motivator was to be recognized—not with more money but through regular praise, honest feedback, opportunities to grow, and awards when they were deserved. We say she "confessed" because it was not an easy admission on her part. In her last job, her boss had asked what he could do to improve her work experience. What a considerate thing to ask, she thought, and he seemed so sincere. So she replied, "The most important thing for me in a job is to be recognized." He did a double take and then hooted with sarcastic laughter. A dozen times during that day he walked by her desk firing off wise-cracks like, "Hey, thanks a million," and "Thank you, thank you, thank you" while shooting finger gun bullets at her. She ultimately decided to leave; what an opportunity lost for him and a boon for us. She was a fantastic employee!

Yes, some of the Reward-Driven may rub managers and their colleagues the wrong way. And of course they must be careful not to be obnoxious in their score keeping or in blowing their own horns. But wanting recognition and rewards for work well done should not be perceived as needy, or greedy. Our studies of workplace engagement have shown that recognition in particular is a remarkably powerful tool for increasing the engagement and happiness of an entire workforce.

THE REWARD-DRIVEN

SCULPTING STRATEGIES FOR THE REWARD-DRIVEN

How to Enhance Your Value and Accomplish More

Develop a softer side. For a lot of Reward-Driven individuals, the soft stuff can be the hard stuff. Some in this identity readily admit they are so focused on winning rewards that they don't have time for warm-and-fuzzy stuff at work. But to build stronger relationships with coworkers and eventually be able to effectively lead others (and earn more money, prestige, and recognition) it's important to spend some time to enhance the softer side of the ledger. As such, the Reward-Driven may consider training or self-study in relationship- or team-building, communication, or servant leadership. We always say the simplest place to start is by learning how to show sincere appreciation to others, which includes letting coworkers know they are truly valued. Those who wield this skill the best look for incremental improvements in others' performances and appreciate small and large steps; and in turn, they build more trust in their relationships. One of the biggest complaints we hear about the Reward-Driven is, "He/she hogs all the credit around here."

THE REWARD-DRIVEN

Have a piece of cake, would ya? When we counsel with those in this identity, we often tell them it's important to stop work and socialize a little more than they may be comfortable with. It's not that these individuals aren't gregarious, they certainly can be if they need or want to, but some have a tendency to be so driven in the pursuit of their desired rewards that they can fail to connect with others on a deeper level. That means they might need to stop and go to lunch or get coffee/soft drinks with coworkers now and then, rather than working through every break as they may be apt to do—making them seem aloof to teammates. A fellow college classmate of ours, a very bright student, was recruited by a government agency out of university and put on a fast track to take over as a regional director when the current general manager retired. The position offered a sizeable salary and considerable prestige in the community, and our Reward-Driven friend wasn't going to do anything to jeopardize his chances of winning that big prize. While the others in the office were, in his mind, "goofing off in the break room at lunch," our friend stayed at his desk, typing away. When the team left early in the summer to play in an evening softball league, our young friend kept the lights burning at the office. The result of all this diligence? When the agency director was about to retire he recommended an outsider be brought in to

THE REWARD-DRIVEN

take his job. He felt our former college classmate was estranged from the team, wouldn't have the necessary support of the staff, and didn't understand office politics. Ironic that it was working too hard in pursuit of the reward that killed our friend's dreams.

Shift thinking. Instead of just focusing on daily to-dos or task lists, which will hardly ever satisfy their need to win, we advise those in this identity to spend time now and then thinking about those bigger rewards they are seeking—what they really want from life—and then apply those to their work tasks right now, whatever they're doing and wherever they do it. This way, instead of chores that have to get done, like a day spent in a training session or cold-calling prospects, these activities become opportunities to develop and try out skills that they will use to achieve those bigger goals: perhaps winning a sales contest, or earning a promotion, or running a team as a manager. Those rewards are only possible with the right skill set, and work is more fulfilling and engaging when those in this identity believe they are making incremental progress toward ultimate rewards.

Be grateful. Another comment we make to some of the Reward-Driven is to stop comparing themselves with others who have more. Instead, those with strong reward-drives will be happier if they regularly express gratitude for the talents, resources, and relationships they do have, not to mention their health, their friends, their own brilliance, their motivation, and their family who inspire them. Everyone is happiest when they are thankful for the gifts they have been given, and that gratitude also should be offered up regularly to those around them. Psychologists are only just beginning to understand the healing and strengthening mental power of grateful attitudes. Every person has a lot to be thankful for—especially for those who support them and help them thrive—and the most successful and happy are frequent and specific in their verbal appreciation of not only their colleagues but also family members and friends.

Reward yourself. Some of the Reward-Driven get frustrated when they accomplish something big and don't see rewards from their bosses or company. Even those who work for more aloof managers can still feel a great sense of reward for their accomplishments. It may seem a little over-simplistic, but the happiest people in this identity often give themselves something tangible when they've worked hard and reached a goal. They might take themselves to a good lunch, buy something fun they've been wanting, or, if it's a really big deal, go away on vacation. Forgetting to reward yourself is a subtle form of sabotage. If no one else will do it for them, the Reward-Driven need to do it for themselves.

THE REWARD-DRIVEN

When individuals reward themselves their motivation remains higher, and in turn they tend to accomplish more and spread rewards to those around them, too.

Serve. Some of the happier Reward-Driven people focus their efforts in service of others. With some, it may mean they sell more and achieve more because they truly believe in their products or services and genuinely believe they are serving their customers by putting those goods in their hands— versus those who are simply striving to win a deal and make a buck. It's a subtle change in thinking, but it's important. Psychologists also say people with a reward-drive do better when they focus their energy toward serving their families instead of themselves. What that means is reward-motives based on the pursuit of power, narcissism, or overcoming self-doubt are less rewarding and less effective than reward-goals based on the pursuit of providing security and support for one's family, or being able to give of one's gain to a worthwhile cause.

Take something from everyone. There is a secret of this life that the most successful people in this identity have discovered: while most of us humans may appear a boring and mundane lot, every one of us can be wonderfully interesting and funny, compassionate and inspiring, helpful and stimulating. The trick is in knowing the right questions to ask to get us out of our shells. Some Reward-Driven people admit they are often too busy to develop deeper relationships at work. We tell them they'll be more likely to achieve greater success long-term if they take a genuine interest in others. One way to begin is by writing down a few simple conversation starters and seeing how much they can learn from their coworkers by asking questions such as: What's the most interesting project you are working on? What do people usually complain about over in your team? How did you end up doing what you do here? I'm reading a book about motivation; what would you say motivates you at work? And even more personal questions like: Where are you from originally? What music do you listen to? What's the last book you read? By being a little more interested in others, the Reward-Driven will inevitably gain relationships that will help them in their careers, but it's also just a nice thing to do.

Turn energies outward. Another effective way for those in this identity to develop and grow and earn more sought-after rewards is for them to step outside of themselves, which means becoming more genuine-ly open and friendly and developing positive listening

THE REWARD-DRIVEN

skills. Of course, we recognize that the harder someone tries to be someone he is not, the more likely he'll fall flat. We don't recommend all the Reward-Driven try to memorize a string of knock-knock jokes, heaven's no; we do encourage them to try empathizing and connecting with those around them. Most people are pretty savvy when it comes to intention; they can usually read what's on another's mind—especially someone trying to sell to them. Adrian learned this while working his way through university selling window-washing services door-to-door in the summers. He needed to win at least two jobs a day. "The more I tried to be animated and excited, the more the people at the door seemed to see the desperation in my eyes," he says. "I found if I sold in the afternoon—right after I'd already washed dozens of windows on a couple of houses—I was a lot more successful than if I waited and started fresh the next day. It didn't make sense. I was exhausted and really didn't care if I ever saw another window again. But I suppose I was more at ease, more myself." Our intent is for the Reward-Driven to understand the real business and personal advantages of connecting with people—creating stronger relationships at work with coworkers and clients, having more people in their corner, building a greater sphere of influence, and gaining a perceived ability to take on new roles including leading others.

THE REWARD-DRIVEN

Develop a good close. "It was nice to meet you" or "good to see you again" are standard goodbyes after conversations, but they are instantly forgettable. Instead, the most memorable individuals shake hands and say something specific and affirming to close, "You know, I really enjoyed your thoughts on the Bornstein project. You have some really creative ideas. Thanks for sharing." And then they smile—not a cheesy salesperson's toothy smile, but an authentic, appreciative grin. Making a great first impression is important, but so is making a lasting closing impression. All this sounds simple, right? But it's not so easy for some in this identity. We all have to accept that change can be hard. But when the Reward-Driven become a little more deferential, a little more genuine, a little more complimentary, and a wee bit more vulnerable, they help people around them feel better about themselves, which makes them more likeable. It's a virtuous circle.

THE REWARD-DRIVEN

How to Address Blind Spots and Potential Conflicts

Reduce the expectation of others' opinions. Winning can sometimes come at a cost: heightened stress, tension, and anxiety. Those driven to win rewards often spend inordinate amounts of time working and can report a higher incidence of failed relationships with their significant others and children. Some of the Reward-Driven find themselves pushed not by a healthy desire to compete but by an overriding fear of failure, which means they find fault, first and foremost, in themselves. There is a difference between a healthy need to please and an unhealthy one. A healthy need is not dependent on a particular response. For instance, if a person cleans up the supply cabinet at work because he or she knows it will be helpful to the team, but are not expecting any reward in response, then he or she most likely has a healthy need to please others. That's natural. On the other hand, if they expect their boss and coworkers to praise or reward their work, and know they'll get upset if these people don't thank them, then they may have an unhealthy need to please. We point this out only because the former response has less anxiety while the latter response offers great anxiety. Overcoming the need to please others takes time and practice. As an important first step we recommend people stop the negative self-talk such as, "I'm not good enough" or "They don't appreciate me." By reducing the expectation of others' opinions, people gain freedom from living their lives to please others, which greatly reduces their stress levels.

Curb the need to win. Many of the more über-competitive Reward-Driven admit that when they first meet people they can fall into an odd form of pissing contest. A crude reference but one that instantly calls to mind a time you saw two people arguing about something you thought was incredibly trivial. The most savvy of these individuals have actually taught themselves to lose, are complimentary of others' abilities, and are impressed by the successes of their peers. In his autobiography, Benjamin Franklin admitted he was arrogant and annoying as a young man. He was crushed when a friend confided to him that while he was unquestionably brilliant, winning every argument, no one liked him. To force himself to become more humble and likeable, he introduced phrases into his vocabulary such as "I conceive" and "I apprehend" rather than words he had been using such as "certainly" or "undoubtedly." Franklin wrote that he afterwards started enjoying conversations more, and became a man of greater compassion and humility. Like Franklin, the Reward-Driven can most likely stand to add a measure of humility to their conversations, use self-deprecating humor to appear less threatening, and display vulnerability by admitting their own failings or weaknesses now and then. Thus, if an acquaintance says,

THE REWARD-DRIVEN

"I just purchased a new mainframe," the enlightened Reward-Driven individual won't try to win a debate on the role of mainframes in modern technology, but will steer the conversation to something that intrigues them and won't alienate such as, "I'm pretty lousy at getting large purchases approved. How did you pull it off?" People sincerely like genuine interest in their work.

Beware of self-promotion. Advertising one's accomplishments can get the Reward-Driven recognized and promoted early in their careers, but at some point they have to outgrow it or it can backfire. As people rise to loftier levels of experience and authority, they are expected to be mentors to others, leaders who shine the light on those around them. Boasting is often seen as a negative in senior staff members or managers. This can also include self-promotion on a person's own social media sites. It's great to have a professional blog or to utilize other ever-evolving online tools to communicate a message, but as our wise moms told us, "Don't brag. Let your actions do the talking." Writing interesting, authoritative online posts about an area of expertise will do more to build a person's reputation than sharing a litany of personal accomplishments on social media pages. The only time it's really acceptable to brag is when someone is in a performance review or job interview, and then it should still be done with grace and humility.

THE THINKERS

Autonomy
Creativity
Excitement
Impact
Learning
Variety

WHO ARE THE THINKERS?

The motivators clustered within this identity are:

- Autonomy
- Creativity
- Excitement
- Impact
- Learning
- Variety

Some people are drawn to jobs with clear responsibilities; they feel comfort in following a set of rules. Studies have shown that this preference develops early in life, and that at some point between grades three to five many students become more interested in following set guidelines than in being independent and imaginative. After all, rules are easy to understand and follow, and they keep you out of trouble. Coming up with your own way of doing things and creating original work exposes you to a risk of failure.

But for some people, being allowed to exercise their imagination is much more appealing. They long to be autonomous, free to take risks, and follow their own interests now and then. These people are the Thinkers, those who tend to challenge the status quo, who crave opportunities to explore and discover, and who can grow bored and frustrated if their work becomes routine.

THE THINKERS

As a group, these people are resourceful and more artistic, and many we've interviewed say they can become unhappy and uninspired when they aren't creating. That can mean trouble for their careers. Thinkers need to constantly put new stuff out into the world; and they do their best work when they get to try out new tools and techniques of thinking and developing.

Once, when we visited a Fortune 100 consumer products company, veteran employees looked back and told us about a time of unprecedented innovation in the organization, during which some bold, highly creative changes in marketing occurred, including a memorable series of consumer head-to-head challenges and some surprising celebrity endorsements. A maverick marketing team had crafted all of these; and they led to the company making incredible gains on its largest competitor with resulting upticks in revenue growth and stock appreciation. But within a few years many of the old guard in the venerable company began to be more and more bothered by these marketing upstarts. "We are an operations company," became the mantra, and ever-tightening restrictions were placed on the Thinkers. Budgets were cut, fewer outlandish ideas were approved, and one-by-one the Thinkers trickled away. Since then we've met about a dozen of this company's former marketing superstars in other firms around the world, many of them now in successful leadership roles. As for that consumer products company? It settled back into a much slower rate of growth.

THE THINKERS

The moral of the story: Creative Thinkers can be the lifeblood of innovation in an organization, and unless companies learn to get the best out of them they will sooner or later stem the flow of great ideas. Yes, some can be a handful to manage, but giving them time to discover and pursue ideas, and making some exceptions for them amid the rigid rules, tends to pay off in many surprising ways.

The Characteristics

- **They dislike bureaucracy.** Some managers tell us their Thinkers balk at deadlines, but that's usually not completely accurate. Most we've interviewed say in fact that they do need and crave structure—understanding timelines, project strategy, and so on. But what they hate is red tape, obstructionism, and silly rules that get in the way of doing new, better things. When leaders give them clear goals, keep them intellectually engaged on the journey, and help remove obstacles from their way, they'll usually shine for them.

- **They want to know the "why."** Thinkers tend to want to know why something is important. They are not the type to just accept that what a boss or organization wants makes good sense without compelling reasons why it will benefit customers or coworkers. After all, understand they are drawn to discover if there might be a better way, so they need all the details they can get.

THE THINKERS

- **They value novelty.** Thinkers are often described by their friends and family as adventurous, which means they generally crave jobs with a little pulse-pounding excitement now and then. Few things are worse for them than to be stuck in a rut, and they thrive when forced to learn something new, tasked with breaking new ground, and when their work changes regularly.
- **They like to see the impact of their innovation.** Coming up with new ways of doing things or developing new product ideas is very satisfying to most Thinkers, especially when they can actually see the final improvement they've brought about.
- **They think before they act.** Thinkers tend to want to play with different possibilities for a while before making a decision. They typically like to ask lots of questions and to test various scenarios, and this often leads them to push the envelope on deadlines, or even to blow past them if they aren't careful.
- **They like to draw on a wide range of experiences.** Those in this identity tend to be good at making unexpected connections, and they like to bring even seemingly unrelated information to tasks at hand— maybe a movie or play they just saw, a recent climbing trip to Yosemite, or a sermon they heard at church.
- **They don't like being told *how* to do their work.** Thinkers usually want the freedom to figure things out

THE THINKERS

for themselves and like to be their own bosses, even when they work in traditional organizations. They don't do their best work with onerous oversight, and tend not to believe in preconceived notions of how work gets done.

Where Thinkers Thrive

Thinkers are typically happiest and most successful working with fewer bureaucratic strictures placed on them, in places where they're not always required to follow established processes. Many believe they'll only find true happiness as their own bosses, but in reality they can absolutely thrive in corporations when they are given a little latitude about how things get done and are encouraged to bring out their creative sides. Environments that are best for them encourage unconventional thinking, where people take the quality of their work they do very seriously but themselves not so seriously.

The head of marketing for Facebook, Rebecca Van Dyck, seems to be a true Thinker. Named one of the world's most creative people in business by *Fast Company*, Van Dyck reads three newspapers daily to get multiple perspectives on the world. Her career has been called "a chronicle of cool": she shepherded Nike's "Just Do It" campaign around the world, launched the iPhone and iPad as head of marketing communications at Apple, and helped update Levi's global brand identity. Her

THE THINKERS

advice for Thinkers like her: "Don't let fear be a deciding factor in your career."

Now as a leader of other Thinkers, her philosophy is to create an environment where highly talented people can feel safe, where they can be wildly bold and take risks. She tells them, "Don't worry about the linear path. Instead collect experiences as if they are tools or treasures that you store in your backpack for future use. The more gadgets (experiences) you have, the better equipped you are for life's adventures."

SCULPTING STRATEGIES FOR THE THINKERS

How to Enhance Your Value and Accomplish More

Incubate ideas. Many Thinkers tell us they are most productive when they have multiple projects going at once. Remember, part of the creative process is incubating ideas, and Thinkers often tell us their best ideas are nurtured when they research an assignment, do a few hours of work, and then stop and move on to something else. They may have hit a wall and suddenly they are waiting at the auto mechanic and kapow— they think of something brilliant. That's because many imaginative brains do their best work when they work on multiple problems over time. This type of variety also can help keep them from burning out, but more importantly gives their brains time to focus on bigger problems and innovative solutions. With that said, we do see many Thinkers who work evenings as well as weekend after weekend to get their projects done and make an impact with their clients. It's more important for Thinkers than anyone else to take their vacation days, turn off the computer for at least twenty-four hours on the weekend, and go out regu-

THE THINKERS

228

larly with friends or family to recharge their batteries. Thinkers must learn to balance; and another part of that means getting enough sleep. Studies show that creativity declines the less sleep a person gets.

Push for specifics. Few things frustrate a Thinker more than statements from bosses or clients such as: "That's not it, but I'll know it when I see it." Or, "Something is missing, I'm just not sure what." Those in this identity will accomplish more when they gather the courage to push, and push again if necessary, for clarifying feedback—all with a positive, receptive attitude, of course. We recommend they start with affirming statements such as, "I want to do great work for you, and I find that the more specific you can be at this point will help me get this that much closer to perfect for you." Then we have them explain what their intentions were with each area of the assignment and ask if each part is on target or off. However, if they still aren't getting clear feedback, we'll have them try a Hail Mary such as, "If you were pushed to give just two suggestions for improving this, what would they be?" As they receive feedback, Thinkers need to be open and not defensive. We've noticed there's an equal and opposite reaction that happens: as Thinkers reduce the amount of self-justifying comments they utter, the more others around them begin to trust that they have a thick skin and can actually receive honest, constructive feedback in order to improve their work.

Chase down rabbit holes. Thinkers can boost their value and impact by making sure their imaginations get regular exercise, at least so say Shelley Carson, a professor at Harvard University, and composer Bruce Adolphe. These two luminaries suggest Thinkers should frequently play "what if" games—imagining some difference in the normal world; for instance, what would happen if all the grass turned red, or what if all cars could suddenly fly? What would the consequences be? They suggest Thinkers give themselves planned time every day to think like this, daydream, and turn off the critical, self-censoring parts of their brains. Carson and Adolphe say also to shut off anything electronic during these creative interludes, allowing the brain time to digest and synthesize what it has seen and experienced recently. The most creative people we've met look for ideas in a wide variety of fiction and nonfiction books—about their industry and the world at large. Talented Thinkers are typically not myopic, but are willing to look far and wide for inspiration: they read a variety of newspapers and magazines, chase ideas down various rabbits holes online or at the library, and attend varied cultural events. Rather than simply collecting information, they let their brains play with it. For instance, a non-creative person might see a horse standing in a field and think it is a magnificent looking animal. But a curious Thinker who has honed her craft might take the time to wonder what the horse thinks about all day in the field. She might notice that the horse is hanging out by the fence near a field where another horse lives and wonder how two animals that do not speak might bond and what kinds of friendship they might have. Cultivating that type of curiosity in all aspects of life drives innovation in the workplace.

Grasp the latest trends. Yes, there are Thinkers who don't own or even understand the latest technology, social trends, or popular culture, but they are rarely the most successful. Learning-driven people ensure they continually embrace the modern world and know what others are talking about when they rave about their new smart phone or the latest social media craze. If Thinkers have no idea what a popular trend is when coworkers bring it up, or have no desire to find out about it because it's outside their comfort zone, they aren't enhancing their value to their organization. The most successful

THE THINKERS

in this identity understand the modern consumer and what their world is all about to solve real problems on the job, and they take time to read, learn, and experiment in their work. Thinkers, to be effective, must gather ideas and store them mentally before they are needed.

Rate what is boring. A great idea for Thinkers comes from Jill Leviticus of Demand Media, who recommends those in this identity write down each of their job functions and rate them on a boredom scale. She suggests they rate tasks that are very interesting as fives, and jobs that are completely uninteresting as ones. The chart will help people identify which tasks they find the most dull and uninspiring, helping them devise ways to complete boring work quickly, find a way to make it more interesting, or avoid monotonous projects in the future if given a choice. Of course, part of sculpting is asking a supervisor for projects in areas that do interest them, or volunteering to help on a committee or with a new project. Even taking a break during the workday to attend a seminar or read a book about the latest advances in their field, or taking ownership of office tasks that *are* interesting to them—from running brainstorming sessions to watering plants to teaching coworkers how to use software.

THE THINKERS

Understand what motivates. When Thinkers are dissatisfied at work, we encourage them to understand not only what they do well but also *how* they do it best. Here's an example: Certain Thinkers respond well to healthy competition and tight deadlines, while others prefer having a long leash and time to really create something amazing. As an extreme illustration, years ago we heard the story of an editor at the *New Yorker* who gave assignments to his writers when passing in the hallway. He might pause, look thoughtfully to the ceiling, and mumble something cryptic like, "Coca-Cola," and then walk on. Nothing more would be said about the hoped-for article on the soft-drink giant—even if it took months or years to develop. That kind of autonomy, we're afraid, is unrealistic, but Thinkers can still dream can't they? Back in the real world, we suggest Thinkers learn how they do their best work by answering questions such as: "Under what circumstances do I do my best work?" and then pushing themselves with, "Why exactly do those circumstances make me better?" Their jobs may not always be able to meet those preferred requirements, but they'll have a better grasp of what makes them tick, which will help when assignment choices do come along.

THE THINKERS

Develop a passion to learn. Consider Thomas Jefferson and Halle Berry. We know, it seems like a huge leap—what with Jefferson and his dazzling good looks and all—but despite their very different professions and backgrounds both can be classified as strong Thinkers. Driven to learn, Jefferson was a practicing circuit lawyer who brought an ongoing passion for study in rhetoric and persuasion to the continental congress in 1776. Perhaps no other person in the colonies could have phrased the Constitutional argument like Jefferson, forming the now famed syllogism: (1) governments that are destructive of people's rights to equality, life, liberty, and the pursuit of happiness ought to be abolished or altered by the people; (2) the government of King George (Great Britain) is guilty of such destruction; and (3) therefore, the Government of King George should be abolished. As for Berry, a method actor, she uses a vivid imagination and a love of learning to construct a backstory for each of her characters—an ability that won her a Best Actress Oscar for her portrayal of a death-row inmate's wife in Monster's Ball. The actress arrived on set for her debut film role as a crack addict in Spike Lee's Jungle Fever having spent time with the homeless, and even decided that the best way to get into her character was to not bathe for two weeks. Here we see a

Father of American Democracy and an Academy Award Winning Actress using their passion for learning to make an impact in their work—with very different, but very successful results. (But no, we can't explain Catwoman.)

Share crazy ideas first. We've found most Thinkers tasked with a big project usually have a few sets of ideas to present when they meet with their bosses, the team, or clients. They have first a set of conventional ideas that will work within the established order, and second they usually have a few less conventional ideas—the kind that come out of left field. Smart Thinkers present them in reverse order: crazy first, conventional second. Why? While no one is ever going to be laughed at for coming up with an idea that is in keeping with the norms of the culture (whether it is society, school, or a workplace), then again very few boring, conventional ideas have ever changed the world for the better. When sharing the outrageous, we suggest Thinkers set up the reviewers to listen with a receptive spirit. For instance, they might preface the idea by saying, "I have some solid ideas that I think are going to work well in our system. But I want to start with a wild and exciting idea that might really break some new ground if we are willing to take a chance on it." Then they'll passionately explain why this idea would resonate

THE THINKERS

with the intended audience. Linda Kaplan Thaler, chairman of advertising giant Publicis Kaplan Thaler, once told us of a pitch meeting she and her team made to the Lifetime Network for a national breast cancer awareness campaign. While they had some traditional ideas ready, the first idea they threw out on the table was from one of the firm's young interns who had said that when she and her friends sign off their texts to each other they always ended with "You are my bra"—meaning their support, their lift. It was certainly a little outrageous at the time. After hearing everything, Lifetime decided that crazy would win the day, and "Be my support. Be my strength. Be my bra," became a series of TV commercials starring Whoopi Goldberg that touched the lives of millions.

Ask the right questions. While we might tend to view Thinkers as free spirits who wear cool, thick-rimmed glasses as they sit around in coffee shops, there is a large group in this identity who are highly logical. Reason, not emotion, rules for these people. The very traits that make some of these logical Thinkers so successful in fixing computers or balancing books for instance, can make them struggle at times relating to other people. And that is why analytical departments like IT can have more than their share of individuals who prefer to hang out by themselves. Some of the more analytical

THE THINKERS

Thinkers—often in STEM positions—have told us point blank they care deeply about the emotions and opinions of the select group whom they respect, but perceive most others they meet as dull or boring, perhaps because they can't hold a conversation on the same cerebral level. As the saying goes, they don't suffer fools gladly—or at least, those they perceive as being foolish since they don't have a working grasp of quantum physics or cloud computing or Occam's razor. However, we've found many successful Thinkers who are not only logical but have evolved their more sensitive sides to become, gulp, likeable. People who are likeable are masters at Social Jiu-Jitsu, the art of getting people to talk about themselves without ever knowing it happened. Likeable people use their social graces to cast a spell on others, and get people to like them for it. It begins with asking the right questions and allowing room for description and introspection. In other words, they ask how, or why, or what. So, as soon as they learn about a person's specific accomplishments, they ask *how* they did it, or *why*, or *what* they liked about doing it, or *what* they learned from it, or *what* they would do differently if they were in a similar situation.

THE THINKERS

How to Address Blind Spots and Potential Conflicts

Learn patience when pitching. Thinkers must be sold on their own ideas before they have a hope of selling them to others. After all, people are drawn to those who have a genuine passion and belief in what they do. Now, with that said, the minute a Thinker shares one of his cherished ideas he needs to be less shocked when audiences don't jump up and say, "Let's do it!" Sometimes less-creative people need a little time to realize that a brilliant idea is, ahem, brilliant. The most successful Thinkers are patient when making a pitch. They give others time to think about their unconventional ideas. But if they believe enough in their concepts, then they are respectfully persistent. Patience is important for a Thinker, but patience with persistence is most effective. After all, it took Christopher Columbus—a Thinker if there ever was one—a decade to convince Queen Isabella to finance his mission. We suggest Thinkers ask smart follow-up questions to better understand their audience's concerns, and also spend time further clarifying their vision.

Don't be a rebel without a clue. Thinkers can often be some of the most wonderfully unique people—following their own rules. As such, it's great for a Thinker to look and sound creative, but that doesn't mean they should try to look or sound like a *rebel*. There's a difference. Great Thinkers challenge the status quo in positive ways, while rebels are difficult, defiant, and cynical. Here's an odd but true example: In a conservative one-hundred-year-old organization we met a very creative marketer who was not able to get many people to take him seriously for the simple reason he insisted on wearing shorts and a T-shirt most days. We know, that sounds like a ridiculously silly problem, right? He thought so, too, which is why he refused to give in to the stodgy old guard. But the fact was he worked in a place where

most people still wore ties or skirts. Those people looked at him and talked about him as if he'd just stepped off the moon. It may have been completely unfair from his perspective, but no matter what profundity spewed out of this man's mouth there were certain people who didn't really listen. Their loss, we know, but the point is: Thinkers get more accomplished, get more buy-in, and impress a lot more people when they bring incredibly creative ideas to their workplaces in a workman-like manner. Successful Thinkers are creative inside the box, if you will.

THE THINKERS

Consider smart criticism. One common mistake of Thinkers is to filter out everything but the most positive comments that reinforce their own points of view. Yes, all of us have to avoid negativity from the born pessimists around us, but enlightened individuals are always open to constructive comments from customers and coworkers that make their work better. After all, it will cost much less in time and money to listen to and fix problems in the prototype stages than to start over when an idea is already in production. When others do offer advice, we recommend Thinkers take a note or two, not only for later reference but to show respect. Also, we counsel against any form of criticism during this idea phase such as, "I understand, *but* ..." or "In my opinion ..." And we tell them to use the tried but true method of repeating back what's been said to ensure they are really clear on the thoughts being suggested.

Don't be domineering. Nobody is a saint when it comes to being overbearing, and everyone can have a tendency to bully other people at various times—maybe when they know something in great detail, or they are in a position of authority, or they may just feel a little pushier than usual due to anxiety or pressure. We hate to say it, but Thinkers can fall prey to the know-it-all-ism syndrome more than other identities. We advise them to recognize

THE THINKERS

when they are being overly controlling at work or home and try to understand the reason behind the behavior and especially notice the reactions of other people when their domineering behavior appears. When they do see it happening, we recommend they back up and if necessary apologize to the person whose boundaries they crossed. This can cultivate healthier friendships and relationships in their lives. Most importantly, it helps to analyze why the controlling behavior is rearing its head—is it insecurity or fear, or has another party truly acted inappropriately and needs to be corrected?

THE THINKERS

END NOTES

Chapter One

Research on Michelangelo comes from:

Shaikh, Saad and James Leonard-Amodeo. "The Deviating Eyes of Michelangelo's David." *Journal of the Royal Society of Medicine*, February 2005.

"Michelangelo's David: A Tale of Two Noses." *Globus*. http://www.globusjourneys.com/travel-stories/Italy/michelangelos-david.

Jacobsen, Aaron H. "Michelangelo from The New Book of Knowledge®." *Scholastic*. http://www.scholastic.com/browse/article.jsp?id=3754421.

Sonya Lyubomirsky and Jessica Pryce-Jones's research comes from:

Salemi, Vicki. "Start Smiling: It Pays to Be Happy at Work." *Forbes*, August 8, 2010.

The Gallup research quoted is from:

Bruzzese, Anita. "Meaningful Work Helps Keep You Happy After You've Gone Home." *USA Today*, June 9, 2010.

The Conference Board and the additional Gallup data is from:

Adams, Susan. "Americans are Starting to Hate Their Jobs Less, Study Shows." *Forbes*, June 28, 2012.

Crabtree, Steve. "Worldwide, 13% of Employees are Engaged at Work." *Gallup.com*. October 8, 2013. http://www.gallup.com/poll/165269/worldwide-employees-engaged-work.aspx.

The sections on motivation theory include research from:

Deci, Edward. *Why We Do What We Do*. New York: Penguin Books, 1995.

Pink, Daniel H. *Drive: The Surprising Truth About What Motivates Us*. New York: Riverhead Books, 2011.

Herzberg, Frederick. "One More Time: How Do You Motivate Employees?" *Harvard Business Review*, January 2003.

Steven Reiss is quoted from:

Grabmeier, Jeff. "New Theory of Motivation Lists 16 Basic Desires That Guide Us." *The Ohio State University Research News*, June 28, 2000. http://researchnews.osu.edu/archive/whoami.htm.

Chapters Four and Five

Andre Agassi's story comes from:
Agassi, Andre. *Open: An Autobiography*. New York: Vintage, 2010.

Jane Hutchinson and James Waldroop quotes were culled from:
Vu, Uyen. "Is it a Manager's Job to Understand What Makes Employees Tick." *Canadian HR Reporter*, September 25, 2006.

Chapter Six

Marci Alboher's story and the MetLife research comes from:
Alboher, Marci. "A Switch at Midlife, to Make a Difference." *New York Times*, December 8, 2012. http://www.nytimes.com/2012/12/09/jobs/switching-careers-at-midlife-to-make-a-difference.html.

Arthur Brooks's story comes from:
Brooks, Arthur. "A Formula for Happiness." *New York Times*, December 14, 2013. http://www.nytimes.com/2013/12/15/opinion/sunday/a-formula-for-happiness.html.

Joseph Campbell's work was culled from:
Campbell, Joseph. *The Hero With a Thousand Faces*. Novato, California: New World Library, 2008.

INSEAD research comes from:
Ibarra, Herminia. "How to Stay Stuck in the Wrong Career." *INSEAD Alumni Newsletter*, January 2003. http://www.insead.edu/alumni/newsletter/january2003/herminiaibarraHBR.pdf.

Randall Hansen's research is quoted from:
Hansen, Randall S. "Career Change Do's and Don'ts." *QuintCareers.com*. http://www.quintcareers.com/career_change-dos-donts.html.

Chapter Seven

Lynn Robbins was quoted from his talk:
Robbins, Lynn. "Making a Living, Making a Life." Presentation at BYU-Idaho, October 12, 2010.

Identity Reference Guide

The Achievers section includes research from:

"What is Achievement Orientation and Why is it Important?" *Coventry University CURVE Open Research.* Last modified June 1, 2010. https://curve.coventry. ac.uk/cu/file/e4f25ab7-9574-d874-a82b-35543b1e5e66/3/achievement.zip/ index.html.

Saunders, Elizabeth Grace. "Make Time for Growth Assignments in Your Daily Work." *Harvard Business Review Blog Network,* July 4, 2013. http://blogs. hbr.org/2013/07/make-time-for-growth-assignments-in-your-daily-work/.

DiSalvo, David. "The Five Hallmarks of Highly Respected Achievers." *Forbes,* June 21, 2012. http://www.forbes.com/sites/daviddisalvo/2012/06/21/the-five-hallmarks-of-respected-achievers/.

Burns, David D. *Feeling Good.* New York: Harper, 2008.

Greenspon, T. "'Healthy Perfectionism' is an Oxymoron!" *Journal of Secondary Gifted Education* 11, no. 4: 197-208.

"Research Suggests Perfectionism and Work Motivation Contribute to Work-aholism." *Science Daily,* August 29, 2013. http://www.sciencedaily.com/ releases/2013/08/130829110423.htm.

The Builders section includes research from:

Schwartz, Arial. "People Want Jobs That Make A Difference, Even If It Means A Pay Cut." *Fast Company,* May 23, 2012. http://www.fastcoexist. com/1679904/people-want-jobs-that-make-a-difference-even-if-it-means-a-pay-cut.

Johnson, Emma. "How To: Become a Servant Leader." *SUCCESS.* http://www. success.com/article/how-to-become-a-servant-leader.

The Caregivers section includes research from:

"Leading Teams: Be a Caring Leader." *Managing People at Work.* http://www. managingpeopleatwork.com/Article.php?art_num=3982.

Rabin, Roni Caryn. "Talk Deeply, Be Happy?" *New York Times,* March 17, 2010. http://well.blogs.nytimes.com/2010/03/17/talk-deeply-be-happy/.

Frick, Walter. "The More Time We Spend Online, the Less Time We Spend Working." *Harvard Business Review Blog Network,* October 22, 2013. http:// blogs.hbr.org/2013/10/the-more-time-we-spend-online-the-less-time-we-spend-working/.

The Reward-Driven section includes research from:

Chamorro-Premuzic , Tomas. "Does Money Really Affect Motivation?" *Harvard Business Review Blog Network*, April 10, 2013. http://blogs.hbr.org/2013/04/does-money-really-affect-motiv/.

Hammond, Christine. "How to Overcome the Need to Please Others." Life-Works. http://ezinearticles.com/?How-to-Overcome-the-Need-to-Please-Others&id=6559166.

Franklin, Benjamin. *The Autobiography of Benjamin Franklin*. SparkNotes: http://www.sparknotes.com/lit/franklinautobio/.

The Thinkers section includes research from:

Lidsky, David. "Most Creative People 2012: Rebecca Van Dyck." *Fast Company*, April 27, 2012. http://www.fastcompany.com/3018185/most-creative-people-2012/2-rebecca-van-dyck.

"Halle Berry: Biography." *Answers.com*. http://www.answers.com/topic/halle-berry.

Weintraub, Karen. "Brain a 'Creativity Machine,' If You Use it Right." *USA Today*, November 9, 2013. http://archive.news10.net/news/national/262839/5/Brain-a-creativity-machine-if-you-use-it-right.

Leviticus, Jill. "How to Prevent Job Monotony." *Houston Chronicle*. http://work.chron.com/prevent-job-monotony-5947.html.

Bernell, Laura. "The Declaration of Independence: A Lesson in Logic." *Suite*. https://suite.io/leah-abramovitz/3qrc26w.

Haden, Jeff. "6 Habits of Remarkably Likable People." *Inc.* http://www.inc.com/jeff-haden/6-habits-of-remarkably-likeable-people.html.

Put Your Passions to Work™

The authors are founders of The Culture Works,® a global firm that helps many of the world's most successful organizations with leadership and employee motivation keynotes, training, and culture consulting and assessment.

If you are interested in learning more about this process, please review the resources on the following pages and contact The Culture Works team at:

(844) MOTIV88 or (844) 668-4888

(toll free in the United States and Canada)

or email

Info@TheCultureWorks.com

or visit

TheCultureWorks.com

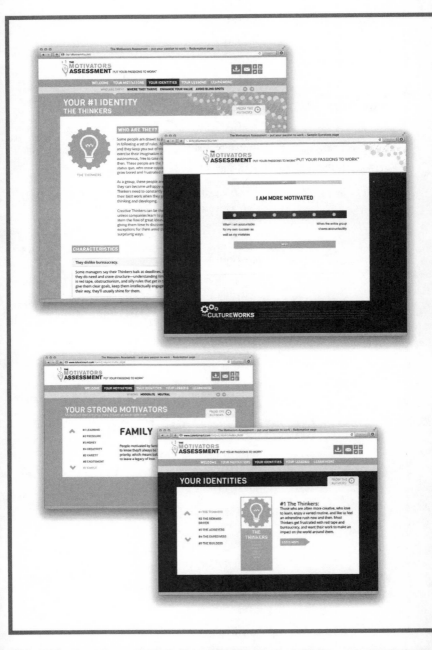

MOTIVATION TOOLS FOR INDIVIDUALS

Personal Workbook

Packed with introspective sculpting exercises and worksheets, this valuable workbook will help anyone shape their work to align closer to their motivators and identities.

Personal Workbook: $24.95

Volume, government, education, and nonprofit discounts available

Coaching

Always-confidential mentoring is available through our expert coaches at The Culture Works, helping you:

- Gain one-on-one, personalized insight into your motivators and identities.
- Better understand your Motivator Profile.
- Create a high-impact Action Plan to sculpt future work and take control of your career.

Pricing available upon request.

Public and Virtual Seminars

Whether you are just starting out in your work life or you are a mid-career professional, the fun and highly experiential What Motivates Me Public or Virtual Seminar is intended to help you develop the knowledge and skills to Discover, Sculpt, and Empower your career. The half-day seminars help you:

- Learn how to sculpt your job by blending your motivators and identities.
- Create an empowered Action Plan that will sustain your efforts to work in greater alignment with your passions.

To order online, visit
TheCultureWorks.com or call
(844) MOTIV88 or (844) 668-4888.

MOTIVATION TOOLS FOR MANAGERS

Public or Virtual Seminars for Managers

The What Motivates Me Public or Virtual Seminars help leaders empower themselves and their people to greater success. The seminars teach leaders:

- How to act on their team's Motivator Profiles to unleash drive, and increase productivity, empowerment, and satisfaction.
- Enhance accountability by helping team members create sustainable, empowering Action Plans.
- Integrate job sculpting into daily management.
- Features the Manager Workbook, full of illuminating and insightful exercises to gain a clear understanding of how to job sculpt as a team leader.

Executive Coaching

For those who manage people or projects, for new or seasoned leaders, the confidential What Motivates Me one-on-one mentoring is available with an expert leadership coach from The Culture Works, helping you:

- Better understand the Motivator Profiles of each of the team members in your care.
- Create Action Plans for each person on your team—helping motivate, engage and empower their success.

Pricing available upon request.

MOTIVATION TOOLS FOR ORGANIZATIONS

Trainer Certification

Certify your trainers to deliver the What Motivates Me Training Workshop for managers and individuals—helping empower everyone within your organization to take control of their careers. Each participant will have the opportunity to teach-back and receive personalized feedback from a seasoned Culture Works facilitator.

Onsite Seminars

Based on the latest research and case studies, The Culture Works trainers offer highly experiential seminars that take participants on a journey of self-discovery and transformation, and also help them lead positive change within work teams. Sessions are available in various lengths, for manager and employee audiences.

Keynotes

Have one of the *New York Times* bestselling authors of *What Motivates Me, The Carrot Principle,* and *All In* deliver a dynamic presentation to your organization that will help managers inspire greater engagement and empowerment within their teams.

*Visit **AdrianGostick.com** or **ChesterElton.com** for speaking reels and availability.*

Executive Retreats

Solidify your organization's talent strategy through exclusive What Motivates Me Executive Retreats for leadership teams wishing to integrate advanced job sculpting and career planning strategies to retain and energize their talent.

Talent Screening

Understand your candidates' motivators and cultural fit before you extend an offer. Vet your candidates' cultural and motivational fit to achieve your strategic objectives.

TOOLS FOR CONSULTANTS

Consultant Certification

Grow *your* leadership- or HR-consulting business. Independent consultants worldwide can become certified to deliver the full range of exciting What Motivates Me products and services to their clients. Attend the three-day certification seminar as the first step in becoming a What Motivates Me Certified Consultant.

- Deliver the What Motivates Me Seminar for Managers, Mentors, and Individuals.
- Debrief Motivator Profiles with individuals, managers, and teams.
- Help executives job sculpt within their teams.
- Help individuals build effective Action Plans.

This exciting program offers exclusive access to a wide array of world-class, turnkey products and services. Getting started is easy.

To order online, visit
TheCultureWorks.com or call
(844) MOTIV88 or (844) 668-4888.

About the Research Team

In 2014, Adrian Gostick and Chester Elton, along with a team of scientists, unveiled the online Motivators Assessment, which is based on findings from employee engagement surveys of 850,000 people and developed with rigorous testing. Included on the research team were:

Steve Gibbons, MS

President and partner of The Culture Works. A seasoned consultant, certified project management professional, and engaging training facilitator, Gibbons oversees client solution development and engagements, including custom assessment, consulting, and education life cycles—developing positive and sustainable behavioral changes in organizations among leadership and teams. He holds an MS degree in instructional design and technology from Utah State University.

Dr. Travis Bradberry and Dr. Jean Greaves

Drs. Bradberry and Greaves are the cofounders of TalentSmart, and the award-winning authors of the #1 bestselling book *Emotional Intelligence 2.0*. Their bestselling books have been translated into twenty-six languages and are available in more than 150 countries. Drs. Bradberry and Greaves have written for, or been covered by *Newsweek, BusinessWeek, Fortune, Forbes, Fast Company, Inc., USA Today, Wall Street Journal, The Washington Post,* and *Harvard Business Review.*

Dr. Greaves holds a PhD in industrial-organizational psychology and did her undergraduate work at Stanford. Dr. Bradberry holds a dual PhD in clinical psychology and industrial-organizational psychology and did his undergraduate work at the University of California, San Diego.

Melissa Oates, MS

Director of programs and assessments for TalentSmart, Oates oversees assessment services including client implementation, research and development, and customized assessment development. She earned an MS degree in industrial-organizational psychology at San Diego State University, where she won the Rebecca Bryson-Kissinger Memorial Award for Outstanding Thesis.

TalentSmart® is the world's number one provider of emotional intelligence tests and training, serving more than 75 percent of Fortune 500 companies. The company's assessment expertise is unparalleled, and it offers a variety of assessment tools that are powered by proprietary assessment technology. TalentSmart builds customized assessments for Fortune 500 clients and business thought-leaders including Adrian Gostick and Chester Elton, Jerry Porras, and Ken Blanchard. To learn more, visit TalentSmart.com.

Additional Thanks To:

Noreen Gibbons   Andrew Gibbons Sr.
Christopher Kendrick   Andrew Gibbons Jr.
Karen Fay   Anthony Gostick
Emily Loose   Yufan Chen
Kevin Small   Andrew Hahn
Christy Lawrence

About the Authors

Adrian Gostick is coauthor of the *New York Times, Wall Street Journal,* and *USA Today* bestsellers *The Carrot Principle* and *All In.* His books have been translated into thirty languages and have sold more than a million copies around the world. As a workplace expert, Adrian is a regular columnist for *Inc.* magazine and has been called a "must read for modern-day managers," by Larry King, "creative and refreshing," by the *New York Times,* and "fascinating," by *Fortune.* He has appeared on NBC's *Today Show* and CNN, and has been quoted in *The Economist, Newsweek,* and the *Harvard Business Update.*

Adrian earned a master's degree in leadership from Seton Hall University where he is a guest lecturer on workplace culture. He is also a founding partner of The Culture Works, a global consultancy focused on helping organizations build high-performance work cultures. He consults with companies such as General Electric, Rolls Royce, American Express, and California Pizza Kitchen.

OCT. 2000

Revelation 3:20

OPENING CLOSED DOORS
Keys to Reaching Hard-to-Reach People

C. Richard Weylman, CSP

McGraw-Hill
New York   San Francisco   Washington, D.C.   Auckland   Bogotá
Caracas   Lisbon   London   Madrid   Mexico City   Milan
Montreal   New Delhi   San Juan   Singapore
Sydney   Tokyo   Toronto

McGraw-Hill

A Division of The McGraw-Hill Companies

Cover photo: Gary Gruby, Atlanta, Georgia

Sponsoring editor:	Carol Rogala
Project editor:	Rita McMullen
Production manager:	Jon Christopher
Interior designer:	Heidi J. Baughman
Cover designer:	Mike Schnell
Compositor:	BookMasters, Inc.
Typeface:	11/13 Palatino
Printer:	Book Press

Library of Congress Cataloging-in-Publication Data

Weylman, C. Richard.
    Opening closed doors : keys to reaching hard-to-reach people / by
C. Richard Weylman.
       p.   cm.
    Includes index.
    ISBN 0-7863-0154-6
    1. Market segmentation. 2. Selling. I. Title.
HF5415.127.W49 1994
658.8'02—dc20

93–43011

Printed in the United States of America

8 9 10 QPV 02 01 00

To all sales professionals and business owners who are frustrated by the new barriers to the marketplace and the old ways of dealing with them: May each of you be able to get so close to the people in your market that you can hear their hearts beat.

Preface

Sales professionals and business owners are fed up. As I crisscross North America and several foreign countries on business each year, I listen to the concerns of thousands of sales professionals and business owners and hear a groundswell of frustration about how inaccessible prospects have become. They find that people are jaded, skeptical, and cynical from the typical mass marketing and prospecting techniques used by out-of-touch marketers, and, as a result, sales professionals and business owners are caught between the pressure to produce sales and this increasingly hostile, hard-to-reach buyer.

"Americans trust marketers about as much as the UN trusts Saddam Hussein," concludes *American Demographics*. A recent Roper poll indicates 70 percent of US adults believe marketers often exploit children, 71 percent believe marketers exploit women and minorities, and 70 percent say marketers often mislead people. How does anyone succeed in this environment? Sales professionals and business owners that are prospering in today's skeptical marketplace have discovered they must reduce and remove the wall of skepticism and caution that surrounds potential buyers. To accomplish this, they are focusing on ways to build quality relationships with prospects from the very first point of awareness or contact. This is a much different approach than in the past. As an example, in the 1980s, whoever got to the prospect last with the best price got the sale. Now, however, it's the person who gets to the prospect first and builds a solid relationship founded on respect that earns access to the prospect and ultimately gets the sale.

This need for quality one-on-one relationships to gain access is necessary, and the process is successful, because of the three axioms of today's prospects: they see and buy from (1) people that they know or know about, (2) people that they trust, and (3) people to whom they relate and feel relate to them.

Unfortunately, while companies both large and small are building quality into products and services, many are still using archaic approaches in marketing and prospecting. Today's buyers are looking for more than just quality products and services. They want quality in the way they are approached as well. They are responding to updated marketing and prospecting approaches based on ethics, honesty, and mutual relationships. In every industry, companies with quality merchandise are struggling to increase sales and market share. Typically, they are using outdated marketing and prospecting approaches that focus only on building relationships after the sale. Conversely, there are companies that offer second-quality goods and services that are steadily producing increases and profits. They are focused on building quality relationships before and after the sale.

Further, some sales professionals who work for the same company acquire a great deal more market share than others, often in the same territory. The clear difference is their ability to initiate and build better prospecting relationships. This, in turn, enables them to approach more people in the market on a favorable basis and deliver increased volume. Ultimately, it's the quality of the one-on-one prospecting relationships they build that determines their level of success. My conclusion is that the greatest sales come from the greatest prospectors, not the greatest salespersons.

I have come to know the frustrations of sales professionals and business owners firsthand, not only as a professional speaker and marketing consultant but also from my own personal sales experience and business ownership over the years. I have sold a wide range of products and services ranging from cookware door-to-door to Rolls-Royce automobiles to the most affluent buyers in the land. I've sold laundry supplies and magazine advertising business-to-business as well as to a wide range of individuals. I've observed both retail and wholesale sales professionals and business owners in all types of industries, including insurance, direct sales, manufacturing, services, transportation, distribution, utilities, and communications. One message is clear throughout all these experiences: People typically do not fail because they can't sell or have nothing to sell; they fail because they did not have access to enough buyers.

That's why this book is written specifically for you, the sales professional and business owner. Others can benefit; however, it is in your language and from your perspective. By following the strategies and tactics given here, you will learn how to unleash the power of relationship-building in your marketing and prospecting efforts.

In turn, your prospecting efforts will be enhanced, thus reducing your frustration with out-of-date concepts and slick techniques to simply "get your foot in the door." In addition, you spend a great deal of time, effort, energy and dollars trying to reach people. By building quality relationships from the first point of awareness or contact, prospects will be more willing to see you and do business with you. This will help lower your cost of customer acquisition.

The relationship marketing and prospecting ideas in this book will be of use to you over and over again. I would encourage you to read the book and then to reread it, to write in it, to underline in it, to circle and mark it with enthusiasm. Use this as a tool to create your own relationship marketing and prospecting plan. As you move forward, use it as a valued reference book and revisit it to refresh your memory, to renew your enthusiasm, and to spark your creativity. Share this book with a friend and meet together on a monthly basis to discuss these and your own ideas.

As you read, I would encourage you to ask questions of yourself such as:

- How can I use these ideas to my advantage?
- What strategies and tactics will make an impact on my market?
- How can I be more effective marketing and prospecting one-on-one?
- What can I do to improve my ability to build a relationship with the people in the marketplace even before the sale takes place?
- How can I add value to the relationships I have with my existing customers?

Many sales opportunities exist for those who create a groundswell of marketing and prospecting activity based on building quality relationships. With this in mind, invest enough time, effort, and money in your efforts to get to where you want to be. For to dream of the person you want to be and not do something about it is to waste the person you are.

Market and prospect smart.

C. Richard Weylman

Acknowledgments

To God for my wife, Jackie, who has taught me more than she will ever know about relationships with others.

To Bob Gibeling, my chief organizer and encourager through most of this project, for his thoughtfulness, dedication, and intellect.

To Kathy Doud, for tirelessly typing and retyping these words so many times that we lost count.

Contents

I

FOCUS: THE FIRST KEY TO OPENING CLOSED DOORS

"Concentration is the key to economic results . . . no other principle of effectiveness is violated as constantly today as the basic principle of concentration . . . Our motto seems to be: Let's do a little of everything."

Peter F. Drucker

Trying to be all things to all people and attempting to reach them with a shotgun approach puts your career and your business in jeopardy. This has been illustrated in the past by some of the largest corporations in the world. With a lack of focus, they put themselves and their employees at risk.

American Express once tried to reach everyone with its credit card slogan, "Don't leave home without it." This indicated that it wanted to do business with everyone. Now its revised, targeted approach is "The right card for the right people." This indicates that it now realizes that it is more important and effective to reach the *right* people than it is to reach simply *many* people, according to *Business Week*.

AT&T once touted that it was the only telephone company nec-essary in the United States. After the division of the communica-tions industry by the government, AT&T now rightly proclaims, "One size no longer fits all." That says that AT&T, too, recognizes that it must focus if it hopes to capture the specific segments of the market where it knows it can be effective and profitable.

The same holds true for you as a sales professional or business owner. Your objective should be to focus on specific niches or groups of people within your territory or local marketing area. This will allow you to focus on the prospects and build the quality rela-tionships with them necessary to gain favorable access. Unfortu-nately, though, when you talk to the average sales professional or business owner and ask "Who is your customer?" or "What is your market?" most respond, "The whole world is my market; we deal with pretty much everybody." While it's true that we now operate in a global economy or world market, taking a whole world ap-proach to marketing and prospecting is not the way to penetrate it successfully. That kind of approach demonstrates to customers that you are trying to be all things to all people at a time when they want to do business with people who relate to and specialize in people like them.

Most sales professionals and business owners skip from market to market to market, jumping from prospect to prospect. Even though it increases overhead, there is a strong tendency to do this because they have not been taught any differently. Most are just try-ing to get their feet in the door somewhere. What the most *success-ful* people do, however, is *focus* on specific niche or target markets and then work those markets deep. Figures 1 and 2 depict the dif-ference in approaches, with and without a focus.

On a personal level, a lack of focus not only increases your frus-tration as a sales professional or business owner, it reduces your ef-fectiveness as a prospector. By focusing on specific niche or target markets, you obtain a clear vision of where you are, where you are going, and how to get there. In fact, Peter Marshall wrote in *Mr. Jones Meets the Master*, "Give us clear vision that we may know where to stand and what to stand for, because unless we stand for something, we shall fall for anything."

If you think about it, even as a child you learned the power of concentrated energy. We all remember how great sunshine felt in

FIGURE 1
Skipping from Market to Market
(Horizontal Growth and Increased Overhead)

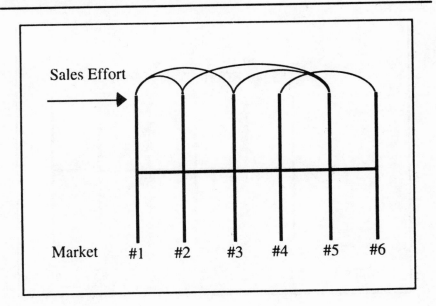

the summer and how it never seemed to really hurt us. However, if you had a magnifying glass, you quickly realized that by focusing that sunshine, you could burn holes in leaves, chase the family dog, and even catch slow ants in the driveway. In the same way, your prospecting energy, when focused, gives you a whole new set of results.

If you're spreading yourself all over the market, you're diffusing your energy and you're not burning through the clutter that prevents prospects in the marketplace from knowing about you and buying from you. Gaining focus, then, should be your primary consideration. It is the beginning of a dynamic process.

For the experienced sales professional or business owner, gaining focus means uncovering hidden markets and relational prospecting opportunities within your current business activities. For those just starting out, it means defining your best markets early in your business or career. This enables you to focus on building the quality one-on-one relationships necessary to open closed doors. In all

FIGURE 2
Focused Effort, Working the Markets
(Deep Vertical Growth and Increased Profitability)

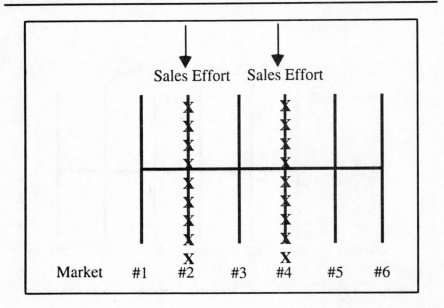

cases, achieving your focus is the first step in reaching those hard-to-reach, skeptical buyers. Without it, you cannot gain maximum access to the people within your own local market area.

As you move forward toward identifying what your best niche market or markets could be, consider the experiences of my father-in-law, John Nicholson.

John is a first-class fisherman. Although he is 82 years old, it is common for him to catch his limit in just a few hours. John fishes in Lake Lanier outside Gainesville in north Georgia. His approach to fishing is unlike those of his friends and friendly competitors. They launch their boats and troll all over the lake, looking for just the "right catch."

John uses a totally different strategy. He launches out in his small bass boat, moves along the shoreline, and visits his personal fishing holes. While the others cast all over the lake, attempting to hook a big one, John simply drops his line into his fishing holes and repeatedly catches fish.

When I questioned him about his renowned fishing ability, he simply stated, "I fish in my fishing holes because it's easier to catch the big ones, and besides, why would I waste my time fishing all over the lake?" John understands the power of focus. He clearly illustrates that it is far more productive to find and fish in fishing holes than it is to fish the whole lake, just as it is more profitable to determine and prospect specific niche markets than to prospect the whole marketplace.

A recent article by Tom Stanley, author of *Marketing to the Affluent*, suggests that there are actually two ways to "fish" for prospects. One traditional method is finding, chasing, and landing the prospect. Another is the "chumming" method, which is based on the principle that the prospect will find, chase, and land the sales professional or business owner.

Dividing your marketplace into definable segments or groups of people allows you to receive the benefits of both methods. You are better able to find, chase, and land the prospects because you know where they are. Coupled with your efforts to become known to your prospects through relationship-building strategies and tactics, your prospects find it easier to find and land you as their supplier. Prospects will be comfortable with both methods because, through your marketing and prospecting efforts, they will become confident you are the individual who relates to them and knows their needs and the best solutions for the situations they face.

Regardless of the industry you're in or the products or services you sell, there are many different niches or "fishing holes" available to you. If you're responsible for finding your own customers, such as most real estate agents, office equipment sellers, financial services people, direct sellers, small-business owners, advertising agency account executives, salespeople for radio and TV time, and so on, your marketplace can be divided for easier access.

If you're working a preselected corporate list of markets, such as pharmacies and physicians to sell medical supplies, garden stores and landscapers to sell fertilizer products, or even consumer goods for grocery stores, dividing your marketplace will work for you as well. No matter who determines who your prospects are, you can define, redefine, and segment your markets to build the quality relationships necessary to gain even greater access to your prospects.

As you move forward, the questions you should be asking your-self are:

- What are my best markets?
- How do I select them?
- How can I take the list of markets I (or my company) already have to the next segmentation step so I can prospect more effectively one-on-one?
- How can I qualify these markets to be sure they have enough potential for my product line and me?

The following three chapters give you the strategies and tactics necessary to divide, understand, and select your best market segments or niches. After reading these, you will be able to make an informed decision and know that you have selected the right niche or niches that will work for you. You'll then be ready to put into practice all the other relationship marketing and prospecting ideas in the subsequent chapters to open closed doors successfully.

Chapter One

Strategy: Define Your Target and Find Your Niche

Objective: To divide the marketplace into definable segments or groups of people so you can gain favorable one-on-one access.

F or years, the goal of marketers has been to focus on the whole marketplace and then segment it through demographics, psychographics, and, in some cases, even consumer attitudes. Although segmentation by demographic or psychographic code gives you insights into market potential and is important for strategic planning, it does a poor job of allowing you to find and build relationships with prospects one-on-one.

To market and prospect successfully, you must gain access to the people based on how they relate to and interact with one another, not just what their demographic grouping happens to be.

As I mentioned earlier, in many industries the reason business failures and sales professional turnover is high is because of an inability to reach prospective customers. This is often caused by a lack of focus on specific accessible segments by the leadership. There is a continued push to simply market and prospect to selected demographic profiles in hopes that the sales professional will find a way to reach and sell the people.

As a case in point, IBM has historically assigned its sales representatives to geographic areas. Its 62 geographic areas were clearly defined, and a myriad of demographic and psychographic information was available for each of these areas. However, faced with customer demands that it try to do a better job of relating to them and presenting solutions they could use, IBM has now redefined its markets and restructured its sales force. It is now selling to specific industries, not geographic areas or a demographic profile. This, in turn, has helped it build relationships with and gain access to prospects based on their specific industry affiliations, not demographic profits.

No matter how you or your company have segmented your market or territory in the past, it is ultimately your responsibility to adjust the way you see and define the marketplace now. Successful sales professionals and business owners know you cannot earn the right to see people based on a demographic profile.

To segment and build quality relationships with prospects requires that you think about and see them differently. To demystify and break through the demographic or psychographic code, look at how people interact and build mutually rewarding relationships with one another. You will quickly realize that they usually organize or associate with one another based on what they do for a living (i.e., their profession, type of business, or occupation) or what they do for recreation (e.g., play sports or join clubs). Many also organize and associate based on their social, charitable, cultural, or community interests and ethnic backgrounds. Remember the old truism, "Birds of a feather flock together." People associate and communicate with other people like themselves. For instance, people in the same type of business or profession join together in an association. People who play golf associate at country clubs. To gain access to the marketplace, we should then divide it based on what our prospects do for a living, for recreation, or where they have special interests. The advantage is that by segmenting your market into niches in this way, you can reach out to prospects that associate and communicate with one another. This means you can find and associate and communicate with them. They, in turn, can find and associate and communicate with you. Without these two factors, your marketing and prospecting efforts will continue to be frustrating and expensive. Think about it:

- Isn't it likely that trial attorneys will associate with other trial attorneys or orthodontists will socialize with other orthodonists?
- Wouldn't the members of a country club, tennis club, or ethnic social group compare notes with one another about how satisfied they are with a product or service?

- Don't the parents of children in a particular school relate and communicate with each other on a regular basis?
- Isn't it true that people who own convenience stores belong to a common group with their peers? Don't fast-food operators follow the same path?
- Is it fair to say that executives belong to a group of their peers as well?
- Most assuredly, plumbers, welders, electricians, and others in the trades have their own groups and associates, don't they?
- Homemakers in a neighborhood know other homemakers in their neighborhood, and don't they often have watch associations or activities together?

The objective is not to segment the marketplace just so you can divide and conquer, nor is it just to get a more defined mailing list of prospects. You should divide the marketplace into segments or niches, to, first, better understand the people in the markets and build solid relationships with them—relationships based on mutual respect, honesty, and integrity. Second, by focusing on how people in the specific markets interact with one another, you can target your relationship marketing and prospecting efforts specifically to them and for them. This combination of targeted efforts founded on ethical relationships will give you favorable access to them and others like them.

Even a company such as General Motors has changed its marketing focus to capture this principle. One of its latest advertising slogans is, "We don't just build cars, we build relationships." General Motors is no longer segmenting for the sake of segmenting. It is now segmenting so it can earn the right to its prospects' business by relating to and building a sense of relationship with them.

With this understanding, you can see how continued prospecting to most demographic groups is frustrating and counterproductive. It is not good enough to just know about your prospects. You must know how they relate and communicate with one another. For example, people 35 to 55 years of age making $75,000 don't know each other, nor is it likely they communicate with each other solely because they fit in this databased statistical demographic definition. They may be a great group of prospects; however, you must resegment to reach them. Small-business owners with sales over $5 million a year may be an attractive market for computer workstation sales. Yet they are not likely to associate and communicate with each other because they have sales over $5 million. Thus, it is hard to focus on them, get to be known by them, and build quality relationships with large numbers of them. However, if you focus and segment these same prospects by their industry or business affiliations and associations, they are readily accessible to you.

The same holds true in nearly every product or service category. There is a critical necessity to segment or resegment your marketplace based on how people associate and communicate with one another so you can focus your energy and reach the people.

To get started and get a grasp on the various niche segments available to you, look at the marketplace as a large target with a bull's-eye. There are two parts to this bull's-eye, simply to enable you to work through the process step-by-step (see Figure 1–1).

As you can see, part 1 of the bull's-eye is your existing prospects and customers. It's important to analyze these first because you need to know where you *are* before you can determine what new markets you may need or want to develop. For some of you, just identifying and reaching more people like your existing customers or prospects will give you the increased growth you seek. Others of you will realize that you must expand into new markets.

The new markets represented in part 2 of the bull's-eye could be markets you have always wanted to pursue, markets where you see growth opportunities, or markets where you have products or expertise that are needed.

The following tactics will enable you to find and redefine both your existing and new markets so that you can focus on the people in those markets.

Let's begin by examining the first half of the bull's-eye—that is, how you should segment your *existing customer and prospect base* (see Figure 1–2).

TACTIC 1   Divide the market into groups of people who have much in common.

Those of you who are working from a corporate preselected list of markets have a very clear idea of whom you're going to be calling on. For example, if you are working for an organization that sells

FIGURE 1–1
Define and Analyze Your Opportunities

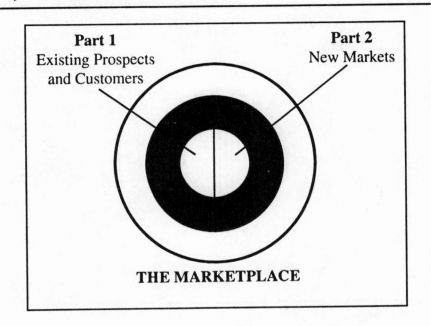

stationery supplies, you are calling on people who retail your products. If you are selling automobile aftermarket parts, you are calling on people who own auto parts stores or various garages. Whatever the particular product or service you are selling, you're typically selling to a preselected list of markets and prospects. However, this should not prevent you from rethinking how you can reach your prospects.

Resegment these customers and prospects into definable groups of people that have more in common—that is, their specific type of business, recreation, or interest. Begin by dividing your existing customer and prospect base into specific, definable groups. For example, if you are selling hardware supplies to retail stores, divide and list all of your customers and prospects by specific types of stores, such as department stores, chain hardware stores, discount stores, mom and pops, and so on. If you are selling auto parts, as mentioned earlier, divide your existing customers and prospects into groups such as auto parts stores, auto wrecking yards, new car

FIGURE 1–2
Analyze Your Existing Business

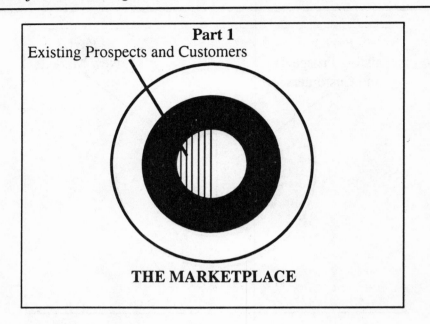

dealers, used car dealers, and so forth. As you will quickly realize, specific groups have more in common with each other. It is also much more likely that they will know and interact with one another. This, then, is the way you will want to segment and approach them.

Some of your customers may be tax attorneys, real estate attorneys, litigators, or corporate law firms. Avoid grouping them all together. Instead, divide and list them into specific groups based on specialty. Tax attorneys know other tax attorneys. Litigators associate, communicate, and otherwise interact with other litigators. Convenience store owners know and talk to other convenience store owners much more readily than to the head of a department store. This will help you see your market differently and help you associate and communicate with market members—which, in turn, will lead to favorable access for you.

Here are some examples of segments or niches within broad categories of markets to stimulate your thinking:

Retail Stores	Real Estate Firms	Automotive Market	Medical
Convenience	Commercial	New car dealers	Podiatrists
Chain hardware	Residential	Used car dealers	Psychiatrists
Department	Brokers	Wrecking yards	Pharmacists
Discount	Office leasing	Auto parts stores	Hospitals—
Mom and pops	Apartment leasing	Aftermarket garages	Administration (less than 300 beds)
			Hospitals— Administration (300 or more beds)

Create your own list of segments or groups of people. Be sure to group them based on what they have in common, and you will see the increased market potential. By taking this first step, you will be able to implement the rest of the relationship-based marketing and prospecting strategies and tactics in this book to the fullest.

For those of you who have the responsibility and freedom to choose your own markets, you should resegment your existing list of customers and prospects much the same way. Divide them into definable groups that have a great deal in common—that is, what they do for a living, recreation, or interest.

However, instead of examining your entire list of customers as your colleagues with preselected markets would do, you should start with a tighter focus. Experienced sales professionals and business owners who control their own markets over the years have been told to examine and consider their entire customer list in their decision about the future. The trouble with that idea, for many, is that the people you sold in the early days of your career or business are not the same types of individuals with whom you are working now. In addition, your products or services and the needs of the market may have changed greatly since you began. This has contributed to a shift in your customer and prospect list.

That same thinking has been foisted on new people starting in sales or business. They are often told to list all the people they know and all likely prospects in their area and to sell them. This idea severely limits potential. People you know and prospect in your area have their own affinities and links to other individuals just like themselves. By segmenting your prospects and clients into definable groups, you can reach more people just like them.

To find the people around whom you want to build your future business, look at your past 40 sales and all your current prospects. Reference what industry, recreational, or interest group they are in. Ask yourself resegmenting questions such as, "What type of business are they in?" Be specific. What type of profession do they practice? If you have attorneys on your customer or prospect list, what types of attorneys are they? Identify their area of specialty or commonality. If you have corporate executives, what specific positions do they hold? Vice president of finance? CEO? Be sure you also consider the recreation and cultural interests of your customers and prospects. Even what schools their children attend should be considered. This may be what they have most in common and where and why they associate and communicate with one another.

By grouping the various types of people together based on what they have in common, you will plainly see their potential to interact. Group them much the same as your colleagues who operate with preselected markets would do. To illustrate this further for you, here are several more examples:

Professionals	Small Business	Occupations
Chiropractors	Print shops	Welders
Orthodontists	Auto dealers	Comptrollers
Registered nurses	Used car dealers	Sales/marketing execs
	Fast-food outlets	in the steel industry

Recreation	Special Interests
Country clubs	PTAs
Tennis clubs	AARP chapters
Sports leagues	Neighborhood associations
Car clubs	SCORE chapters
Soccer clubs	Church groups
Little leagues	Korean business league
Football clubs	NAACP members
YMCA/YWCA	Latino Chamber of Commerce
Racquetball clubs	
Ski clubs	
Travel clubs	

For those of you who can select your own markets from existing customers and prospects, the next point is vitally important. After you have divided your customers and prospects into definable industry, recreational, or interest groups, look for those where you feel you have an affinity or link with your own experience or interests. Zero in on those groups of people where you have a common bond or interest. Think about where you enjoy working and with whom you have a passion to sell and serve. This will provide additional motivation to build the quality relationships necessary to deliver you into your best niche markets.

Regardless of whether you have preselected corporate markets or an opportunity for choice, and before you push on to finding new markets, be sure you review the following tactics.

TACTIC 2   Divide your customers or prospects geographically if you are in a large territory.

Once you have segmented your customers and prospects, then think geographically. Working a large territory often means there are separate niches within your geographic area. For example, if your business has grown to cover the entire state of North Carolina, it's important to separate your customers and prospects by location. The corporate executives in Greensboro will most likely know and interact with one another in their local area. The executives several hundred miles away in Greenville will do likewise in their area. The two groups in the same state could have entirely different needs and priorities. Remember, you're looking to define segments of people who have a great deal in common and thus associate and communicate with one another.

TACTIC 3   In business-type markets, segment more broadly in rural areas.

In a rural area, you may not need so many breakouts of specific types of business or professional markets. Instead, as you segment, include everyone in the same type of industry. As an example, instead of podiatrists, psychologists, and orthopedic surgeons, each assigned to a separate niche, group them as the doctors in a certain geographic area. This type of situation occurs if you market in the broad expanses of the Midwest or the great western plains of Canada or Australia. You may wish to group auto dealers by their synergies with others, such as transportation companies, instead of by themselves. Unlike in urban areas, people in rural areas interact and interface with one another more frequently in broadly defined categories. The retailers usually know each other and probably belong to the chamber of commerce, while the farmers are likely to belong to the grange. In the case of recreation or special interests, you should still segment using a narrow focus.

TACTIC 4   Identify potential groups by the specific products and services your current customers have purchased.

This can give you insight into how your customers and even prospects may be connected to one another. For example, if you have several customers who have all bought a particular high-end type of copier, identify what types of business they are in. You may find very quickly that you have a group of people that is somehow tied to each other. They may do business with one another or supply the same industry. They may even belong to the same industry or supplier group.

Similarly, if you find a group of customers in the same age group that buys a particular product or requires a specific service you provide, you may be able to identify a peer group or association to which they belong.

TACTIC 5   Use a college intern to help you define your current market segments or niches.

If you do not already know what specific type of business, recreation groups, or interest groups your customers belong to, you need to find out. Discover the connection points of current customers or prospects by using a college intern to do the research. Provide the resource material, such as customer lists and information sources, to a college student who has an interest in marketing or research. Have the student call your existing customers to "update your files." Have the student ask your customers in what type of occupation, specific business, clubs, and associations they are involved. Then divide your customer base and assemble them into definable segments or groups of people based on that information and your market focus. Contact a local business college placement office to get guidance on how to find the right person.

Let's turn our attention to the *second half of the bull's-eye*, which is determining opportunities in *new* markets (see Figure 1–3).

Whether you are working for a company that provides you with a preselected list of new markets or have more flexibility in selecting your own new markets, there are many new market opportunities to be found. The desire to find and reach into new markets to expand your sales and business is limited only by your desire for growth.

TACTIC 6 Look for market niches where your product or service could do well.

Take a hard look at where you are currently selling or where your business is currently operating, and ask yourself, "What are some other places where my products could be delivered into the market?" For example, if you're calling on wholesalers of nursery products, look for opportunities with landscapers or large lawn care companies who need your product. If you're selling surgical supplies to medical schools, step back and look at emerging markets you may not have thought about before. Can your product be used somewhere else? Could it be repackaged to fit into a new niche?

In their book *Making Niche Marketing Work* (McGraw-Hill, 1991), Robert E. Linneman and John L. Stanton, Jr., give an excellent example of this way to identify a spin-off market.

Convatec, the manufacturer of Stomahesive, a large adhesive dressing to attach colostomy bags, found that hospitals were buying Stomahesive in large quantities. They were buying so many that Convatec realized they had to be using the product beyond its original purposes. Nurses were cutting up the big sheets of adhesive and using them for other medical conditions. So Convatec came out with a new product, Duoderm, which was nothing more than the original Stomahesive cut into strips.[1]

FIGURE 1–3
Analyze Your New Business

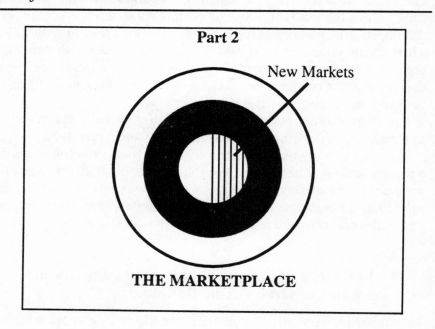

Convatec was able to market Duoderm to other niche markets within the medical profession that needed smaller adhesives.

As you think about new market opportunities, deliberately look for an adjacent niche market. If you're selling copiers to publishers, it may make a great deal of sense to call on printing companies. If you're marketing services of a travel agency that specializes in apparel manufacturers, you might find that buyers for apparel are also a good market because they travel frequently to merchandise shows. Think bigger and define your opportunities.

TACTIC 7   Use Dun & Bradstreet's *Census of American Business.*

Dun & Bradstreet lists businesses by Standard Industrial Classification codes, which divide the marketplace into a system of two- and four-digit numbers, commonly called SICs. The two-digit codes are assigned to broad industry categories such as transportation, chemical products, fabricated metal products, apparel, furniture and fixtures, and so on. The four-digit codes are assigned to very specific types of businesses within the broader two-digit categories. For example, within the two-digit SIC category for transportation, there are many different types of transportation companies listed. These would include everything from automobile manufacturers and shipbuilding companies to manufacturers of aircraft engines and railroad equipment. Each would have its own four-digit code.

Use the *Dun & Bradstreet SIC 2 + 2 Directory* to help you identify potential spin-off markets that you may want to pursue. By reviewing all the businesses within the two-digit SIC category that your existing customers are in, you may have a magic moment and find a potential spin-off. The Dun & Bradstreet address is 3 Sylvan Way, Parsippany, New Jersey 07054, or call toll free 800-526-0651. Dun's census is also usually available at large public libraries as well as business-oriented schools and universities.

You may also find much of this information in the *Standard Industrial Classification Directory*, published annually by the US government, Office of Management and the Budget. The SIC directory is also available at many libraries and may be purchased at US government printing offices, found in many large cities.

TACTIC 8   Ask existing customers where you can or should grow.

You'll often find your existing customers own or serve on boards of other businesses. They may suggest that you expand into those market niches. They can help you gain favorable access as well, through their relationships and influence. Ask your customers what markets they think would be good for your products or services. Ask for suggestions about where they think you could be effective.

TACTIC 9   Make a list of the types of businesses or people that could prosper from your products or services.

This list could be based on something these businesses or people have in common with your current customers or a unique need they have that your product or service could satisfy. Then segment the marketplace based on how you think they might associate and communicate with one another. Remember to base your thinking around what people do—that is, the type of business or industry they're in, how they recreate, or their areas of interest.

TACTIC 10   Use *The Occupation Finder* for brainfood.

Dr. John Holland's *The Occupation Finder*, published by Consulting Psychologists Press in Palo Alto, California, gives a long, systematic list of various types of occupations. Scan this list to help find new occupations that could use your product or service or help you recognize groups with whom you have something in common and may have overlooked.

TACTIC 11   Use *The Lifestyle Market Analyst* to help identify lifestyle markets.

If your goal is to sell a product or service to people in specific recreational groups and lifestyles, this is a helpful tool. It will help you understand how people group themselves by their lifestyle. This extensive reference manual is available from Standard Rate and Data Service. It gives descriptions of 58 separate lifestyle interests, hobbies, and activities. Ask your local library for availability, or call 800-323-4588.

TACTIC 12   Contact your local board of tourism, trade, and conventions.

These are often an excellent source of new industries that are coming to an area and new clubs or service groups that haven't been announced to the public yet. You may find spin-off business opportunities. Check with them periodically to stay ahead of the competition.

TACTIC 13   If you have control over the selection of your new niche market, choose a new market niche in which you would like to expand or build your business or career.

Start with a fresh piece of paper and follow these three steps:

Step 1.   Examine yourself. Consider these questions: What is your background? What are your interests? With whom do you enjoy working? What type of people do you have a passion to service? What is your educational background? How do/did your parents and grandparents earn a living? What type of work experiences have you had? Where can you and your products and services make a real impact on the people in the niche?

Look for answers that trigger a positive response in your mind and that point to a common element or direction. This will help you get a sense of the type of people with whom you would like to work. From your analysis, pick market types such as professionals, small-business owners, or people in certain types of occupations. If you are more at home with a lifestyle or interest group market orientation, select a market type such as families, sports-minded individuals, or ethnic markets.

Step 2.   Select the specific segments or niches you would like to target. For example, if you want to work with professionals, determine what specific type of professional people. Is your choice neurosurgeons, tax attorneys, or chemical engineers?

Similarly, if you want to work with ethnic interest groups, choose the segment or segments on which you wish to focus. A Latino business league or a particular NAACP chapter are some specific examples. If you have chosen small-business owners, what type of small business? Are they welding shops, air-conditioning retailers, or gift shop owners? Make a specific choice. Remember, in a rural area, defining your niche as simply attorneys or doctors may be narrow enough. In a metropolitan area, however, you should be more specific and focus on a particular type of attorney, doctor, or engineer. Remember, birds of a feather flock together.

Step 3. Be sure you truly have something in common with the people. It's important for you to work with people with whom you have an affinity or link. It's very difficult to choose and work in a market where you feel you have little in common with the people who are a part of it. Not only will they be uncomfortable with you, but you will be with them. The penalty will be a longer access time or no access at all.

The most remarkable example I know of choosing a niche where you have something in common is Karen Officer, from Foster City, California. Karen, who is profoundly deaf, sells insurance and other financial services to the hearing-impaired community, which totals 30,000 people in the San Francisco Bay area. Because of the general difficulty hearing people have in communicating with hearing-impaired people, very few of the latter have ever been contacted by someone with the ability to help them plan their financial future.

Karen, on the other hand, communicates well by using lip reading and American Sign Language. Working for Link-Allen & Associates, she brought in a record number of new clients in her first 90 days. As Peter Evans, her supervisor, states, "This has got to be the quintessential market. If you are not deaf or able to communicate [with the deaf community], the market is impenetrable." Ask yourself what you have in common with your market that will give you a passion to work with the people in it.

TACTIC 14   For those of you with freedom to choose but no idea where to start, utilize checkbook marketing.

Look at your check register and examine the people to whom you have recently written checks for a service they have provided. You may find individuals who are supplying you that could be an entree into a new market. For example, your doctor, dentist, or dry-cleaning shop owner might be a valuable source of information about people you want to target. Be systematic in your approach. By peeling away the layers of information, you may find a hidden jewel of opportunity.

Whether you are working with assigned markets or have the freedom to choose your own, the outcome of the focus and segmentation process is the same. Dividing your existing business and new market opportunities into definable segments and groups of people that are likely to associate and communicate with one another gives you a much clearer idea of where to focus your efforts. Now you can move forward to get important qualifying information to be sure existing and new markets are profitable and the people accessible to you. After you have that information, you can make a good decision about these markets and whether you should pursue them. These two steps are the subjects of the next two chapters.

Chapter Two

Strategy: Determine Whether Your Niche Markets Have True Potential

Objective: To collect enough relevant information and insights into your existing and new niche markets to be sure they are and will continue to be profitable and accessible targets.

F rancis Bacon's oft-quoted prose "Knowledge is Power" certainly applies to prospecting and marketing. To be effective, you must know all you can about your niche market and its prospects. Particularly useful is information on how profitable the market is and how you can reach and relate to the prospects. Information gathering does not just apply to new niche market opportunities, it also applies to your existing market niches as well. It also does not just apply to individuals who can choose their own markets. Those of you who work in preselected company markets need to know more about those markets and why you're in them. You need to be sure of their potential and how to access them so that you have a vision for the future.

In all cases, because you are resegmenting existing markets as well as new ones, gathering profitability and accessibility information will help you make a good decision about whether to continue to pursue a particular niche and how to do it.

Specifically, knowing in advance whether markets have continued potential gives all of you an important competitive edge. Most sales professionals and business owners rely on six to eight months of effort in a new niche market before they know if it will pay off for them, or they continue to pursue existing markets long after the signs of decline are clear. This is a costly mistake, both in effort and financial resources. Information gathering about existing and new markets allows you to make a wide range of decisions based on market intelligence, not just experience.

The information-gathering process will give you great insight into how to relate to and reach your prospects in new ways. You will also find that as you know more about them, they will be more inclined to see you and buy from you. Peter Drucker stated this so clearly when he said, "The aim of marketing is to know and understand the customer so well that the product or service fits him or her and sells itself."

The people in the marketplace today demand that you know about them before they are open to knowing about you. They want to be sure you speak their language and understand their perspective. They want the sense of mutual relationship to start even before they meet you personally. They want you involved in their organizations and associations. All the more reason to know about them and how they associate and communicate with one another. You can meet them where they meet with each other. Without market information, it is impossible to convince them that you know and understand them.

In the past, those people who spent their time concentrating on gathering information have sometimes been given unflattering names like *nerd* and *bookworm*. Is there any wonder, then, that the frequent reaction to any research-type project is, "Research? Give me a break!" Yet, gathering the niche market information you need to build your business or career can be one of the most stimulating and rewarding activities you've ever pursued.

Research allows those of you who can choose your own markets to move ahead with confidence. The same holds true for those of you who work in corporately defined markets. Your market intelligence and identification of a new market or new approach to an existing market may be just the power point you need to move up in the organization.

Information gathering, then, not only gives you the facts you need to make a quality decision about your niche, it also enables you to know how to gain maximum results from your relationship prospecting and marketing efforts.

For these reasons, it is important to maintain your focus on what type of information to gather. The two overriding issues are the *profitability of the market* and the *accessibility of the people in the market*. You want to know if it makes good business sense for you to continue to pursue this market, and you must be certain you can relate to and reach the people in it.

To choose smart:

Consider these market profitability issues

- Is the market growing or declining?
- Are the sales and/or incomes of this market in growth or decline?
- How can you position yourself and your company in this market?
- What opportunities are there for spin-off markets?
- What are the employment or membership projections for this market?
- Will more businesses, professions, clubs, and people like this move into the area?
- Who among your competitors is currently selling these people, and how are they positioned?
- What is the potential dollar volume you can sell in this market?
- Does the market have a need for your products or services?
- Could you repackage your products or services to fit the needs of this market?

Consider these market accessibility issues

- What is their common culture—ethnic, business, recreation, or interest?
- How do they associate with each other—through associations, clubs, or special-interest organizations? If so, which ones?
- Do they have newsletters, trade magazines, bulletins, or other means of targeted communication with their colleagues?
- Do these people have a word-of-mouth network and refer suppliers to one another?

- What words are common to them as a group?
- Are they heavily screened or hard to reach because of secretaries, voice mail, or electronic mail?
- Are there targeted lead sources available for this niche?
- How often do the people in this niche meet or recreate with one another?
- Do you feel an affinity, link, or connection to the people in the market?

You can add other issues that are appropriate to your situation and market as you get a clearer picture of the people and processes in your targeted niche(s). You might even use the same college intern mentioned in Chapter 1 to do the actual information gathering once you have existing and potential new niche markets defined. To begin the process, keep the following points in mind so you can have the right information to make a good decision:

- Set the time aside to do this information gathering. A day or two spent in the beginning saves you headaches and heartaches long term. As Abe Lincoln said so eloquently, "If I had six days to chop down a tree, I would spend five days sharpening my axe!" Remember, learn from market intelligence.
- Be sure to make a list of the information you are seeking for each niche market segment before you start. This will help you stay on track. What is more important, you will be able to evaluate all your existing and new opportunities equally. Remember to key in on how prospects and customers associate and communicate with one another. Use and expand on the profitability and accessibility questions in this chapter. To stimulate your thinking as to what other questions to ask, a quick review of Harvey MacKay's *How to Swim with the Sharks without Getting Eaten Alive* would provide additional brainfood.
- Avoid being distracted. If you spot another market opportunity, research it separately. Keep yourself focused on each niche to expedite the process.
- Avoid using written materials as your only sources of information. Interaction with people who can offer their insight and opinions will be vitally important to you and will help you make a good decision.

- Ask your sources questions in a way that promotes discovery. You want your discussions with reference librarians, custtomers, and prospects to be a dialogue.

Finally, the most important thing about doing your background research is to have a passion for it. You cannot just outwork the competition, you must also *outthink* the competition. Good information helps you to think well *and* choose well.

The following tactics are designed to help you gather the right profitability and accessibility information quickly. After you have worked through these tactics, it will be time to move to Chapter 3 and make a decision about whether your niche markets will deliver or continue to deliver results for you.

TACTIC 15   Ask your existing customers and prospects to verify profitability and accessibility issues.

If you already have customers in the particular market segment you are trying to approach or you have a list of prospects, talk to them one-on-one. You can do this on a formal basis by calling them on the telephone and asking them to help you by answering a few marketing and prospecting questions. Tell them of your desire to specialize in their industry or interests and become more involved.

Create and use your profitability and accessibility list to stay on track. Be sure to ask them to what clubs, organizations, or associations they belong. Find out how you can better relate and interact with them. Most people are receptive if you ask with a gracious demeanor versus a demanding one.

If you want a less formal approach, ask a few questions from your profitability and accessibility list as you make your normal sales calls. Be sure here that they understand that you're not looking for just another sales opportunity but a long-term, mutually profitable, and rewarding relationship with them and other people in their niche.

Either way, over the course of two weeks you can collect much valuable information.

Most importantly, be open to their suggestions. Paul Shevlin, a client from Philadelphia, suggested that I attend a trade show and get involved in a national organization that supported him and other decision makers in his industry. I nearly forgot my own advice as I told him why I couldn't, even though I was asking him for his advice. Thankfully, I came to my senses. Taking his advice opened a whole new market to us.

TACTIC 16   Call the membership chairperson of the local club, association, or organization that services your market for information.

Whether you are targeting special interest groups, social clubs, recreation clubs, or professional or industry groups, the local organization is an invaluable source of information and favorable access. The very existence of a formal organization indicates that the people in your niche market probably associate and communicate with one another. Call membership chairpersons and build friendly relationships with them. They have a very good sense of the characteristics of their members. They might have a member profile of the people you are considering as a target market. They will certainly be able to tell you how accessible these people are. They will be able to advise you as to whether you can join their organization and become involved. Further, you can gain profitability information such as whether the organization is growing or not and whether competitors have a presence there. Most, if not all, of the information on your profitability and accessibility checklist is at their disposal. You should meet with them one-on-one to begin or to continue building a relationship with them. They will be valuable allies in your relationship marketing and prospecting efforts.

TACTIC 17   Meet with noncompeting suppliers already in your existing or new niche.

Sales professionals and business owners working in your targeted niche not only can give you answers to the questions on your profitability and accessibility checklist, they can give you fresh insight and ideas you could not acquire any other way. Be sure to ask how they access your niche market for the sale of their products. Find out what associations or organizations support those same buyers you're trying to reach. Write them down for use later.

To encourage this dialogue with you, volunteer to share with them all the information you gather. You should also offer to meet occasionally to update each other about the market and its prospects. Whether you are reexamining and resegmenting an existing market or selecting a new niche, this reciprocal interaction can provide you with special information and a competitive edge.

TACTIC 18   Use your public or college library for a wealth of information.

Instead of spending hours in the stacks groping for information, be sure to work with research librarians or reference desk staff. They are very familiar with the best sources and how to access information quickly. By building a personal relationship with these people, it will be as though they are part of your staff, in effect, even though they're not on your payroll. It's important to give these library researchers respect and treat them as colleagues. Let them know what you are doing and that you would like their help because you see them as experts at gathering information. A little personal attention and respect can go a long way.

There are many different tools to use within the library. Among them are:

- Electronic, computer-based search terminals that will locate articles about target market groups. These articles will give you insight into areas of interest and market language.
- Modems to library databases showing books available about your niche markets.
- Current trade, club, or special-interest magazines that those in your niche markets read.
- Lifestyle and industry directories and catalogs listing leads and niche lead sources.

Learn from the library staff which ones can give you what you need.

With the ongoing fragmentation of the marketplace and the increased need to segment the marketplace by industry, recreation, or interest, there are new tools available to you almost daily.

TACTIC 19   Find the appropriate industry magazines or special-interest publications by using SRDS.

To help you determine if the people in your niche communicate with one another and how they relate to each other, you should identify what, if any, publications they read. If you know the names of key trade magazines or special niche publications aimed at your niche market, look them up by title at the reference or periodicals desk of the library. However, if you only know the name of your niche market group, such as florists, advertising executives, or pharmacists, you can find the title of the industry or professional magazine that reaches them by looking in *Standard Rate and Data Service* (SRDS), *Business Publications*.

For recreation or lifestyle niche markets, such as antique auto enthusiasts or snow skiers, consult *Standard Rate and Date Service, Consumer Publications.* Both of these directories list the names of magazines that people in your niche are likely to read and use to make purchase decisions. The magazines are listed under their respective industry, business, or lifestyle categories. They may be found at many large libraries (and are also available from Standard Rate and Data Services, 3004 Glenview Road, Wilmette, Illinois 60091; telephone 708-256-6067).

TACTIC 20   Use the *Pocket Media Guide.*

This is another good source of names of publications read by the people in your market. It lists 700 trade and professional magazines and provides names, addresses, and phone numbers. You must use a company letterhead when requesting a copy (provided free by writing to Media Distribution Services, PRA Group, Department P, 307 West 36th Street, New York, New York 10118).

TACTIC 21   Call the specialty or trade magazines and request a sample copy and a media kit.

Ask the advertising representative to send you a media kit and a demographic profile of the people the publication targets. This will provide you with information such as average income, average age, what types of products they buy, and what types of services they render or need.

If you feel uncomfortable calling the advertising representative, use this telephone presentation:

Receptionist:

Hello, ABC Publishing.

You:

I need to speak with advertising sales, please.

Marge:

Advertising sales, this is Marge.

You:

Good morning, Marge. This is Linda Smith with Quality Products Company. How are you today?

Marge:

I'm just fine Linda. How can I help you?

You:

Marge, I'm interested in finding out more about your magazine and its readers. Would you please send me a media kit with a demographic profile so I can determine who I would be reaching if I purchased your mailing list or placed an advertisement? I would also like the two most recent issues of your publication as well as one older issue. What is your current circulation and what was it two years ago?

Marge:

6,000 statewide, and it's been fairly static for the last five years. Is there any other information you need?

You:

Yes. What other surveys or research regarding your readers do you have?

Marge:

We have a new survey that shows the buying habits of our readers.

You:

Great. Here is my address so you can send me the media kit, the sample copies, the demographic profile, and the new survey. Thanks.

TACTIC 22　Know how to extract every bit of information from key publications.

Once you receive copies of the trade, cultural, or lifestyle consumer-oriented magazine or newsletter that is read by the people in your niche market, you have a gold mine of information and insights at your fingertips. To be effective, however, you must know what you're looking for. Here are four easy steps to mine that information for your own use.

1. Look at who publishes the magazine. Is it a trade, cultural, or lifestyle organization? If so, who are the officers? Do they have a local chapter in your area? Call the headquarters to get more information and a profile of the membership. You'll want to join key groups that serve your target market, as they represent a dynamic way to reach your prospects one on one.

2. Read the articles and editorials with an eye for reader insights. First, scan the titles and introductory sections to discover what key challenges are facing this group of people. Notice who the author is and how he or she fits into the picture. Is the writer a professor, permanent editorial staff of the magazine, or successful executive from the business? Read further and ask yourself, "How do I relate to the issues that are discussed in this article?" Check the size of the recent publication against the older issue. Are there fewer pages, or more?

3. Examine the advertising in the magazine. Who are the prominent advertisers? Focus on the benefits they are selling to discover what's important to this audience. Is it saving time? Image? Quality? This helps pinpoint the hot buttons in your niche market. Notice key phrases and themes the ads and articles use. What are the key words used to describe the people or their processes? Are they members, owners, partners, or associates? You can learn to speak the language of your market very quickly this way. Using the right words and topics in conversation will help you appear knowledgeable and part of the group you're trying to reach. Be sure to count the number of ads in the old issue against those in the most recent issue to determine potential viability. Are there more, or less? Is the market in growth or decline?

4. Find a calendar of events. Look for industry-related meetings, trade shows, social events, and charitable and community support events. These are excellent opportunities for
you to make good decisions regarding the accessibility issues
facing you in this market. The events on the calendar provide a natural gathering place for the people in your niche
market. An excellent opportunity for you to demonstrate
your desire to know them is by joining them there.

Keep in mind all the issues on your profitability and accessibility
list as you glean information from these publications. Review your
list. Reading industry and specialty magazines, newsletters, bulletins, and other niche market communications media helps you
know what the marketplace wants and how strong the opportunities are to deliver it.

TACTIC 23   Use your local library to find the places where members of your niche markets associate with one another.

Of the many criteria on your profitability and accessibility list, the
ability of market members to associate and communicate with one
another and you is vital. If they associate formally or informally,
you need that information. In addition to asking the prospects and
your customers directly where they network, here are several published sources:

The Encyclopedia of Business Information Sources (EBIS). This
source covers industry, trade, and professional association listings. It is valuable if you know the general type of business you
would like to target but don't know the name of associations or
publications that serve the people in the market. The encyclopedia lists trade associations, on-line databases, trade publications, and books by topic area.

Gale Encyclopedia of Associations. This reference source lists the
names of all types of US associations in alphabetical order. Do
you need to know the association orthodontists belong to? Simply look up orthodontists. The same is true with golf course su-
perintendents or school principals. It also gives one- to
two-paragraph synopses of the organization, including addresses, telephone numbers, names of key national officers

(who can give you the key person at the local chapter), membership statistics, and number of local chapters.

The *EBIS* and *Encyclopedia of Associations* are both published by Gale Research Inc., Book Tower, Detroit, Michigan 48226. Both are often available at many large libraries as well.

The Salesman's Guide, Inc., 1140 Broadway, New York, New York 10001. State association listings are available for all types of niche groups and organizations.

Associations Yellow Book. This lists not only the same information about national associations as Gale's, it also includes local chapters with contact names, addresses, telephone, and fax numbers. Call 212-627-4140 for more information from them.

In Canada, look for *Associations Canada*, which is a volume of listings much like the *Gale Encyclopedia*. Outside North America, contact your local library to gain more information.

TACTIC 24   Call your secretary of state's office, local chamber of commerce, or state legislator.

Ask for information on the size of the niche market you are working or considering. Request gross dollar volume statistics within the industry and size of labor force. This will help you get a feel for the profitability of the niche. To be sure you have access to prospects where they associate and communicate with one another, ask for a list of clubs, associations, and nonprofit organizations. Most states offer free or nearly free lists. This will help you narrow your search for the right places or networks to reach your prospects.

If you are based outside the United States, contact your local legislative or ministry officer, most of which can provide similar listings.

TACTIC 25   Scan the yellow pages for local recreational clubs and interest group listings.

To verify profitability, call the publications director and ask for a copy of the club or group magazine or newsletter. Explain to them that you currently are, or are considering, specializing in people like their members. Request several copies of their newsletter or club magazine. They may also have some demographic information about their members, so ask for that as well. Be sure to request membership information. To determine accessibility, find out who their members are, how often they meet, where they meet, and the purpose of the organization. Ask specific questions to find out if the association or organization serves your niche market.

TACTIC 26   Be sure niche lead sources exist or can be built so accessibility is possible.

Unfortunately, profitability is usually emphasized and accessibility is overlooked. However, a great market that is inaccessible is of little value. You must identify lead sources to ensure that the people can be reached. The more the people on the list interact with one another, the better. The less they do, the more difficult they are to reach, which makes it likely you will abandon the market and find another. Be sure you have access to niche lead sources and names. Over time, you will develop a wide variety of targeted leads, and you will develop your own prospecting lists. Here is a list of niche lead sources from which to work:

- Your existing client and prospect lists, resegmented by what they do for business, recreation, or interest.
- Referrals from current customers to other prospects in their specific niche.
- Chamber of commerce membership lists segmented by type of business.
- Membership lists from social clubs, industry or trade associations, lifestyle groups, cultural or special-interest organizations, and neighborhood associations.
- Yellow Pages listings of industry groups, clubs, associations, cultural organizations, and so on.
- Yellow Pages listings by industry, profession, or trade segment.
- Friends you know in the niche market.
- Sales professionals or business owners who sell a different product to the same niche market you're considering and who are willing to share leads.

- Specific industry lists from companies such as Dun & Brad street or the Salesman's Guide, Inc.
- Subscriber lists from niche market publications and journals.
- Prospect lists from list brokerage houses, especially if they are segmented into well-defined, homogeneous groups such as SIC codes in the US or SIC and SOC codes in Canada. Ask if the list house can custom make the list to fit your segmentation needs, and be sure you request telephone numbers.

Finally, look for unique opportunities to market and prospect to businesses in your specific niche that are in close proximity to each other. The same holds true for people with similar recreational interests who may live in clusters, such as a country club or tennis club. Develop a list of prospects within cluster communities, and find out how they associate and communicate with one another.

TACTIC 27   Find out all you can about the area where the people you want to target will live, work, and play.

To determine market profitability, particularly growth and decline issues, call your local real estate board or regional planning board. They can give you up-to-date information about growth potential for a particular market, industry, or geographic area. If you are targeting ethnic groups such as Latinos, they can tell you how much that particular group is expected to grow in a specific area. If you are targeting retail hardware stores, they can usually tell you their estimate of how many more will be opening in your area.

The planning or real estate board should also be able to tell you a great deal about your area. Ask in which geographic areas population growth is projected. If you're starting or moving your small business, ask about physical accessibility issues such as how road-widening projects or new exit ramps from freeways will have an impact on a particular area. A change in one-way streets or putting in medians could make a significant difference.

TACTIC 28   Call the heads of research or planning for local advertising agencies and take these people to lunch.

One of the great untapped sources of market information is an advertising agency. Call the people who head research or planning and acknowledge their expertise. Describe the niche market you are seeking to penetrate and ask them if they are familiar with that market. If they are, ask them to breakfast or lunch to discuss it. Tell them your objective is to find out whether the market is or continues to be profitable and accessible.

There are several reasons why they may want to help you. First, you can offer to share information that you collect from other sources. That way, you are both receiving something from each other. If you are a small-business owner, you may need an advertising agency sometime in the future. If you do eventually plan to use an agency, you can mention it—not as the only reason, but as an additional reason. Be forthright and offer to share with them the knowledge you gain.

When you meet, ask them how much potential growth they see for this market. What do they suggest would be a good approach to take to reach the people? Probe to discover their insights into the market. Go with your profitability and accessibility checklist and an open mind, and take good notes!

TACTIC 29   Contact the research or advertising department of your local newspaper.

Take the same approach as in the previous tactic. Meet with the heads of research or advertising sales and ask the same questions about your niche market, growth potential, and best approaches to take. By offering to share information with them, you can develop a group of people who will supply you with valuable information. The more you know, the more effective you can be in choosing or continuing in the right market and knowing how to approach the prospects in an effective and ethical way.

TACTIC 30   Contact your local department of labor or the US Bureau of Labor Statistics.

Ask for publications that indicate the growth projections for a particular industry, occupation, or profession you are considering as a target. This will show you if your targeted niche is projected to shrink or grow in numbers.

TACTIC 31   Read everything you can about your market.

There are many good books and periodicals available in bookstores and libraries that help inform you about your niche. Some are fairly broad in definition; however, they will still help you gather information so you can make a good decision about which groups of people are right for you. Here are a few of the best:

The Clustering of America, by Michael J. Weiss. This is "a vivid portrait of the nation's 40 neighborhood types—their values, lifestyles, and eccentricities." It is a 406-page book based on the premise "you are where you live." It has become a classic in defining lifestyle demographic market types. Although it doesn't indicate segments that associate and communicate, it gives you plenty of ideas and fresh perspectives. (Harper & Row Publishers, Inc., 10 East 53rd Street, New York, New York 10022; $10.95.)

Almanac of Consumer Markets, by Margaret K. Ambry. This is a factual guide to today's more complex and harder-to-find consumers. It contains 403 pages of customer profiles and is an excellent source of statistics that can be used as background information for a consumer or lifestyle niche market group. (American Demographic Press, 108 North Cayuga Street, Ithaca, New York 14850; telephone 800-828-1133; $29.95; order book 605.)

The Sourcebook of Demographics and Buying Power, for every ZIP code in the United States. Volume I gives age, employment, detailed housing, and income profiles. Volume II gives social, demographic, housing, and income profiles. Good for building background information and a sense of potential about your niche. Both volumes cover every ZIP code in the United States. (Published by CACI Marketing Systems and available through American Demographics, Marketing Tools; telephone 800-828-1133; $295 per volume; order book 611-A for volume I and 611-B for volume II.)

Lifestyle Market Analysis. This is a 1,000-page book loaded with information about your niche. Be sure you focus on how people associate and communicate as you view this information. (Available from Standard Rate and Data Services, 3004 Glenview Road, Wilmette, Illinois 60091; telephone 708-256-6070; $245; or may be found at many large libraries.)

American Demographics. Don't let the title fool you—this is a great tool because this is a monthly magazine that often focuses on definable segments and groups of people who associate and communicate. It features current articles and statistical analysis of the population, primarily in North America. (To subscribe, call 800-828-1133.)

Chapter Three

Strategy: Choose Well So You Can Prosper

Objective: To choose which niche markets offer the best opportunities for you to build long-term, profitable relationships with the people in the market.

O nce you've divided your existing and new market segments and researched for profitability and access, you need to make the right choices regarding which markets to continue to target for expansion.

The information you have gathered will have opened your eyes to shifts in existing and new markets. It will also help you adjust your view of the prospects and how to reach them.

As a case in point, in the mid-1970s I was a general sales manager for a Rolls-Royce dealership in upstate New York. Our company had developed a marketing profile of a qualified prospect. One early afternoon, a couple drove up to the dealership in a 1952 Studebaker. This couple got out of the car, he in his bib overalls and she in a tattered housecoat. They certainly did not fit our profile of qualified prospects. I immediately prejudged their ability to buy and decided not to spend any time with them.

You can imagine my surprise when, after they looked at the various models, they asked me how much a new Silver Shadow sedan would cost. I sat them down in my office, worked up the price, and found, much to my delight, they were not trading the 1952 Studebaker. They decided after a few moments that the Silver Shadow was the car they had been looking for. They then counted out the entire purchase price in cash on the spot and proceeded to tell me that they owned their own plumbing supply business, and this was their reward for years of hard work. That opened my eyes to a whole new market. No, not people with 1952 Studebakers, but owners of companies in the trades. It also taught me to adjust my view of prospects. Too bad I had to learn from experience, rather than from market intelligence. The value of your market intelligence is immeasurable. It will help you see the potential in your marketplace. It will prevent you from prejudging your opportunities.

Another example of the power of the information you now have gathered is best illustrated by this next story. I was working with a group in the insurance industry to help them increase their prospecting activity. The company had chosen farmers as their new niche market because of their need for disability insurance. The sales force followed up on leads from advertisements and direct mail campaigns by calling the prospects on the phone. To offset their skepticism that this was a good market, they asked so many qualifying questions that they talked the people out of the desire to meet and buy. Only after I suggested they be shown the market information did they realize the potential of this new market. Not only did it change their outlook, it changed their methods of approach, which led to many more appointments. No longer were they trying to talk people out of seeing them.

Ultimately, the information you have gathered and your decision about which niche markets to pursue will have a tremendous impact on your ability to be productive, profitable, and satisfied for the long term.

To pull together all your information and make the right decision, organize it in such a way as to be sure you're dealing with all the facts. Compiling all the information on one sheet will help you see the entire picture. Then you can make your decision based on the variety of input sources you have used.

If you are a sales professional or business owner choosing your own niche markets, this exercise will help you feel confident about each market and its opportunities for you. If you are a sales professional selling in a market or markets selected by the company you work for, it is important to work through this process so you can explain your resegmentation or recommend new market opportunities and the reasons why. Figure 3–1 shows a worksheet you can use as a model. It highlights the most important information you need to make a quality decision regarding each market segment. Create

FIGURE 3–1
Market Information and Decision Worksheet

Profitability
Size of market _____
Current income or sales of market _____
Growth signs and trends _____
The common needs of the market _____
The business, employment, or membership projections of this market:
　　　　　Good _____ Fair _____ Poor _____
Benefits the market can receive from my products or services _____
Potential spin-off markets _____
Potential dollar volume I can sell _____
Who is my competition? _____
How are they positioned? _____
How can I position myself in this market? _____
Is there a need for my products or services?　Yes _____ No _____
Do I need to repackage?　Yes _____ No _____
Can I fit in with these people because I have
something in common with them?　Yes _____ No _____

Accessibility
What is their common culture? _____
Level of interaction among people in the niche: _____
　　(Circle a number from 1 to 5, 5 = strong, 1 = weak　　5 4 3 2 1
How extensive are the sources of targeted leads?　　5 4 3 2 1
What sources have I identified? _____
The type and means of written communication between prospects ___
_____
How do they associate with one another? _____
How often do they associate with one another? Can I attend? _____
Do these people refer suppliers to one another? Yes _____ No _____
Are these people accessible by telephone? Good __ Fair __ Poor __

a separate worksheet for each niche market you are considering. Be sure to expand it to meet your own particular needs.

Recognize that each of these issues is a decision point. Obviously, your objective is to choose to continue in or access new markets where you have the highest degree of profitability and accessibility. In the final analysis, profitability is ultimately determined by accessibility. For without access, no matter how strong a market is, a sale cannot be made.

To further shape your decisions and add perspective to your choices, consider these tactics as guidelines to a good decision. I believe they are vitally important for success in any market.

TACTIC 32   Be sure your niche market has a legitimate need for your product or service.

It's imperative that you see clear evidence of this need. Too much time, effort, and energy is spent by sales professionals and business owners trying to twist a particular product or service to fit into a market where there is no legitimate need. This is usually done when they perceive the buyer has money and they simply want to extract it. If you feel you're putting a square peg into a round hole, stop and refocus. For instance, you don't want to be promoting a telephone system with 25 stations to a small-business niche that typically has five employees. That kind of effort is not only counterproductive, in most cases it is unquestionably unethical.

TACTIC 33   Determine what benefit people will derive from doing business with you.

Today, people don't buy just the best price, products, or presentations, they buy the best solution to their problems. They want to know, "What's in it for me?" Be sure this is clear to you as you make your market choice. If you cannot articulate a benefit your prospect will receive, you will always question your purpose and find yourself searching for the motivation to continue. Michelin is an excellent example of knowing what it can do for its market. It has been highly successful in promoting the "safety to the family" niche by its slogan, "You've got a lot riding on your tires." Know what your benefit is as clearly as Michelin does!

TACTIC 34   Verify that the people in your market have the financial power to acquire your products or services.

Does the purchasing power of people in your current or potential niche market match up with the price of the goods or services you're selling? Mercedes Benz is an example of a company that is changing to meet new customer information. It is now targeting a new market of people who are less affluent than those who purchase their top-of-the-line automobiles. It is introducing a new line of cars that is more in line with this less affluent market. Thus, it is aligning the product with the purchase power of its new market. It makes very little sense for you to merchandise a product to a market that cannot afford your product or services. You need to either repackage or rethink your choice.

TACTIC 35   Be sure the prospects associate and communicate with one another.

Regardless of whether you work in markets preselected by the company or you choose your own, this will help ensure that you gain favorable access. As you resegment your company or your own markets, be sure to group by what they do for a living, recreation and/or interest, industry, or business. Then verify through your information-gathering process that they interact with one another frequently. Be sure you find out the methods they use. They can associate through a range of venues such as clubs, associations, organizations, and other networks. They can communicate through journals, bulletins, newsletters, magazines, and word-of-mouth networks. If they associate with each other, you can associate and build a quality relationship with them. If they communicate with one another, they can talk about you in a positive way when you're not there.

TACTIC 36   For those of you who can select your own markets, be sure you have an affinity or link with the market you choose.

Motivation comes from within. If you truly have a passion and a desire to work with the people in your niche markets, you will succeed.

There should be a sense of belonging that you can use in your efforts to build quality relationships. Can you truly relate to these people? Are you comfortable with them? Can you speak their language? Your affinity or link is important so that you come to the market as an insider, not an outsider. Most assuredly, the people in your chosen market or markets will see your genuine interest—or lack of it.

One of my favorite verses is Proverbs 14:23: "In all hard work there is profit, but mere talk brings only poverty." Despite all the discussion you hear about working "smart and not hard," there is no substitute for putting forth effort to reach your individual and business goals. Once you make your niche market choices, you must be willing to put forth the effort needed to establish solid, ethical, high-quality relationships to access the people. To choose well is important. To work your choice well is equally important.

II

POSITIONING YOURSELF TO OVERCOME SKEPTICISM

"You cannot always control circumstances. But you can control your own thoughts."

Charles E. Popplestone

C learly, in today's skeptical environment, people buy people long before they buy products or services. Even with the best intentions, people often do not buy simply because sales professionals do a lousy job of positioning or presenting themselves before the sale takes place. Recently I was on vacation with my family, and I went into an antique shop. Browsing for just the right piece, I found one I thought was especially attractive. I mentioned to the saleswoman that I had some interest in the particular piece, and I told her I would like to come back with other members of my family later in the day.

Several hours later, we returned to the shop. As we were looking at the piece, I turned to my son and said, "Jeff, how do you think this would look in the dining room?" The saleswoman then interrupted me and said, "You're not going to let someone else decide what goes in your dining room, are you?" Needless to say, we decided that regardless of how much we liked the piece, our desire to buy from her had evaporated. Skepticism overcame our sense of value and we simply took our business out the door and down the street.

How you position and present yourself to your customers and prospects during the marketing and prospecting process determines how much access to the marketplace you can ultimately achieve.

Some misguided sales professionals and business owners try positioning and presenting themselves through a slick ad campaign or prospecting technique that they hope will capture the prospect. A vice president of sales told me that his company had developed just such a new prospecting technique. When I asked him to define it, he quickly described what he called the Porcupine Approach: Pump the customer up to gain access and then stick it to them. What a wonderfully archaic concept! That is the usual short-term thinking with long-term consequences. This type of approach does not fit into a society of individuals driven by their sense of relationship and need for respect.

Knowing that people want quality relationships, how can you position and begin to present yourself effectively to the people in your niche markets from the first point of awareness or contact? To be seen as the right person, the right supplier, and the right organization to do business with, you must begin by focusing on the buyer's perspective. No matter the tomes written about focusing on yourself and dressing for success, or adjusting your personality to fit the situation (all of which may have their place), the first step must be to focus on the buyer. You must step back and ask, "What does the customer, what does the prospect in this marketplace want to see in someone like me?" People give you access to themselves based on *their* perspective, not your perspective. It is essential that they see in you the characteristics they are looking for to open their door to you. On a corporate level, we have seen this demonstrated by many companies.

McDonald's is no longer promoting the fact that it has *sold* several billion hamburgers; its signs now read that it has *served* several billion burgers. Why? Because it wants to position itself as an organization that is focused on what people want—service! Toyota has also done very well positioning itself by focusing on the buyer with its ad campaign, "I love what you do for me." This ultimately says, "We know how important your car is to you and we will make sure it's right for you!"

All of this says that, by focusing on the buyer, you achieve the right frame of mind to display the characteristics that help build the quality relationships necessary for access. Sadly, most sales professionals and business owners have been taught to reveal little of themselves to the prospect or customer. Nothing could be further from the truth. What, then, do people want and what are they looking for in a sales professional or business owner? What relational characteristic will position you as someone with whom they will want to build a relationship?

On the basis of recent research by *Sales Management* magazine, *64 percent* of the decision makers in America will schedule an appointment with a sales professional or business owner based solely on their perception of the person's positive attitude. Furthermore, projecting a positive attitude about yourself, your products or services, and your customer translates into likability and eventually opportunities to generate *trust*.

We need not look any further than Thomas I. (Toby) Hull to determine what the prospect's perspective is. Hull is a founding member of Top of the Table, an elite group comprised of 300 of the top insurance sellers in the world. His keen insight is, "Once you establish that you care about or are interested in an industry, [Industry members will] tend to stick with you even after the competition arrives." Why? By demonstrating a positive and genuine attitude of interest in the people, you encourage prospects to be open to knowing more about you, which leads them to trust you.

Psychologist Allison Cohen, senior vice president of Ally and Gagano Advertising Agency, finds that today's customers are clear in what they want before they give you access. They are saying, "Show me what you've got before you earn my trust." In a real sense that means, "Reveal yourself to me and that will help you prove yourself trustworthy."

We have reached a point where Christian Dior suits and Gucci shoes are no longer effective to gain access. Now the demonstration of a positive, caring attitude and trustworthiness from the first point of awareness and contact have taken over. Of course, not everyone who likes you will trust you—nor will everyone like you.

In a marketplace where the products and services are perceived as equal, a positive, caring attitude and trustworthiness will position and present you as someone who is different. The prospects that recognize these traits will give you access to themselves because they perceive you as different.

How, then, do you go about creating a positive perception and demonstrating trustworthiness? The following two chapters will give you the strategies and tactics necessary to meet your prospects' and customers' expectations.

Chapter Four

Strategy: Tap the Power of Positive Perceptions

Objective: To position yourself with your prospects and customers as having a positive, caring attitude.

I t is readily apparent today that in all relationships, *positive* builds and attracts, while *negative* destroys and repels. For this reason, a positive, caring attitude is known to remove skepticism from the minds of prospects. They quickly perceive that a person who is enthusiastic has their interests at heart and will respond to their problems effectively. This phenomenon accompanies positive perceptions.

Conversely, the more the negative is emphasized, the more repelled people become, the less likely they are to have a sense of confidence in you as an individual, and the less likely they are to see you. As an example, I made an error that created a negative in the mind of one of our prospects. The chairman of the board of The Tom James Company spells his name in a very unusual way. It isn't a difficult name, just one that can be spelled several ways. Without checking (mistake 1), I selected one of the incorrect versions. Sometime later, I sent a letter to him with the incorrect spelling of his name. He graciously sent us a note asking us to correct it, which we did—or thought we did.

What we didn't know is that his name was inadvertently placed on our prospect list twice (a second mistake), once under his industry category and once by his name. Of course, he received another piece of mail with his name misspelled. The result was he had some pretty negative exposure to us through this, which created a negative experience for him. His perception may be that we have an

I-don't-care attitude. We do care and it was an honest mistake; however, that won't completely erase his negative perception.

Your attitude also effects how a relationship with a prospect progresses. Whether you want to admit it or not, your attitude is very visual. People can see immediately what your attitude is about them because you demonstrate it through your emotions, opinions, and actions. Prospects really do mirror you and mirror the attitude that you seem to project, which positively or negatively affects their acceptance of you.

Furthermore, your attitude is demonstrated in your outlook as it relates to the results you think you might or might not obtain from calling on prospects.

As an illustration, I was speaking at a National Sales meeting for a particular group on competitive differential. An old pro leaned over at the break and said to the young sales professional sitting next to him, "Where are you going to be going tomorrow for prospects?" The young man said, "Well, I'm going to be calling on the people in the office building next to us." The older fellow said, "I wouldn't bother doing that. I called over there two years ago and there's not one good prospect in the whole building." The young man thought about it for a moment and said, "Yeah, you're probably right, maybe I'll just stay in the office and get some paperwork done." Your attitude can definitely affect your outlook. In my early years it affected mine.

My parents died when I was very young, and I lived in a variety of foster homes. I had a sizable chip on my shoulder, and I really struggled trying to get ahead for several years. Finally, I recognized that I had a negative attitude and outlook. I also discovered I was making a choice even though I didn't know it. My attitude was negative, which made my outlook negative, guaranteeing negative results.

In contrast, a good friend of mine, Roger Crawford, had to make his choice about attitude and outlook early. He was born without hands and with one usable leg. His view has always been, "I'm going to have a positive attitude about this because I do have a usable leg and two usable arms." He has gone on to become not only an excellent speaker but a tennis pro, all because of his choice of attitude and outlook.

Of course, like you, I realize that you can't control everything. You cannot control all the people, circumstances, and things in your market or in your life. However, you can control the way you respond to them. To be perceived as a positive individual, you must work hard to address every issue from a positive perspective. You must consistently convey a positive perception through the emotions, opinions, and actions you demonstrate to your prospects. It's attractive to the people and they are looking for it. It's not easy. A lot of things get in the way. A lot of people get in the way. A lot of circumstances get in the way. Just avoid letting yourself get in the way.

The challenge, then, is how to develop and keep a positive, caring attitude. You can't project what you don't have or lose sight of. Here are several tactics to help you develop and keep a positive attitude so you can project it into the hearts and minds of your buyers.

TACTIC 37   Keep things in perspective.

Things happen that can knock you off track. If you're going to keep a positive attitude, you should ask yourself these four questions when things go wrong:

- How serious a setback to my long-term objectives is this situation?
- How serious is this situation when I compare it to what others around me are going through?
- How upset will I be about this one month from now?
- What is the one good thing I can focus on in all of this?

If you will ask yourself these questions, you will be able to keep things in better perspective. Typically, a negative attitude results when you lose your perspective and focus only on the individual circumstances versus the overall picture of what you are trying to accomplish.

TACTIC 38   Concentrate on thankfulness versus entitlement.

As you focus on your niche markets and gain increased success, sometimes a feeling of entitlement can invade your attitude. This is particularly true as one becomes more credible within a market. Nothing can destroy relationships faster than conveying an attitude of entitlement. Avoid coming across to others as if they owe you a favor or they owe it to you to see you. To develop and keep a positive attitude, focus on being thankful for the opportunities and the business. Being thankful keeps you in the right frame of mind and thus earns you respect in the eyes of the buyer.

TACTIC 39   Think about the consequences.

Whether you are building a business or a career, it is very easy to become focused on what's happening right now. For this reason, too many people think and act from a short-term perspective. This can lead you into negative reactions. If you focus on the short-term, you think about what's happening now and how you feel about it. Then you decide to take some action or no action. The consequences of your decisions follow. It's more important, when negative things happen, to consider your overall plan for this market and your desire to build quality relationships with the people in it. First, think about the consequences of your actions. Second, take the appropriate actions. You'll then feel good about your decisions and the outcome. When you think about the consequences of your behavior and focus your attention on long-term relationship-building versus simply short-term events, you can overcome "what's happening."

TACTIC 40   Avoid using negative self-talk in your personal and professional life.

Negative self-talk reduces your ability to be positive. Too many sales professionals and business owners talk about themselves, the conditions of the market, and their ability to move ahead in a negative way.

Self-talk is powerful. I was speaking in Salt Lake City at a national convention for a direct sales company. At the conclusion of my presentation, a man and wife in the audience told me about how self-talk had made an impact on one of the foster children in their care.

They were caring for a young boy. Soon after he came to their home, they asked him what he wanted to be when he grew up. He said, "I want to be a truck driver because my Dad was a truck driver." They told him that was fine; however, he didn't have to do the same thing his Dad did because he could be "anything he wanted to be." His eyes lit up, and over the next few months he told himself and others he could be anything he wanted to be. When the social worker came to move him to another home, she asked him if he was still going to be a truck driver. "No," he said, "I don't have to because I can be anything I want to be." Self-talk creates self-perception that translates into prospect perceptions.

If you've had bad experiences, you can educate yourself to respond positively to them. Speak to yourself in ways that reinforce your effort and esteem. Attitude is a result of education and experience. Talk yourself through negative experiences and rejection with positive self-talk.

TACTIC 41   Practice self-control. Learn to limit your depression.

Certainly things will go wrong. However, by practicing self-control and not self-indulgence, you learn to limit your depression. Recognize that every time you walk into a prospecting situation, every time you sit down to create a letter, every time you pick up the telephone, you're on stage. It's important to practice self-control. Even though you may be seething over a situation, the way you respond is a choice you make. Taking it out on others can devastate you in the marketplace. Think about your long-term objectives. Think about what it is you're trying to accomplish. Feel bad, shake it off, and prepare for your next opportunity. Your opportunities are in the future, not in the past.

TACTIC 42   Keep an open mind.

Several years ago, I was speaking at an advertising federation dinner meeting in Chattanooga, Tennessee. I was speaking about being open minded and creative in marketing, and a young girl, perhaps nine or ten years old, approached me after my remarks. She said, "I am here with my Dad tonight and I know what an open mind is. A mind is like a room with a door. When the door to your mind is open, you can let things in and you can let things out. But if you have a closed mind, you've closed the door and nothing can get in and nothing can get out." Pretty profound for a nine-year-old. I could have taken a break and let her do some speaking. Keep your mind open and avoid falling victim to a closed mind. Your open mind will help you open doors.

TACTIC 43   Surround yourself with motivated people.

If you're going to develop and keep a positive attitude in the marketplace, you must associate with motivated people. Charlie "Tremendous" Jones, a legendary insurance agent and speaker, has perhaps one of the most famous quotes regarding this idea. He simply says, "The books you read, the messages you listen to, and the people with whom you associate will have the greatest impact on who you are five years from now than anything else you do."

My wife and I have taken this to heart. Each year, we make a list of people that we no longer want to involve in our social circle. We eliminate the people who are always accentuating the negative, who are continually down in the mouth, who are mad most of the time, who are depressed about where they're going with their life or not going. You too should begin to make a list, not only about people you want to remove from your social circle but people that you want to begin to include. If you want to build mutually rewarding relationships with your prospects to gain access, you must guard your mind and your associations.

TACTIC 44   Listen to one motivational and inspirational message each week.

As a business owner or sales professional, day after day, week after week, you're continually pumping out all types of messages to relate to people, to persuade people, to service people. You cannot continue to pump yourself out without pumping something back in, or eventually you're just going to run out of you. You'll become exhausted within, which will ultimately be projected outwardly. To help keep a positive, caring attitude, provide yourself with positive energy. Listen to at least one inspirational or motivational message at least once per week. This may be at your church, temple, synagogue, or on a videotape or audiotape. The impact of having some positive reinforcement for yourself helps you to continue to be a positive force in the marketplace and thus to produce pleasant perceptions in the minds of your prospects.

TACTIC 45   Read books by and for successful people.

What you put in your mind eventually is what comes out of your mouth. If you put positive reinforcement in through the books that you read, your attitude will reflect the difference they make. One way I helped turn my own attitude around was through regular reading of good material. By reading the right things, I began to reshape the way I was thinking, which enabled me to move forward even in the face of negative experiences.

Mylon Le Fevre, a well-known gospel artist, reinforced this idea again for me several years ago. He and I have a great deal in common, including our many nights on the road each year. He can identify with some of the challenges that constant traveling can bring. He encouraged me to spend time each day in devotional reading and prayer. This was great advice. That daily form of rejuvenation has increased my already high enthusiasm for life. Most importantly, it helps sustain it.

TACTIC 46   Face challenges with a sense of opportunity.

As a sales professional or as a business owner, the things that occur outside your control can be negative and frustrating. They can sometimes make you think that you are in the wrong place or in the wrong market and convince you that you should quit. On the contrary, these challenges are often good opportunities to demonstrate diligence, perseverance, and persistence to the prospects in your niche market. An individual who can overcome negative situations and negative circumstances, including skepticism, is respected in the market.

Look for the good in all ideas, situations, and circumstances. Run your thoughts to advantage versus disadvantage. Focus on the goal of victory versus defeat.

TACTIC 47   When the competition runs you down, expect sales to run up.

Often, competitors will talk about you and how bad you are as their way of gaining a competitive edge. Nothing could be further from the truth. Prospects see this archaic tactic as evidence that competitors are terrified of you.

As a case in point, I was looking for a pedestal to display a particular plant that my wife had purchased. When I saw a roadside stand selling pedestals, I thought it would be a great opportunity, not only to see a good variety but perhaps to secure a fairly good price, so I stopped. After I got out of the car and began to look for a moment, a woman who identified herself as the owner said to me, "We have all different types," and she quoted me some prices. Then she said, "Now, one thing you need to know is the department store here in town (and she mentioned the name of it) is going to be selling these same pedestals because I supply them. They're going to charge you three times as much, so you really can't pass up this opportunity. This is the opportunity of a lifetime because, after all, I'm saving you a lot of money, and they're just ripping you off."

I thought to myself, "She's speaking about her own customer that way. These are the people she sells to wholesale." It also occurred to me that if this is the only way she can build value, by running down the competition and their pricing, maybe I should go shop the competition to really see if they're overcharging me as much as she says they are.

Another example of this occurred when I was shopping for art with my wife in Carmel, California. Many of the sales professionals and business owners in the various galleries we visited talked about the fact that their prices were significantly lower than Simic Galleries, the largest in town. They told us time and time again that Simic was overcharging, it was simply asking too much money, its artists were too expensive, and if we just wanted a good painting, we ought to buy from their gallery, not Simic. In addition, most were crying about how bad things were and that the economy was tough, so they had cut back on marketing to save money.

When I spoke to the gallery director of Simic, his comment to me was that business was booming. Simic had just opened its third gallery within a one-block area in Carmel, California. I mentioned the fact that other people were talking about Simic and running it down. Simic's director said he really appreciated it because it was sending him more business than he could handle. The prospect knows that if you are the subject of the competitor's presentation, you are probably worth opening the door to.

TACTIC 48   Look past prospects' faults and see their needs.

It is vitally important to recognize that customers and prospects are not perfect. To do this, it helps to keep in mind that you're not, either. Sometimes you'll see things in the marketplace you don't like. You'll not like the way people act towards you or the way they do things. Don't let this discourage you from working with them. Don't let this put you off in such a way that it shapes your attitude and outlook about them in advance.

Even though people have faults, look beyond them to find what their individual needs are. Discover what they're trying to accomplish and how you might be able to help them. Quality relationships cannot be built if you are prejudging prospects in advance because you see all of their faults. It's essential that you focus on their needs and demonstrate enthusiasm for solving them.

The result of projecting a positive, caring attitude and creating a sense of trustworthiness is that you earn the right to see the prospect. The character traits that prospects perceive when they see or hear about you should convey the message that you are a quality person. Quality prospects throw open the door to quality people.

Chapter Five

Strategy: Demonstrate That You Are Trustworthy

Objective: To position yourself with your prospects and customers as having integrity, not just expertise.

M y very first sales position was with an organization selling cookware. All the salespeople were taught that the most effective way to sell the product was to simply work door-to-door in neighborhoods and ask people to buy it. We didn't have many people calling in to buy cookware, particularly stainless, waterless cookware. It was fairly expensive compared to what you can buy in a store, so we had to take the product to the prospects.

As I went through these neighborhoods, however, I found out very quickly that you could not just stand at the door and talk to somebody about cookware to get them to buy it. They simply didn't understand the value. They didn't really have any true feel for what it could do for them, how they could use it, or why they should pay that kind of money for pots and pans. They could get a perfectly good set, they reasoned, right up the street at the local hardware or department store for a lot less money.

I recognized very quickly that the way to sell cookware was to demonstrate it. That simply meant that I had to begin to plan events where I could cook meals for the individuals that I was calling on so they could see the value. I could demonstrate that the food tasted better and had a better flavor than food cooked in traditional cookware. Because it tasted better, prospects would never argue with the fact that the food was healthier for them because no nutrients were lost. I began to put on small dinner parties.

Prospective buyers, nearly all of whom were women, would invite five or six girlfriends over, and I would cook a full meal using the waterless cookware. When I demonstrated this cookware, several things happened. One, many women bought, I believe, simply because they were so amazed a man was cooking dinner for them. Second, all kidding aside, they bought because the value was real, because I was demonstrating the cookware, not just standing there "talkastrating."

The same holds true in nearly every other type of sales. Sales professionals selling copiers know very quickly that if the can get that copier into the office for a demonstration, it's going to sell much better than if they sit and talk about it. For people who want to buy an advertising campaign for their business, you put together story boards that demonstrate the campaign's concepts. This makes it clearer what the campaign is going to do for the customer versus just trying to describe it to them.

When people are selling automobiles, their goal is to get you to drive one. The reason is that once you get behind the wheel, you feel the experience. That's much more powerful than someone telling you about what's going to happen. This is the same reason that architects use models versus just trying to get you to perceive or conceive something from a blueprint or a piece of paper.

Clearly, the power of demonstration works much better than all the words you can use to describe something. With this in mind, ask yourself, are you demonstrating trust or are you simply talking about it? I know some sales professionals and business owners say, "I tell people right up front, the last thing I'd ever do is rip you off." Sad to say, this still happens. Others will assert their trust in an offhand remark. They say things like, "Well, let me be honest with you for just a moment" or simply, "Trust me, it's okay." All of these things will work against you almost all the time.

To position yourself in the marketplace and build effective relationships with your prospects, you must demonstrate trust. People need to have a good sense of who you are and what you stand for. The questions the prospect needs answers to are, "What is your reputation in the marketplace? Are you someone I can trust? Do you change your ethics based on the situation? Would you tell me anything to get the sale?"

Even though your company may be known for certain principles in the marketplace, the customer today will decide to see you based on how you personally demonstrate those principles and those you call your own. They judge this based on how they are treated from the first point of contact with you. They can trust you if you can demonstrate that you are trustworthy.

It's vital to realize that most customers and prospects in your niche are so focused on their immediate tasks that they don't have time to study the nuances of a product or a service. They must feel as though they can rely on the character and integrity of the individual with whom they are going to do business. Being perceived as trustworthy will give you a competitive edge. Ann Boe, the author of *Is Your Net Working?* asserts that sometimes it is customers' trust in you that enables them to keep going, to take a risk that they otherwise would not attempt. Trustworthiness will encourage many, many people to do business with you because they will feel comfortable revealing their personal needs and wants to you.

Randy G. Pennington, the author of *On My Honor, I Will,* speaks about the positive power of integrity in the marketplace. His suggestion is that the integrity-driven organization takes its marketing, public relations, and communications very seriously. Such an organization never makes a statement that cannot be proven or backed up with quality products and quality services.

Faith Popcorn, in the book *The Popcorn Report* (Doubleday, 1991), states that consumers have grown tired of products and services that do not live up to the promises advertised. They demand honesty, integrity, and a sense of duty from the companies with which they do business. In other words, prospects in your niche insist on giving access only to people they can trust.

The message is clear. Doing what's right should be a major thrust of how you conduct yourself and your business. Customers and prospects want to consider themselves respected. They want to know that they are valued. They need, personally and professionally, to have a good working relationship with a sales professional or business owner whom they can trust.

It is no longer possible to simply talk about how you can be trusted. Trust must be earned through demonstration. As you move forward with several tactics to help you, reflect on these three key principles: (1) who we are is more important than what we do, (2) how we treat others is more important than how we are treated, and (3) what we do is more important than what we say.

TACTIC 49   Treat everyone with respect.

I've seen many cases where secretaries, administrative assistants, or members of purchasing teams are treated with disrespect. There are a myriad stories about ill-treated team members and subordinates to decision makers who close the door of opportunity on an individual. Even if they can't close it now, often they are promoted to a position of control later. At that point, they remove the offending sales professional or business owner from the vendor list.

I'm reminded of one fellow who called me from Michigan for help in his business. This was an individual I had met at a conference. He was extremely rude to my secretary and she complained to me about him. When I spoke with him, I mentioned his lack of respect for my employee. His point was that he didn't think she was all that important. Wrong again! If you show respect for all the people in the organization, they will influence others to respect and trust you.

TACTIC 50   Be genuine.

People are looking for a true feeling of genuineness today. They're looking for the real people or, in other words, those they feel are not counterfeit.

One of the things that was promoted by the computer industry in the early years was the concept of "what you see on the screen is what you get as an outcome." Well, that translates here as well. What people see when they observe you, when they read something about you, when they hear about you, or when they meet you all are used to judge your genuineness and ultimately your trustworthiness.

One of the criticisms that I've heard about my industry of professional speakers is that occasionally someone is one way on the platform and totally different off the platform. The criticism is expressed as "he or she does not walk their talk." The greatest impact that you can make is not just in what you say, it's how you act and how that corresponds to what you say. Are you truly genuine, not counterfeit?

TACTIC 51   Be prompt.

Although seemingly a mundane issue to many sales professionals or business owners, it is important. If you're not prompt, it shows a lack of respect and it plants the seed with people that perhaps you can't be trusted to deliver. The larger issue is it will often become a stumbling block that will prevent them from buying now. Some sales professionals or business owners say being late once is no big deal. Tell that to the company or individual who lost a sale because that first impression was a negative one. If you're scheduling appointments too close together, reschedule. Interestingly, a couple we invite to many of the social functions at our home is well known for promptness. This has translated into trustworthiness. The comment most often heard from others about them is, "If they say they'll be there, they'll be on time. You can count on them." Conversely, another couple who is habitually late is often spoken of by others in terms such as, "You can't trust them to be on time."

TACTIC 52   Underpromise and overdeliver.

It's a common criticism in many different circles that sales professionals and business owners alike tend to overpromise. This detracts from trustworthiness and increases skepticism in the mind of the prospect. Be sure to deliver all you say you can deliver. If you underpromise and overdeliver, you will not only separate yourself from the competition by being uniquely different, you will also give an enhanced sense of value to the hard-to-reach individuals you are attempting to reach. That, in turn, will motivate them to want to do business with you.

TACTIC 53   Be willing to walk away.

This is one of the most difficult concepts to practice, because your goal is to bring the relationship marketing and prospecting process to a successful conclusion—that is, a sale. However, occasionally someone will want you to do something such as reduce the price or offer an unreasonable incentive for them to buy. You may also find that they want to buy something or move in a direction that you know is counterproductive for them. In the short term, the money looks very attractive and the sale is one you feel you need to make. Yet, if your goal is a good reputation that will lead to multiple sales and multiple customers, you're better off not making the sale. Suggest to these people that this is the wrong direction for them to go, that it will not meet the needs that they have. Stand firm on your price, explaining that you cannot give different prices to different people in the same position or volume. You'll be better off in the long run.

Of course, the argument against this is, "Well, they're going to buy from somebody else, I might as well sell it to them." Fine, except the long-term consequences can destroy your credibility in your markets. Trustworthiness evaporates with lawsuits and a loss of reputation, while skepticism increases. Avoid selling or marketing products or ideas to people that do not meet their needs, fit their situation, or provide the solution that they're looking for. You must be willing to walk away.

TACTIC 54　Keep all your personal and professional conversations private.

This demonstrates your ability to be trusted. If people hear from others that you've talked about their personal situation or that you've revealed confidential or competitive information to their competitors or suppliers, they will immediately close the door on you permanently. The reputation founded on trust you earn is important. By keeping personal and professional conversations private, both intraoffice and interoffice, you can earn the right to see customers and do business with them.

TACTIC 55　Issue a partnership bill of rights.

One of the best marketing and prospecting pieces to promote trust that I've ever seen was given to me by a former agency manager of The Equitable, Howard Starr from New Hyde Park, New York.

Howard, now retired, adapted his Partnership Bill of Rights from several sources. He distributed this unique document to each of his prospects and customers as a foundation on which to start a relationship. It told them that he or she was entitled to an honest, ethical relationship with him and his organization. He signs it, and they do as well. Starr's Partnership Bill of Rights is reproduced in Figure 5–1.

Now, one of the advantages of this document is that it clearly says without any equivocation that the prospect is most important. It also communicates to prospects where they stand and what is expected from them. This removes skepticism because it is acknowledged they have rights also. This removes any sense of smoke and mirrors.

You probably remember that several years ago, Chrysler had a very successful campaign called "The Customer's Bill of Rights." One of the reasons that particular campaign was so effective was because people were very discouraged, skeptical, and dissatisfied with American automobile manufacturers. Lee Iacocca, Chrysler chairman at that time, perceived the need to reaffirm customers' rights so they felt important. In turn, the campaign helped overcome the skepticism the American buyer felt about Chrysler and created a foundation on which trust, honesty, and thus, business, could be built. Droves of people responded by going to Chrysler dealerships where they had some rights.

TACTIC 56   Avoid stretching the truth even a little.

There's no such thing as a little "white" lie. When you stretch the truth, you create higher skepticism because people then cannot differentiate between what is true and what is untrue. They cannot tell what is right and what is wrong, what is real and what is unreal, what is important and what is not important, what is fact and what is fiction. It all promotes skepticism in the mind of the prospect. If the prospect is confused, he or she will wait to meet you, to talk with you, or to hear about your products and services. It's more important to tell the truth than to tell a portion of the truth and be convicted in the minds of buyers for telling them a lie.

FIGURE 5–1
Partnership Bill of Rights

Partnership Bill of Rights

As my client and partner, you are entitled to:

(1) Professional, prompt and courteous service at all times . . . from me . . . my staff . . . and my company.

(2) Integrity.

(3) An ability to listen to your needs and recommend meaningful solutions.

Once you are my client, I am on retainer for life. I will work for you seven days a week, twenty-four hours a day.

As your partner, these are my rights:

(1) When I call you, please pick up the telephone. If you can't come to the phone, please return my call. Never avoid me, please. I will call you two or three times a year. When I do call, I will have an idea relating to the creation and protection of **your wealth**. I will always have your best interest at heart.

(2) I am entitled to a **yes** or **no**. **A maybe kills opportunity**. Nice people would rather lie to my face than hurt my feelings. I can take a no. The more times I get misled by a **maybe**, the less time I have to serve you or develop new clients. Building and servicing my clientele is my livelihood. To me , a **no** does not mean **never**. It simply means **not now**. So please understand that in all cases, I need a **yes** or **no**.

(3) If I perform to your satisfaction and standards, then I want to meet some of the people that you know. I will never embarrass you. Again, building and servicing my clients is my livelihood, and I want you to feel comfortable working with me this way.

(4) Finally, I am entitled to both positive and negative feedback. Most industries have poor feedback systems. We only hear the bad news. I want to know when you are upset, but I also need to know what's working well.

I look forward to being your partner.

Howard Starr, New Hyde Park, New York. Reprinted with permission.

TACTIC 57   Keep your word.

Keeping your word is practiced so infrequently that those who do keep their word are immediately held in high esteem by others. The cliche, "Say what you mean and mean what you say" has stood the test of time. Sales professionals and business owners who keep their word are perceived as trustworthy. This relates to every issue in your marketing and prospecting efforts. Even if the day you said you would call you don't feel like it or the information you said you would send is harder to put together than you thought, keep your word. This should be a guiding principle on which to build your career and your business. When your word is reliable, you are counted as reliable.

TACTIC 58   Have a personal code of ethics.

When you talk about demonstrating trust, it really translates into what you consider to be ethical behavior. To ensure that you have a foundation or base from which to work, develop a personal code of ethics. A code of ethics helps you avoid making decisions based solely on emotion. It will help you be more principled in the way you approach your niche markets. Let your prospects and customers know what your code of ethics is and it will increase their confidence in you. It will open doors of opportunity.

An organization that can send you information on how to develop a personal code of ethics and help you get started is Executive Leadership Foundation, 2193 Northlake Parkway, Building 12, Suite 107, Tucker, Georgia 30084; telephone 404-270-1818.

CREATING VISIBILITY
IN A MURKY
MARKETPLACE

"No man is an island." [and neither is a woman]

John Donne

Networking is so common a subject these days that it has taken on a wide variety of meanings. You can hear *networking* used to mean everything from "talking to your friends" to "one of the 10 major trends transforming our lives," as defined by John Naisbitt. However, target networking has its own unique and clear definition. It is the process of identifying and getting involved in the associations, groups, clubs, and other organizations where your niche market prospects and customers associate with one another. Through your involvement, you achieve the visibility necessary to build quality relationships and gain favorable access. In addition, the visibility you gain is perceived as part of the relationship-building process, thereby reducing your prospecting time.

THE NEED FOR VISIBILITY

Sales professionals usually do not acquire or see enough people because of a lack of visibility with prospects. Similarly, businesses do not have enough customers as a result of low visibility in the marketplace. Essentially, most salespeople and small businesses fail because no one knows they are in business.

As a case in point, a small automotive wholesaler in the northwestern United States decided he wanted to go into the retail automotive business. He specialized in luxury vehicles and invested all his efforts and capital in the latest facilities, from the service department to the showroom door. He spent a tidy fortune buying everything from marble inlaid floors and crystal chandeliers to fresh roses every day to create a sense of ambiance. He failed, however, to address the most important issue facing him in order to be successful: achieving visibility in the retail marketplace. Because he spent all the money he had in facility and inventory instead of marketing and prospecting to more affluent people, he went out of business. He blamed his failure on a lack of capital.

The lack of visibility in your niche markets not only thwarts your prospecting efforts and sales results, but it also frustrates potential customers who are trying to find you. A friend of mine in the boutique business lost the lease on his retail location fronting the main highway. To save money, he took a much less expensive place off the beaten track. Three short years later, he was out of business because prospects couldn't find him and eventually even forgot he was in business. He would have been better off paying the increased rent for the higher visibility at another location on the main road. Some sales professionals do the same thing in a different way. They spend most of their time in their office where they have little visibility and opportunity to build relationships with prospects. With few exceptions, your office is where you store things. Your prospect's office is where you sell things.

In addition, sales professionals and business owners will often invest their time and money learning the latest computer technology or designing the latest promotional gimmick. Instead, they should be investing the majority of their time and money achieving visibility and meeting more prospects in their niche markets.

In a very real sense, the customers of today are demanding that you become more visible to them. Just as your company must be visible in the marketplace, you must become personally visible as well.

In October 1991, *Town & Country* magazine revealed results of a survey among affluent buyers on what influences their selection decisions. One very prominent individual commented, "We make absolutely certain no one, but no one, ever comes up to us by surprise."

This need for visibility, which provides a sense of comfort and security, flows through all types of buyers and markets. Prospects and customers alike want to know you and how you stand out from the competition. They want to know that you position yourself as a specialist and your products as solutions for them. Your visibility reduces their skepticism and creates opportunities for you to build quality relationships with them. They want to be certain that you are clearly the right choice with whom to do business.

Many years ago, when I was in the Rolls-Royce business, I heard of Joe Girard, a very successful automobile salesperson at a Chevrolet dealership in Detroit, who understood the importance of visibility from the start. When he was hired at his first dealership, Joe was given several hundred business cards. Reportedly, his manager said, "Those will last you for years." Joe realized, however, that to be successful selling cars he had to go where the people were and gain visibility.

Joe and his wife would take bushel baskets full of business cards up on the catwalk at Tiger stadium in Detroit and shake them down on the crowds during the games. The cards had special discounts and premium offers to encourage people to come by the dealership. It paid off for him. Joe Girard has become a legend in his own time because he understood the benefit of gaining visibility in the marketplace. Whether you're a sales professional or a business owner, visibility helps prospects get to know you, know about you, and trust you.

THE POWER OF TARGETED NETWORKS

Alexis de Tocqueville, the famous 19th-century French observer of American life, wrote, "Americans of all ages, all conditions, and all dispositions constantly form associations." In the second volume of his great *Democracy in America*, de Tocqueville continued, "They have not only commercial and manufacturing companies, in which all take part, but associations of a thousand other kinds, religious, moral, serious, futile, general or restrictive, enormous or diminutive. The Americans make associations to give entertainment, to found seminaries, to build inns, to construct churches, to diffuse books, to send missionaries . . . in this manner they found hospitals, prisons and schools. If it is proposed to inculcate some truth or foster some feeling by the encouragement of a great example, they form a society."

Statistically, that is true today, as well. According to the Hudson Institute Report on Value of Associations, 69 percent of the population belong to at least one association, 47 percent belong to at least two, and 24 percent belong to at least four. These are primarily associations or organizations that support what they do for a living, how they recreate, or their areas of interest.

Colin Campbell, a columnist for the *Atlanta Journal-Constitution*, wrote recently on this same subject:

> I keep running into Americans who have banded together, volunteered, organized themselves into some *ad hoc* group. A letter arrives: It's from a church or neighborhood association or home-building project, and it's bent on finding jobs for single mothers, alerting me to camps full of Guatemalan refugees, organizing a co-op of carpenters and bankers. The phone rings: Come to dinner; we're lining up English lessons for hundreds of Soviet Jewish immigrants moving to Atlanta. A leaflet appears in my son's lunchbox that says, "News flash—book swap—parents' help needed."

All of this simply confirms that you can still do it for yourself, but not by yourself.

This need for joining together is not exclusive to the United States. A customer of mine, Reggie Rabjohns of Allmerica in Chicago, commented on the need for people everywhere to form networks of common industry and interest. He said, "Successful people are interdependent, not independent."

For this very reason, targeted networking allows you to know more people in your niche markets, which, in turn, sharpens your prospect's or customer's view of you and your products or services. By it's very nature, target networking allows you to break through the clutter, separate yourself from other products and services, and get the name and face recognition in the marketplace you so sorely need.

Your involvement in your targeted niche networks also enhances the dimension of quality in your marketing and prospecting efforts. Your prospects see you involved in their industry or interests, and that suggests to them that you are a quality person. This experience helps shape a quality image of you, which is foundational to building a relationship of mutual respect and consideration with them.

Dr. David Clark, president of KMC Media in Dallas, Texas, is heavily involved in the design of fundraising methods for various nonprofit organizations. His focus on visibility and involvement in niche market networks translates into this simple but powerful phrase: "*Friend* raising precedes fundraising." The same concept applies to marketing and prospecting to hard-to-reach people.

It's important to choose your niche networks carefully. Be sure they support the people in your niche markets. If they do, then select the area of your involvement in those clubs, organizations, or associations so you can demonstrate your abilities best. The more well known and involved you become, the more relationships you will build with potential customers. In turn, they will then give you access and buy from you.

Chapter Six

Strategy: Choose the Right Networks to Gain Access to Prospects

Objective: To identify and select the networks that give you the most visibility and relational access to your prospects.

B y following the strategies and tactics from Part I, you should know what market niche or niches you're targeting. Now it's important to choose the right targeted networks to begin to access your prospects. Consider the following selection factors, as they will ensure that you choose networks that will create opportunities for quality prospect flow.

First, for optimum return on dollars and time invested, you should obviously pick a network that serves or supports your target niche market. These networks could be trade associations, social clubs, or charitable organizations. As an example, if you're selling to nursery owners in western New York, you would target local associations and local chapters of state or national associations to which nursery owners belong in that area. If you're selling college education funding, it would be smart to target parents through their local PTA groups in the geographic area where you want to build your business.

Usually, local niche markets require that you choose local networks. In many cases, you may need multiple local networks to reach all of the prospects. National and state niche markets usually require a mix of local and national target networks to gain access to all the prospects on a favorable basis. The key is to be sure the people in your niche belong to the networks you target.

Second, whatever target network you choose, be sure the people associate and communicate with one another. As you know from Chapter One, one of the reasons you segmented and resegmented the marketplace is so you could group prospects and customers together by commonality. As you remember, this made it more likely that they would associate and communicate with one another. Networking gives you the unique opportunity to build on these characteristics. By associating, I mean that this group interacts on a regular basis. To determine if customers or prospects associate, find out if they meet regularly for discussion, fellowship, or recreation. Do they network because of common cause, industry, or recreational interest? If they do, you have the opportunity to reach many prospects within that network.

By communicating, I mean that members talk with each other. To determine *how* they communicate, find out if they refer suppliers to one another. Do they have a publication such as an organizational newsletter, a trade or club magazine, or even a high-tech audiocassette program that they use as a communications tool? If they communicate regularly with one another, you have the opportunity to communicate with them. In addition, they can talk about you and pass your name along to one another. In other words, you can achieve positive word of mouth much easier. The regularity of association and consistency of communication by members of a niche market network or group are vitally important target network selection criteria. These *core values* give you greater synergy in your approach and access to your prospects.

Reviewing the information you gathered when you were choosing or resegmenting your markets will help you identify to which organizations and interest groups, clubs, and associations your prospects and clients belong. Asking questions of your prospects and customers will further verify that they associate and communicate with one another in these networks.

The third factor to consider when you are choosing the right network to reach your prospects and clients is to be sure you can get involved. Involvement is essential to visibility, relationship-building, and prospect flow. Once you identify targeted niche networks, ask members you know if the local organization has events, committees, and functions in which you can get involved. If you can't get involved and gain the visibility and access you need, reevaluate.

You may need to choose another network to reach your niche market. In other words, the market may be right; however, that particular network may simply not be the right vehicle for you in terms of maximum, long-term visibility.

The fourth and final factor is one of synergy, affinity, and link. Ask for the group's mission statement to find out why they have organized. Is this a network where you are synergistic in values, ethics, and professional focus? Is this really the right network for you? Do the people in your niche belong? Is this really going to be a network you can get behind and support? Can it deliver you into your niche through the relationships you build? Be sure doing business together is not somehow prohibited in their statement of mission or purpose.

As you consider these issues, avoid being too judgmental. Some people see an opportunity but say, "I *probably* should" or "It probably won't work," and "I don't think these people will . . ." Focus on the principle that a positive attitude really delivers positive results. Denis Waitley, author of numerous books and tapes on personal success, says he meets many people who say, "Shoulda, coulda, wish I mighta had." It's important not to talk yourself out of a good opportunity. If you see a niche network that will work for you, get your net working and begin to work in the network.

With these four selection factors in mind, the following tactics will help you organize your choices.

TACTIC 59   Create a list of targeted networks from your market information efforts.

To determine and organize the networks from which to choose, you should refer to your market information-gathering efforts in Chapter 2. In that chapter, I discussed at length the need to identify the groups where your prospects and customers belong. These could range from industry and professional associations to recreational or special interest groups. I discussed many ways to find out where they belong, including asking existing customers about where they associate with one another and visiting the local library to find names of targeted networks.

As you review the information you gathered, make a list of every single targeted network group you can identify. Then rank them based on the four selection factors I discussed in this chapter. The goal is not to choose the biggest, it is to choose the one where you can gain the most visibility and access to the prospects. Multiple local networks coupled together can help you reach all the people.

An excellent example involved a young salesman for a national dental supply house who wrote to me lamenting his lack of success accessing his niche market. By virtue of selling dental products in Chicago, his niche was obviously Chicago dentists. From his perspective and experience, all dentists were potential prospects. After all, he was with a national company. He had decided to go after all 5,000 dentists in Chicago at one time by targeting the entire Dental Association of Chicago. The challenge was that not all 5,000 member dentists associate, nor do they communicate with each other on a citywide basis. For this reason, he was struggling to gain visibility and access. On the basis of only a few calls to Chicago dentists, we found they usually interacted based on their areas of specialty, and they mainly talked to and referred people to other dentists within their own local area of Chicago.

I agreed with the young man that 5,000 dentists was a great market. However, if he was to gain visibility and thus access, he had to focus on local dental specialty groups that associated and communicated with one another within the Chicago area. Taking my advice to heart, he first zeroed in on the orthodontists' association and then the periodontists' association in the Chicago suburb where he lived. He quickly gained visibility and positive word of mouth.

Now he is not only targeting other local dental specialty associations but is rapidly expanding to other areas of Chicago. Eventually, he will gain access to all 5,000 dentists in his niche market, each through the local specialty association where they associate and communicate with one another. He has also stayed involved with the Chicago Dental Association. It helps him to see the big picture and his clients and prospects to "see him everywhere."

TACTIC 60   Avoid selecting lead exchange networks to penetrate your niche markets.

Lead exchange networks simply aren't effective. Too many sales professionals think that by going to the local business lead exchange network or lead swap clubs, they are performing an important networking and business function. These groups may be fine for getting dates and job offers, but rarely do they deliver you deeper into a niche. Most (not all) are simply a gathering of people trying to sell to each other. In addition, they will send you all over the marketplace. The way to get quality prospect flow is to stay focused and work your niche markets deep. Your time is better spent at targeted networking functions where your customers and prospects abound.

TACTIC 61   Remember, members should associate and communicate with one another.

Even if the name sounds good—for example, the National Federation of Conversant Conversationalists—still find out if the people meet and talk to each other. Without this vital factor, it is difficult to gain visibility and prospect flow. A sales professional from Greensboro, North Carolina, had targeted furniture manufacturers for financial sales. He found the local association of furniture manufacturers and verified that his prospects were members of it. Further probing revealed, however, that they didn't meet as a group and rarely talked to one another about business because of their "trade secret" mentality. He regrouped and asked them where they socialized with one another, if ever. Their answer led him to join and get involved in the local country club, where he achieved visibility and access to them.

TACTIC 62   Use creative ways to bring your prospects and customers together.

If you have reviewed all your target network options and you still feel you need a better, more focused way to connect with them, the next chapter will expand your visibility and your network.

Chapter Seven

Strategy: Use Reverse Networking to Create an Opportunity

Objective: To create a network that serves your niche market in such a way that your customers and prospects can interact with one another.

W hat do you do in a situation where prospects associate and communicate casually, yet a structural organization or group doesn't exist in your niche market? What do you do when you want to bring your customers and prospects together for the sole purpose of networking with one another? In both these situations, you can practice reverse networking. This strategy is the process of bringing together individuals in your niche market to form a formal or informal group that will benefit both you and them. It provides a more structured way for customers and prospects to interact with each other. It gives you a unique method to gain visibility and build quality relationships and prospect flow. Reverse networking can take on a wide variety of forms, depending on the needs of the people or companies within your niche.

You could start a trade or professional association for the companies or people in your niche market. You could start an ethnic social club or a charitable group to support an issue or a cause important to your niche market prospects and customers. Or you may simply want to start by creating an informal networking group among your existing customers. You could present this as a special networking event for them.

As an illustration, my company has an annual customer appreciation day for companies using our video learning products. Senior management people from these companies come to this day-long event in Atlanta from all over North America. As a result, disconnected customers are joined together. This reverse networking has created an enormous number of fresh ideas for my customers to use the products in new ways. It has also created cross-sales opportunities for me, as customers share with one another and identify additional needs.

Why should you form an organization or create an opportunity for your niche market customers and prospects to come together? You may not need to. If an organization, club, association, group, and so on already exists that meets their needs and yours by bringing your niche market prospects and customers together—fine. However, if not, or if you want to expand on what is available, reverse networking brings increased relationship-building and prospecting opportunities to you. Forming an organization or putting together a special customer and prospect event also brings those core values of association and communication together—both of which are needed to achieve visibility and access to your prospects.

Mike Jenkins, of Tampa-based Jenkins & Associates, a small estate-planning sales organization, successfully leveraged reverse networking to his advantage. William Ruckleshaus, who was then the director of the US Environmental Protection Agency, was scheduled to speak at the local civic center in Tampa. As soon as Mike saw the ad in the paper, he bought a block of seats in the front of the hall. He invited both customers and prospects in his niche market to attend as his guests and sponsored a networking session, held just before the speech. The networking session took place in a large meeting room at the civic center, complete with refreshments. After the networking function, his guests all enjoyed their front row seats to hear Ruckleshaus. This one sponsored event has since led to several similar reverse networking opportunities for Mike with his target customers and prospects. What is more important, it has solidified his relationships with his customers and given Mike increased favorable access to his prospects.

There is an old saying, its author lost in the annals of time: "Whenever three or more people are interested in the same thing, they start an organization." However, for any occasional reverse networking event or more formal niche network you put together to be successful, it must first meet the needs of the members, not just your needs. Notice, I said first meet *their* needs. Once that is accomplished, *your* needs will be met.

Another case includes Liz Medley, a marketing consultant in Manhattan. She started a sports medicine newsletter as the first step in reverse networking with her targeted niche market of sports medicine specialists. There was a very large need for a concentrated source of sports medicine information. No association or group existed for these individuals to acquire the specific information they needed. By starting a newsletter, she is meeting that need, and it has become a fine vehicle on which to build her visibility and reputation. Having accomplished that objective, she is now working to establish a formal network to encourage new, improved ways of treating and preventing sports injuries. Why did she start this newsletter and subsequent niche network? So she could associate and communicate with her disconnected customers and prospects in the same industry more effectively. Her success was a result of focusing on their need for targeted information.

Zig Ziglar, perhaps, said it best: "Help people get what they want and you will get what you want." Your customers and prospects need to feel a sense of benefit, encouragement, and direction before they will become involved in your reverse network. The following tactics will assist you with the implementation of this strategy.

TACTIC 63　Avoid creating the new group solely for your own gain.

Promote the reasons why others should join and become involved; namely, benefits they will receive. As a sales professional or business owner, you've heard the old acronym WIIFM: What's In It For Me? Usually we talk about the organization or event in terms of what it is. What people want to know is, "Why should I spend my time networking with these people"—that is, what will this do for me?

People will buy into the organization or reverse networking event and invest their time based on *their* perspective, not *yours*. Determine what prospective members will gain, and make that the driving reason for coming together. It's very important to promote from their perspective. Focus on the OPBs: Other People's Benefits.

Your Perspective	Their Perspective (OPBs)
Talk with colleagues	Learn new techniques from colleagues
Share ideas	Spot the latest trends
Meet interesting people	Expand your industry contacts
Hear about what others do	Capture proven business ideas

If people in your niche market recognize they have something to gain by getting involved in the group or event you are organizing, you will motivate them to do business with you because they see you have their best interests at heart.

Fellow speaker Alan Cimberg comments, "When you *sell* someone, you do something *to* them. When you *help* someone, you do something *for* them."

TACTIC 64   Be sure your purpose and mission are clear.

If you are unsure of what the network or event you are helping to form or organize is all about and what it will do, then you cannot communicate the message to others. If the mission is unclear to potential members or participants, they may well decide that the only reason you are trying to set up a network or have a function is simply to sell more people at one time. Keep your customer perspective message very clear.

TACTIC 65   Assemble a list of the names of current customers and prospects in the market and form a steering committee to help guide the development process.

Whether you are creating a formal network that will meet on a regular basis or a large singular event, select several influential people and create an advisory group to help you organize. To be successful with reverse networking, it's essential for you to commit to the

process of creating the organization or event by serving as the cata-
lyst. You will benefit greatly from the organized contact. Prospects
and customers alike will buy in because of their involvement in the
development. It can be your idea, but it will blossom only if they are
part of the process.

TACTIC 66   Ask your customers and prospects what they want and when they want it.

Poll your nonmembers, customers, and prospects. Find out the best
place and time to meet. Determine whether they want a breakfast,
lunch, or dinner meeting. Ask what times are best and second best
and what days of the week are preferred. How often do they want
to meet? How do they like to receive notices of meetings or events?
Be sure to get their fax numbers and assistants' names, so you can
use these as means of communication.

TACTIC 67   Once you're up and running, avoid being the captain of the ship, or the king and queen of the ball.

If you're starting a formal network and it's now meeting regularly,
take a secondary position of leadership instead of becoming president. An example of a secondary leadership position would be serving as a membership chairperson. This position is more valuable
than being president because it avoids the appearance that you have
simply created the network for your own interests. Besides, the industry president can attract other high-profile industry leaders that
you want to know.

Also, by taking a more formulative secondary position, you are
able to guide and shape the organization in a way that is of benefit
to the members and a benefit to you.

Dick Biggs, a friend in the automobile leasing business and a fellow speaker, enjoys the sport of running. He helped start an organization of runners in Atlanta, which has now grown to several
hundred members. After he formed the club, he took a secondary
position and was involved in producing a newsletter. He was later

elected president because of how he had served. His secondary position allowed him to build the relationships necessary to gain positive visibility. People recognize those who invest in them.

TACTIC 68   Choose a name that conveys the benefits or the needs of your potential members.

I belong to a large church in Atlanta, with 13,000 members. Several years ago, the church's goal was to bring members together into small, local "sharing groups." The intention was to increase the sense of belonging among such a large congregation. However, the name itself was a big turnoff. It sounds like, "Come and share your darkest secrets or problems." Few people wanted to come together and publicly share problems of a personal nature. It would have been better to call them "blessing groups." People would have come together to receive and talk about blessings. Which would you prefer? Choose a name for your event or organization that implies opportunity or clearly illustrates what industry or interest the members share.

TACTIC 69   Promote to your customers, prospects, and the press.

Send press releases, get listed on the meetings calendar of the local newspaper, and send a note to all of your niche market customers and prospects, informing them of the event or new group. Do this consistently. There is no substitute for visibility through cumulative effect.

TACTIC 70   Develop "Smile and Dial" teams.

Just as it has always been, a telephone network among members promotes attendance at meetings and events. It builds strong personal ties within the group as well. Jazzercise, Inc., a very successful international franchise company, has encouraged its franchisees to create a network among the people who attend local classes.

Students actually call other students to make sure they come to class. Each class creates a telephone and class network of its own, which in turn provides increased business for the franchisees and friendships for the students. If you're creating a formally structured network, suggest that teams of people be formed from your founding members to call other members, prospects, and guests every month.

An added note to remember: There is no substitute for persistence. A group of executives who meet monthly in Atlanta has called me to attend its monthly breakfast every single month for nearly the last year. Although I have not been able to attend thus far because of my schedule, I know at some point I will—and so, apparently, does the group.

TACTIC 71   Create a strategic alliance with another organization.

What other group could benefit from putting together a reverse network? Approach that group and ask its members to co-venture. As an example, if you're putting together a niche networking function for conference planners to which you sell advertising specialties, the local hotel association might go in with you and provide free meeting space. Obviously, they would gain a great opportunity to cross-market to the meeting planners firsthand.

You could also call vendors who have a good reputation in your niche and create a strategic alliance. Call a special meeting with them to discuss how you can work more effectively with the prospects in your niche market. Work together with these selected vendors on key accounts. Create a cross-support group. Free-lance writers and other creative people have used this technique for years.

Speaker bureaus, who book public speakers, do this by having a national study group to learn how to work effectively with speakers and meeting planners. You can do much the same in your market.

Chapter Eight

Strategy: Achieve High Visibility in Your Niche Market

Objective: To achieve high visibility and gain the confidence of the people in your niche market.

S o far, your primary objective has been to choose your niche markets and select or create the right targeted networks to position yourself to reach hard-to-reach prospects. Now you need to focus on achieving high visibility, thereby establishing your position in your niche through the targeted networks. Gaining high visibility and a positive, trusted position will ultimately permit you to build quality relationships with more people in your niche markets, resulting in greater prospect flow.

Typically, professionals in sales and business who achieve high visibility in their niche markets have at least five characteristics:

1. They are leaders. They are not afraid to seize the opportunity and step forward.
2. They are rapport builders. High-visibility people have that desire and ability to develop rapport with almost every individual with whom they come in contact. Interestingly, the very word *rapport* seems to be founded on the "today" term *rap,* or a form of communication. Highly visible people are communication builders.
3. They are contributors. They give, not for the opportunity to get, but because they recognize ultimately it will result in more opportunities to give. They realize if they give only to

get, it won't be long before their giving will deliver very little "get."

4. They are idea generators. They are seen as resources, people who can really help move the organization or ideas forward.
5. They become involved in the whole process. People can really appreciate what they do, not because they talk about their intentions, but because high-visibility people demonstrate these intentions with action.

To be a highly visible person requires a commitment to become well known. Sales professionals and business owners who have low visibility have usually not committed to becoming well known to their prospects before access begins. They sometimes are still operating under the archaic concept that they can manipulate a prospect to gain access. These sales professionals and business owners also have five definable characteristics:

1. They confine their activity primarily to joining the network and acquiring the membership list. They may attend a meeting each year to sell something.
2. They are not involved in the organization. They tend to stand in the background. Low-visibility people are not really woven into the fabric of the network. They are not seen as individuals on whom other members can depend or call.
3. They are not reaching out to prospects. They expect prospects to come to them. Sometimes it is from fear, call reluctance, uncertainty, or doubt. In real terms, they do little to initiate contact.
4. They are meeting only a few people. The influence they exert is limited to a small group of prospects they have actually met.
5. They are producing only a few contacts per opportunity. They meet a limited number of people, and they tend not to have much dynamic energy or enthusiasm when it comes to meeting and interacting with their niche market prospects.

On the basis of these two profiles, clearly one of the most effective ways to become well known and achieve high visibility is to meet your prospects face-to-face at their clubs, association meetings, and social functions. That means you have to join and have a presence in your niche market organizations.

As a case in point, I read a story years ago by Scott Walker that I've never forgotten. It appeared in *Daily Guideposts*[2] and was about the power and importance of keeping an active presence.

> Dave had always wanted to play football in high school but, as a fifteen-year-old, he grudgingly realized that he would never be big enough, strong enough or fast enough. Reluctantly, he joined the marching band and learned to play the trombone. If he couldn't *play* football, he reasoned, at least he could support the team.
>
> And his parents supported him. "Mom and Dad never missed a single football game when I marched with the band," Dave told us. "And they never missed a band concert either. And what you need to know is that both of my parents were born *stone deaf!* They never heard a note from my trombone. But they've always been there for me."
>
> We all sat in hushed silence. What a tribute to the power of *presence*. Whether his parents could enjoy his music was not as important as their presence.

For this reason, it is important to make the network work for you by working the network. You already know people buy people before they buy products or services. Becoming well known helps you differentiate yourself from the pricing, product, and service issues. There is no substitute for continuing to meet your prospects face-to-face and establishing yourself as credible. This creates unique relational opportunities from the first point of contact. In addition, it allows you to continually demonstrate a positive, caring attitude to your prospects while also building a sense of trustworthiness.

Here are tactics that will help you become well known for the right reason.

TACTIC 72   Join the group and heighten your credibility.

The best money that can be spent to become well known is money you invest in joining the niche network group, club, affiliation, or association you have selected. Not only does this give you access to members who are in your niche market, but it also gives you opportunities to get involved in their functions and meetings. In addition, you will usually acquire the use of the organization or club's logo, which allows you to present yourself as part of the network even before you become well known. You can use this on business cards, stationery, name badges and so on. Finally, you will acquire the membership list, valuable because you can use it to track your contacts, gather referrals, and maximize your public relations efforts for all types of events. You may find it helpful for occasional mailings, premiums, and offers as well.

TACTIC 73   Find out what all your membership benefits are.

Often, when you join a group, you get some added bonuses. For example, when you join the Direct Sellers Association, as I have done, you also get a trade show booth at their annual exhibition. The space for the trade show booth is part of the membership fee. Another example is the Georgia Speakers Association, which includes registration for a one-day speaker school as part of its membership dues. Speakers and vendors alike are invited to attend.

Many times, membership gives you benefits that leverage you and your company far beyond the logo, the membership list, and the usual visibility benefits. Take the initiative and ask, "What else is included?"

TACTIC 74   Avoid presenting a laundry list of the things you think you deserve.

When you join a network, avoid making too many requests too fast. Even if you think you want labels and a list of suppliers plus an article published in the newsletter, slow down. Remember the Marathoner's Creed: "Inch by inch, everything is a cinch. Yard by yard, everything's hard." Ask for one item at a time. Don't position yourself as someone who is trying to take control and who needs too much care and feeding, or you will become well known for all the wrong reasons.

TACTIC 75　Attend as many meetings as possible, sitting with different people at each meeting.

Marilee Marshall, a sales professional in Phoenix, Arizona, sells to people in the advertising industry. Every month, she attends the Phoenix Ad Club meeting and sits with different people each time. Sitting at a round table of eight, she picks three or four people with whom she would like to develop a relationship over the next 30 days. She asks for their business card and invites each of them out for lunch to hear more about what they do. This is the type of proactive, high-visibility approach that it takes to become well known.

Make sure when you invite prospects to a follow-up lunch that you avoid pulling out your presentation folder and video recorder for "just a second" to show them your latest product or service. Use the opportunity to continue to build a quality relationship; then, once that is in place, move forward into the sales phase.

TACTIC 76　Choose where you sit carefully.

People who are followers tend to sit in back. Sit in the front with the leaders of the club, organization, association, or interest group. There you can maximize your efforts and become well known among the centers of influence. The people you associate with affect your credibility.

TACTIC 77　Avoid using your automatic business card shooter.

Your objective in going to a niche network meeting is not simply to pass or collect business cards, or to ask qualifying questions as a basis for conversation. Collecting or passing out an occasional card is fine; it's just not your only focus. Remember why you are there. You are trying to meet people to begin the relationship-building process so you can earn the right to see them and gain their business.

TACTIC 78   Ask rapport builder questions about each person's business.

I remember reading about a couple that people raved about because of their entertaining skills. Everyone looked forward to going to dinner with them. When asked about their skill and how it developed, the couple said, "All we do is ask questions and let people talk while we listen."

People love to talk about themselves. When you meet people, ask how they have become successful in their business or in their sport. Ask what advice they could give to someone working with people like themselves. Find out how many years they've been in business or in the cultural organization. Ask discreet questions about their family. Some things will stick in your mind, which you can use in your sales presentations. If you're not a conversationalist, then create three or four standard questions that focus on your prospects to kick off the discussion. Practice the questions before you go to the meeting or event so your comfort level is high.

I have a client in Roanoke, Virginia, who is amazed that I always ask about his daughter the cheerleader, even though it has been years since she led a cheer. Prospects and customers will tell you it's the simple things that often pique their interest in opening the door to you. The more your questions focus on them, the more people will focus on you. You will become well known as an individual who has a sincere interest in people, not just in the products and services that you sell. Talking about yourself really demeans who you are and prevents your prospect from talking about him- or herself. Remember the old adage: "The sale starts when you stop talking."

TACTIC 79   Demonstrate listening skills versus speaking skills.

Remember E. F. Hutton's commercial: "When E. F. Hutton speaks, people listen"? The commercial should have said; "When you talk, we listen." If it had, E. F. Hutton might still be in business today as an independent company.

Make your prospects feel important by nodding to let them know you are paying attention. Also, avoid the temptation to interrupt when prospects or customers are speaking. I frequently hear sales professionals or business owners interrupt conversations to tell how their products would solve a particular problem. Make it your policy to be interruptible and stop interrupting.

TACTIC 80   Have a 30-second verbal "commercial" ready to describe what you do.

When people ask you what you do, describe what you can do for them. Articulate benefits that you can deliver instead of who you are or just what you do. Use words that paint pictures, such as *proven, increase,* or *maximize.* Be sure you speak *their* language rather than using industry or company jargon. Prospects are not interested in learning your buzzwords. People want you to interpret who you are and what you can do for them by translating these things into words and benefits they recognize.

As an example, instead of telling a pharmacist that you sell pharmaceutical supplies, tell him or her that you help pharmacists provide quality prescriptions to their customers. If you sell life insurance, point out that you help people provide for their families or fund their children's college education. The focus should always be what you can do for your prospects, not on glorifying yourself.

If you sell residential real estate, be sure your prospects hear that you "help people find their dream home." If you are an exercise instructor, talk about how you make people feel better, have fun, and live longer, versus, "I teach people how to exercise." The key is to speak to their perspective with a benefit delivered in their language.

TACTIC 81   Follow up with a note to each person you meet and converse with.

Note the name of each person you meet and with whom you have a conversation. Send each of them a note that is sincere and gracious. Use black ink to handwrite the note, unless your handwriting is as bad as mine. Keep the note no more than three sentences in length. Otherwise, it becomes a short letter.

As an example, a note you could use with people you've met only once and engaged in little discussion would be:

> It was a pleasure to meet you Thursday at the luncheon for the North Dakota Wholesalers Association. I look forward to getting to know you better and seeing you at other events. Please feel welcome to call me whenever or however I can be of assistance to you.
>
> Very sincerely yours,

Here is another example, for situations where you had considerable time to talk at the event or when you have met the person several times at group functions:

> It was a pleasure to meet you [or see you again] Thursday at the luncheon for the North Dakota Wholesalers Association. I would enjoy hearing more about you and your business. I'll call you later this month so we can have lunch together.
>
> Very sincerely yours,

TACTIC 82   Send a thank-you note to each officer or customer who introduces you to someone new.

This type of note would typically say:

> Thank you for the confidence you have placed in me. I appreciate your introducing me to some of your colleagues last evening. I will always do everything possible to continue to earn your trust and goodwill.
>
> Very sincerely yours,

There are three keys to a thank-you note.

1. Keep it relevant.
2. Keep it short (no more than three sentences).
3. Make it timely. Anyone who waits, loses.

TACTIC 83   Be the first to walk away.

When you are introduced to a prospect by someone at the meeting or event, be the first to excuse yourself and walk away after a few minutes of conversation. This gives people who introduce you an ideal opportunity to tell the potential prospect more about you and what you have done for them and their business.

TACTIC 84   Exhibit enthusiasm for your product and your company.

Attitude is the father of all action. In Chapter Four, I described how exhibiting enthusiasm for your product and yourself will lead your prospects to exhibit enthusiasm, also.

One excellent illustration of how this enthusiasm builds relationships and prospect flow is the story of a member of my church who got involved in the Matol dietary supplement organization. He found the people that sponsored him to be very positive and enthusiastic. He, in turn, became positive and enthusiastic about the product and the opportunity the organization afforded him and others. Eighteen months later, his annual income from this network marketing organization is in excess of $100,000 per year. Enthusiasm builds relationships in every type of network.

TACTIC 85   Lean in and speak up.

Yes, crowds can be overwhelming, but think it through. If you are alone at a meeting, focus on others who appear to be alone. Speak up at the hors d'oeuvres table or registration desk. Say something good or positive about anything to someone. George Walther, a fellow speaker and author of *Phone Power*, put good legs on this tactic. He said, "Stand shoulder to shoulder with someone as you watch an event. Lean in and make a comment on the program or ask a question, then introduce yourself." One of the best ways to mingle is to ask a question or make a positive comment. This interaction will lead to introductions, which lead to quality relationships, which will lead to sales. You should also seek out the people you talked to during your information-gathering efforts. They will also introduce you to others.

TACTIC 86   Create a "10 Most Wanted" list.

Create a list of people you want to meet. Begin by asking every-one you meet in your niche market networks if they know any of these people. This helps you to overcome shyness and focus on an outcome. You can use the membership list as a source of these 10 people. Obviously, keep adding people to turn those 10 leads into 100.

TACTIC 87   You don't have to like everyone in the network, just like the target network.

Becoming well known is not a popularity contest. It is simply a mat-ter of taking the time to meet and know people. Demonstrate that you like the people in the network. Let them know you enjoy sell-ing and serving them as your niche market.

TACTIC 88   Avoid being easily offended.

Things will happen that you don't like. One organization to which I belong decided to charge members when they brought a staff per-son or spouse to the monthly meeting. Several members were out-raged and put themselves in a bad light by complaining loudly. The few dollars charged were simply to offset the cost of refreshments so dues would not have to be raised. Keep things in perspective. A little flexibility goes a long way.

TACTIC 89   Create a board of advisers.

Just as marketers use focus groups to find out what consumers like and what they would buy, you could form a board of advis-ers to advise you on how to support, service, sell, and promote to the network. The individuals serving on your board would typically serve on a volunteer basis and meet bimonthly with you, either as a group or independently. Remember King Solomon's advice: "In a multitude of counselors, mistakes are avoided."

Get the members' permission to list their names on your stationery and send out an announcement of your advisory board to your network.

Figure 8–1 is an example of announcement card text you could use.

You could also run an ad in your association newsletter or industry publication using the same text. By creating a board of advisers you say, "I'm here to stay and I'm interested in doing the right thing."

TACTIC 90   Use *we* rather than *I*.

Too often, people go to meetings and repeatedly talk about what *I* did. *I* is the most frequently spoken word in the English language. Whether you're serving on a committee or talking about yourself, learn to talk *we*. You sound larger and, most importantly, you are perceived as larger because you're making *yourself* look smaller.

"It is appropriate because it is, in fact, the truth." Consider how Lanier Motes, a well-known pianist in Gospel music, makes a very graphic and memorable gesture of humility. He always uses the lower case *i* when writing about himself; for example, "Many people think i gave a great performance. If i did, it was only because of the symphony on stage with me." It's a powerful message spoken nonverbally.

TACTIC 91   Create your own color name tag with your organization's logo.

As *i* mentioned before, one of the advantages of being a member of a group is getting to use the logo. If you create a permanent name tag using the logo and wear it to meetings, you also create the impression that you belong there and plan on staying. Often, it will become a conversation piece. Avoid the temptation to put your photo on the tag.

If people ask where you got the name tag, tell them, and ask if they would like you to get one for them. Tell them you'll drop it by their office.

FIGURE 8–1
Sample Announcement Card

Mary Pickens, a commercial real estate specialist and member of the Northern California Developers Association, announces the formation of a board of industry advisers to assist her. The following individuals will provide timely advice on how to best serve you, the developers of northern California:

James Kirby, Community Builders
Diana Barton, Western Commercial Construction
Dr. Charles Riley, Administrator, Sacramento Chapter,
*   American Institute of Architects*

Mary Pickens
77 11th Avenue
Sacramento, California 94514
916-555-1212

TACTIC 92   Avoid being discouraged if not everyone opens up immediately.

Some prospects have been burned in the past and are very skeptical. Becoming well known and earning trust is a process. Realize that some people will open up when the timing is right. Don't prejudge because people don't relate to you immediately. Small towns are often the butt of jokes about acceptance because the residents take their time accepting newcomers. Many of your potential customers in the network will have that same mindset.

TACTIC 93   Lighten up and become a visible light.

Have fun and help others. Sales professionals and business owners take it all too seriously. Become known as an encourager of people, as someone who offers help, hope, and support. You don't have to tell and sell everything to everybody. Keep it fun. "Lighten up and become a light."

TACTIC 94   Let people know you understand them.

Let people in your niche market networks know you understand them, their business, and the way they think. Let them know that you specialize in serving and selling people like them. People often say, "No, I won't buy," because they don't feel you know enough about them. Help your prospects see you as someone who is investing in them so they can have the confidence to invest in you and your products and services.

TACTIC 95   Dress appropriately for each event.

Ask in advance and wear what the majority will wear to an event. Years ago, I was invited to deliver the keynote address at a banquet in Scottsdale, Arizona. I'll never forget the horror of arriving in a business suit with two-thirds of the audience in black tie. I made sure that never happened again. Always ask in advance what the attire will be, and don't ask just anyone—talk to the program chairperson or president to be sure.

TACTIC 96   Follow up every lead you get.

There is nothing more disappointing, from a prospect's viewpoint, than getting no action after saying, "Give me a call." Become well known for your ability to follow up and follow through.

TACTIC 97   Don't pass up an opportunity to serve in your targeted networks.

Even if you feel the opportunity is not exactly what you want to do, start with what you have. More opportunities will come as a result. I have a sign in my office that says, "Start with what you have and give God something to bless. God likes risk." Over and over again, the sales professionals and business owners who step forward and are willing to help out are the individuals who get through closed doors. They achieve maximum visibility and a favored position. Ultimately, they are the people who get the business.

Chapter Nine

Strategy: Participate and Avoid Getting Lost in the Crowd

Objective: To promote yourself to the prospects in your niche markets through participation.

I t's easy to simply join an organization, club, or other group and let yourself get lost in the crowd. There are thousands of sales professionals and business owners who are quite confident that by doing nothing else, they can achieve sufficient access to their market. However, the evidence is overwhelming that by getting involved and participating in the target networks where your prospects are, you reap the harvest of greater access. The very root of the word *participate* indicates you have to be come a *part* of the niche market organization. Participation helps shape prospects' perspective about you because you are working and interacting side-by-side with them. It adds a dynamic dimension to your relationship marketing and prospecting efforts that separates you from all competitors. From your involvement, prospects feel that you are already building a relationship with them even if they haven't met you yet. Harry Hoopis, with Northwestern Mutual in Northbrook, Illinois, got it right when he said, "You know, Richard, the greatest achievement in business is to be considered a part of the customer's network."

As in all things, you will only get from any group or network what you are willing to give or invest in it. Franklin D. Roosevelt said, "Our true destiny is not to be ministered unto, but to minister to ourselves and our fellow men." Your participation utilizes this insight.

A higher level of involvement can also be good for your lifestyle as well as your pocketbook. In 1988, the University of Michigan Survey Research Center released a survey conducted on this subject among 2,700 people over a 10-year period. The study found that regular volunteer work, more than any other activity, dramatically increased life expectancy. Research at Yale, the University of California, Johns Hopkins, the National Institute of Mental Health, and Ohio State University supports the finding that people who get involved not only promote their business but also make a positive impact on their own lives.

To promote yourself and your business through involvement, consider the myriad opportunities available to you.

TACTIC 98   Serve on committees in your target network.

Serving on committees gives you an opportunity to demonstrate talent, ability, interest, and personality. Of course, there are many types of committees. Determine the one that will best showcase your talents and will give you the most favorable exposure.

As an example, if you are in the financial services industry, the fundraising committee would make a great deal of sense. On the other hand, if you are a product representative for a manufacturer, you ought to be on the door prize committee so you have an opportunity to interact with other suppliers as well as all the members. If you are in advertising sales, it would be a logical choice to serve on the publicity or public relations committee to demonstrate your ability. If you sell copiers and office supplies, consider the administrative roles and positions available.

If you are unsure about the best assignment to request, no matter which club, association, interest group, or organization you join, concentrate on one of the two most dynamic committees in any organization: welcoming and membership. They both give you constant opportunities to meet with both old and new members one-on-one. Your service on either of these committees gives you extensive promotional value and prospect access.

TACTIC 99   Be honest about your desire to earn members' business.

Honesty is truly the best policy. Don't be ambiguous. Let prospects know your intent, while making it clear you enjoy working with people like them. It's not necessary to blatantly say "I'm here to sell you." At the same time, avoid being coy and thereby harming trust and credibility. By being forthright and forthcoming, you avoid getting the reputation that you are using the group. Let them know you're there because you believe in the industry or the organization and that they are the type of people you choose to do business with and wish to serve. In time, any skepticism about your intent by some will be overcome by your involvement.

TACTIC 100   Ask the executive director or other officers of the association, club, or organization how best to get involved and support them.

Executive directors and presidents have special needs. They have special projects in mind. They know about unique opportunities and have special access to others. They are a key center of influence. Ask these individuals how you can get involved to best use your talents, meet the needs they have, and promote yourself. Often, you will get an opportunity of a lifetime to position yourself and your company far above the average competitor.

One fellow in the financial services industry in Foster City, California, took this tactic and ran with it. He called an association executive and asked how he could become involved. She replied, "I need a financial editor to give ideas to our members each month and you're it! How soon can you put something together for our monthly newsletter?" And the two of them had never even met.

TACTIC 101   Get involved without strings attached.

A price tag on your involvement reduces it to a ploy. Offer to help or to sponsor an event without specific payment of any kind in mind. *Quid pro quo* is offensive to most. What goes around still comes around. That is not to say you shouldn't derive a benefit. It is only to say that the attitude of "I'll do it only if I . . ." is marketing suicide. And yes, a retraction that says "I was just joking" withdraws the statement but not the impression.

TACTIC 102   Help with a charity cause sponsored by your prospects.

Your involvement can range from cochairing the event and getting "your name up in lights" to simply purchasing or selling tickets. By serving on a committee or purchasing and selling tickets, you punctuate your good intentions with good deeds.

It's important to remember that when you are in charge of an event, let people in your targeted group know who will benefit from the proceeds. Effort and funds come in quicker when the money is known to be for a worthy cause. To maximize event visibility and thus promotional opportunities for you, plan to create publicity in advance. Notify the trade press and the local press as appropriate. Lobby for media coverage before and during the event. Be sure you publicize the event to all the people in your niche market, and be sure they know what's going on. This way, you show your leadership and sympathy for their causes.

Above all, be sure the event doesn't bomb. I recently spoke at a public marketing seminar sponsored by a local business association. The business association's objective was to use the event to raise money for a scholarship fund. A vendor and its sales representative had volunteered to put the event together and make it a "real event." Not only did they fail to organize the event effectively but the association leaders had to take over in the final stages to be sure it was successful. Right intention, wrong impact. Avoid getting in over your head.

TACTIC 103   Offer to organize a vendor or supplier directory.

What an easy promotional tactic this is. It gives you an opportunity to talk with every prospect in your niche market by asking for their recommendations of best suppliers. You gain information that will give you a great competitive edge as well as an opportunity to interact with each of them on a favorable basis. Find out who they value and why. Ask what makes this supplier special to them. This will give you insight on how to build a quality relationship with them even while you enjoy access now. You could organize the directory in a variety of ways, including type of product, geographic location, and alphabetically by name.

TACTIC 104   Buy a ticket to a function and bring people with influence to the event.

Often, organizations aren't focused on publicity and becoming more well known in the community. They may want to grow or increase support, but they don't have much visibility. Use special occasions to help build awareness for them. Buy several tickets and invite a high-profile politician or renowned supporter of worthy causes. Notify the program chairman and president in advance that you are bringing this person so the officers can plan to publicly recognize your guest. Your gesture will increase your own stature within your niche market in addition to creating more publicity for the organization. You will certainly gain immeasurable promotional value.

TACTIC 105   Buy an advertisement in the program of an event sponsored by your network.

Yes, the pass-along readership is very low. However, it sure is the right image builder to those people attending the event. Size is not the most important consideration; a quarter-page ad is usually sufficient. Ask for a right-hand page, to increase readership. Get a graphic artist to design your ad so it doesn't look like something you would see in a high school annual.

For additional promotional value, tie the ad to the theme or reason for the event. Make the message benefit-oriented versus self-serving. Avoid coupons. This ad is an image builder to show your support for the event or project. Begin the ad with a positive headline such as "Congratulations," "Well Done," or "We're Proud of You!"

TACTIC 106   Choose the events carefully so you invest wisely.

If there are too many events in your targeted niche networks from which to choose, select the best events. Seek the advice of someone who already has experience with these charity functions. When I was in the luxury car business in Florida, I sought out a well-known local individual in the jewelry business for advice. I told him that I wanted to participate in the local charity balls; however, I couldn't afford all of them. Then I asked him, "Which ones would you suggest I select?" He listed five that he felt were the most important to gain visibility and to begin building solid relationships in that very closed network-oriented society. It not only worked well for visibility, it created almost immediate prospect flow. You should use the same tactic, whether running an ad or attending an event.

TACTIC 107   Sponsor a speaker at a meeting or event.

Speakers say some things you can't. One customer of mine, Oppenheimer, sponsors speakers at sales and marketing events around the United States for its broker–dealer network. It wants to bring an added value message to its brokers and dealers. These speakers deliver that message loud and clear and have helped Oppenheimer build loyalty among the people and firms in its target group.

On a smaller scale, you can simply bring in an expert to speak on a topic of interest to the people in your niche network. Dave Ford, who sells a variety of products and services to accounting firms in Los Angeles, employs this tactic very effectively. Just before tax season, he invites all of his accountant prospects and customers to a brown bag lunch and a "tax code relief session." Dave brings in a comedian who spends 30 minutes giving them just the kind of relief they need! This has created a steady flow of relationship-building opportunities for him with new prospects, which has resulted in new business for him.

Further, sponsorship doesn't always require your own expense. Often, a simple recommendation of a speaker will be sufficient. One sales professional who was working hard to access Nike executives

suggested to his high-level contact that I speak at their annual bas-
ketball clinic. This event for nationally prominent high school players is held each year at Princeton University. As part of the clinic,
Nike brings in speakers to "coach" the players on off-the-court issues, as well. The year I made a presentation to the players on how
to market themselves, Brent Musberger spoke on media relations
and Fran Tarkenton talked about handling stardom. This was a
great way for the sales professional to sponsor a speaker at no expense to him, yet gain added credibility and access to his prospect.

Of course, the clinic also allows Nike to build an invaluable relationship with top-notch high school players, some of whom will go
on to NBA teams.

TACTIC 108   Provide incentives or rewards to gain promotional advantage.

Rewards and incentives get your prospect's attention. Create a
plaque for a member-of-the-year award. If your niche market network is manufacturing-oriented prospects, sponsor a quality award
for manufacturing excellence. If it is service-oriented, a special customer satisfaction award would work. Have all the members in the
association or organization vote on who gets the award, or form an
awards committee of your niche market customers and prospects to
select the annual winner.

Another way to avoid becoming lost in the crowd is to sponsor
an award for the person who brings in the most new members each
year. You could also offer a prize to help build attendance at a particular event. Be creative. Identify the goals and objectives of the
club, association, or group, and create an award that salutes member efforts. Be sure to participate in the award process.

TACTIC 109   Provide a door prize for meetings.

At a sales and marketing executives meeting I was attending, I saw
a person who was selling advertising for a new sports radio talk
show become very well known and create prospect flow almost
overnight. He targeted the right people with the right tactic. For
door prizes at the meeting, the advertising representative gave

away T-shirts, hats, and other items sporting the radio station logo and the name of the new talk show. This smart marketer gave them away at various times during the evening. This kept his name and the new show's name continuously in front of these highly qualified buyers. He immediately received business from this first effort.

He continued the stream of door prizes several months in a row. He recognized that it's often better to give away door prizes at different times at several meetings than to do it just once. The cumulative effect of repeated exposure is always most powerful. Be sure your name and the name of the company, product, or service is mentioned when the prizes are presented.

Sometimes you may only be able to give one door prize. If that is the case and your prize is one of many to be presented at the same meeting, arrange to have yours awarded last. The name people hear last is more likely to be remembered.

You can also make an impact with one large door prize with proper timing. Years ago, when I was a salesman for a Porsche/Audi dealership in upstate New York, the Western New York Chapter of the Porsche Club of America was my targeted network. Each year at the Christmas party, I offered a prize of a weekend vacation for two in New York or Toronto. To be eligible to win, you had to attend the Christmas party. This had a twofold impact: record turnouts at the party, which helped the club's treasury, and great relationship-building opportunities for me with all the members. No one else at the dealership had that same credible access to the Porsche owners in western New York. The members saw me as someone supporting them and their club.

TACTIC 110   Develop and deliver an educational seminar.

The visibility and potential to build marketing and prospecting relationships with attendees is obviously great. A good example of using this tactic wisely is Jim Yurman of Cleveland, Ohio, who promotes his business by targeting seminars to resident physicians. He recognizes that they are very busy, so he occasionally puts on an hour-long seminar at local hospitals during lunch. This approach gives him an opportunity to showcase his personality and ability. This, in turn, opens the door to reach them on a favorable basis.

You could achieve the same result by conducting a seminar on a particular product or area of interest for the members of your targeted network; for example, "How to buy a copier," "How to maximize your public relations dollars," or "How to reduce labor costs." Work with your targeted organization, association, or club and ask them to be the cosponsor. Let the network promote the educational value of the seminar and encourage its members to attend. To get the support of your targeted network officers, use this approach:

- Meet with the program chairperson to discuss what topics would be of interest. Be certain you outline and focus on the educational benefit the members will receive. Explain why you are qualified to present the topic.

- Be sure you indicate that the presentation will deliver a range of solutions. Avoid proposing only one idea that fits just your product and services. That is self-serving and counterproductive.

- Offer a flexible length for your program. In any case, keep your presentation to a maximum of an hour and fifteen minutes to an hour and a half. Offer to allow time within those limits for questions and answers. Observing this time frame is especially important if you are holding the seminar during the evening or business day, so people can fit the event into their busy schedules. If it is to be held in conjunction with a local convention or other meeting, you will have to adjust your time and material accordingly. So offer flexibility up front.

- Provide the topic title and a brief outline of the program to make the job of putting together a flyer or brochure easier. Include a black-and-white photograph of yourself along with a brief biography outlining your experience and explaining why you are qualified to present the topic. If you are asked to put together the flyer or brochure, call on your free-lance designer or local university marketing department.

Help promote the seminar by the following:

- Get permission from the program chairperson and send press releases about your presentation to the news media. Be sure to include all targeted publications such as trade magazines, newsletters, or, in some cases, local newspapers.

- Send more than one promotional piece to the people in the network. Two are always better than one, and three gives you a sense of importance. Your first could be an event flyer or brochure mailed 14 days before the event. The second and third mailings would be effective if sent as postcards, 11 and then 8 days before the event. Also, be sure the president promotes the event at the network meeting just prior to the seminar.

On the day of the seminar, follow these procedures to maximize the benefits to you:

- Greet everyone as they arrive at the seminar, and "press some flesh."

- Have your introduction printed in large type. This makes it easy to read for the person who introduces you.

- Be sure everyone who comes to the seminar registers so you can follow up.

- Provide name tags to the people who attend. They may know each other, but this allows you to know them, which is one of your key goals.

- Be yourself during the presentation. Don't be afraid to use humor to help the audience receive your message. Avoid saying, "I'm not funny." Involve the audience and ask them to interact with you.

- End on time or even a few minutes early. Bring a clock and place it where you can see it to keep from running over.

- Leave your ego at home. Rather than focusing on yourself, make it clear to the audience that the focus is on them. "There you are" is more effective than "Here I am."

- To get rave reviews, be sure you focus the discussion on specific problems and solutions pertaining to the attendees. Make sure what you promote is what you deliver.

- Provide a program evaluation sheet at the conclusion of the event. Always offer the opportunity for attendees to request an appointment with you, and place this offer prominently on the sheet. Figure 9–1 shows the sample questions to include.

TACTIC 111   Let your imagination work for you.

Carey McNeilly targets chiropractors in North Carolina. One of the ways he gained favorable access to his prospects was by sponsoring a "trick hole" at their golf tournament. This annual event for his tar-

FIGURE 9–1
Sample of Program Evaluation

A) How beneficial did you find the material? Rate it 1 to 5, with 5 being the best.

B) How timely was the topic? Rate it 1 to 5.

C) Would you like more programs on this topic?   Yes ___ No ___

D) What else can I do personally to help you in this area?

Send me: A product sample ___ More information on your services

_____

          Specific information about _____

E) What other topics would you like programs to cover in the future? (Offer suggestions)

_____

_____

F) Who else do you know that should hear this information? (Suggest types of people such as colleagues or suppliers) _____

Name _____ Telephone _____

Address _____

---

get market group is held in conjunction with the annual chiropractors' association convention.

Carey videotaped and photographed the chiropractors as they took a shot at this trick hole. The photographs were processed into color posters that day. The next day, the posters were handed out to the players at his exhibit booth, where the videotape was shown on a large screen TV. This event sponsorship created so much prospect traffic through his booth that it has become an annual event, all because Carey demonstrated his creative ability.

You can apply the same principle by having a special contest or a booth at a neighborhood fair. You could be very creative by sponsoring a booth where everybody gets a prize. What a great way to deliver a positive message about winning with you.

Ask your local luxury auto dealer to provide you with its top-of-the-line vehicle for a hole-in-one prize at the association or club's annual golf tournament. The dealer simply parks the car at the 18th hole. You can purchase hole-in-one insurance very inexpensively. Rest assured, you will get attention and become well known very quickly. Make sure all who participate in the tournament get a photograph of themselves with you and the car even if they don't win. As a note of caution, be sure your advertising and promotional material states the car will be given away only during the tournament to registered participants. Otherwise, any hole-in-one any time could be eligible for your car. It has happened, and the courts awarded the car to someone who got a hole-in-one after the event.

On a larger scale, the local office of CBI copy products in Michigan bought one program slot at the 1991 First of America Classic in Grand Rapids. The company held a contest in conjunction with a miniature golf course to award the slot to the best amateur putter. The media attention was great, according to *Nation's Business*, which quoted Doug Lachniet, the delighted head of CBI's Grand Rapids office. His imagination generated positive publicity. You could do something similar at your local network charity tournament.

TACTIC 112   Send thank-you notes for every invitation you receive and every event you attend.

A thank-you note, much like a picture, is worth a thousand spoken words. One year, after speaking at a Dow Chemical event, I met with a regional vice president of sales at his office to discuss another presentation. Much to my surprise, on his bulletin board I found my thank-you note from the past year. He still had it posted there with a note, "This is the way it's supposed to be done." I realized a note is remembered long after the event is forgotten. A simple, handwritten, three-line note with sincere words makes a great impression and has high promotional value.

TACTIC 113   Help support a sports team.

If the niche market group you are targeting participates in a sports league or has an annual game or tournament, you could volunteer to supply part of the uniforms for the team. Offer to furnish their caps, T-shirts, or other items, depending on your budget. These items could easily include your name and your company name as part of the design. Three things to remember:

- If you use your name, keep it discreet.
- Avoid running the team. Remember, your role is as a sponsor rather than manager.
- Offer to invite the trade and general media to cover the event. This will get you and the organization increased visibility.

If you have no budget for this, volunteer to play on the team.

TACTIC 114   Stand for office in your local target association.

Standing for office means you volunteer or otherwise indicate to the leadership your willingness to serve as an officer. Service gives you favorable access, credibility, and a serious note of confidence and trust.

I heard of a young man who wanted to sell to contractors in Nevada, so he joined the Southern Nevada Contractors Association. Because of his willingness to get involved, association members asked him to stand for nomination and election to the board. He is now a member of the board of directors and has achieved the distinction of being a part of the contractors' network. You can imagine the favorable relational access he enjoys.

TACTIC 115   Write an article for the local newsletter.

Call the local newsletter editor and offer to write an article. Be sure the article is news-oriented, reasonable in its solution, avoids being a sales or puff piece for you, and is written from a third-person perspective. If you think, or know, you can't write, use one of these ideas:

- Record what you want to say on an audio tape and give it to a free-lance writer to edit.
- Find and use a free-lance writer from the International Association of Business Communicators (IABC) chapter nearest you. Look for IABC in the association section of the Yellow Pages.

- Locate a free-lance writer from the English department of a local college or university.
- Contact a service such as Words at Work, a Boston-based editing and writing firm for businesspeople. Founder Susan Benjamin, 617-338-7953, has even established a fax line with 24-hour turnaround time for editing, on request.

To gain promotional value and prospect flow from your article, insist on getting credit in two ways: (1) have a recent photo and by-line with your credentials, and (2) conclude the article with a tagline that states how to contact you. A sample tagline is: "Mary Doakes is the owner of DBS Data Services, which provides custom database management for light manufacturers, including metal stampers." If you can, offer something extra to get immediate access to qualified buyers. As an example, add the following to the sentence above: "For a free, 10-point checklist that reveals how to get the most out of your computerization, fax your request to Mary at . . ."

TACTIC 116   Write a series of articles or a regular column for the local newsletter.

Cumulative effect is very important to gain a continuous stream of prospects. Work with the editors and ask to write more than one article or suggest a monthly column so you can provide readers with multiple ideas. This will also get you repeat exposure. If you don't have the time or resources to write monthly, try to appear every other month. Appearing every other month makes most readers think they are seeing your article or column every month.

TACTIC 117   Write an article for a regional or national publication serving your niche market.

If your territory or market area is such that you need wider visibility, move up to these publications, which have wider distribution. Of course, getting such an article placed isn't as easy as for a local newsletter, where you typically can call the editor, write an article, and simply send it in. Instead, you should call the national or regional editor and inquire about the preferred procedures to get an article placed. Ask what are the topics of interest to their members.

I also suggest you offer to send a query letter regarding your article (you can have your English department writer or IABC free lancer whip this up for you). Evaluate your query letter with this checklist:

- Be sure the article is positioned as a benefit to the reader, not as a self-serving masterpiece.
- Be sure it has a catchy or relevant title.
- Be sure it proposes a length that the publication typically publishes.

After you've reviewed the query letter and mailed it, follow up with a phone call to the editor within two weeks. Ask how you can get the proposed article published in the publication. Be sure to emphasize the value it will bring to readers!

The advantage to you of having an article placed is immeasurable. You cannot run enough advertising to gain the same credibility that one article brings. Recently, a sales professional who has served gas and oil producers for several years had two articles published in the industry's national trade journal. He placed these as an experiment and was startled to find that everyone knew him when he attended the next annual convention.

TACTIC 118   Merchandise any article you get published to maximize its reach and power.

To gain further promotional value and prospect flow from your articles, get reprints made that clearly display the name of the publications where they appeared. You can usually save money by asking the publication to send you a camera-ready copy of their finished pages. You can then have a local quick print shop finish the printing. Send the reprints along with a note to everyone in your niche market. This will help multiply the impact of your article and further establish your credibility and stature in the marketplace. Put the reprint in your company promotional material that you mail out, so future prospects know of your efforts. Whether the article appeared in a local newsletter or national trade magazine, using this tactic will extend the benefits of the article far beyond the normal lifespan of the publication.

TACTIC 119   Start something in your niche market network.

There are many networks out there that need someone to champion an idea or cause, such as a political action committee, a spousal program, or a children's program at their convention. This tactic was successfully demonstrated by Robert Henry, CSP, CPAE, a friend and fellow speaker. He created his own legacy at the National Speakers Association when he served as president. He decided to create a children's program at the national convention, which is now attended by well over 300 children. More people are also attending the convention because of the program. They can bring their children and count on supervision and guidance during the day, so the parents are free to attend various meetings and events.

You could start a professional accreditation society. This would allow people to earn credentials and get accredited within their industry or field.

You could simply support an effort by the community, based on your unique corporate resources. Several years ago, Ken Clary, a friend of mine in Atlanta who sells commercial hot water heaters and boilers, had an opportunity to positively impact the dreams and goals of children in the Atlanta Public School System. Discovering that Jim Irwin was scheduled to be in Atlanta, Ken spoke with him about speaking at several schools. As a result, Irwin spoke and talked about going to the moon, and the importance of having and achieving goals. Although Ken did this as a public service, you could do something similar in your niche. Let your opportunities be limited only by your imagination.

TACTIC 120   Provide an audiotape of the month for the people in your niche market.

Busy people today want convenience. A news magazine format works. I suggest you send an update on the next meeting or happenings with people, places, and things. Load it with news, facts, and member information. A 12- to 20-minute tape would make a favorable impression for a small investment. You also gain an opportunity to get the ear of your prospects and existing customers every month or every other month. To make this easy to do, talk to a local audio recording company or university audiovisual department and work though them to record your tape each time.

Explore ways to barter your time, ability, and effort with the producer and duplication house. If you're in the printing business, give the recording company free stationery for a year in return for a monthly 12- to 20-minute tape. Get the tapes duplicated inexpensively at a local church or school media department for a monthly donation to the department. If you sell office supplies, copiers, advertising, or even investments, offer something in return for services to keep your affordability factor high and expenses low.

You might contact the local association or club executive that supports your niche and make this a joint venture. That way, you share the time and the investment.

TACTIC 121   Share the spotlight with your prospects and clients.

It's important to get others in your niche networks involved so you can build relationships with them and let them share the credit. During the mid-80s, I was invited to a special tour of the White House by a friend who was working on staff there. As I stood in the doorway to the Oval Office and gazed at President Reagan's desk, I saw this sign sitting on the left-hand corner: "A person can achieve anything provided he doesn't care who gets the credit." That tells us that to make a valuable impression in your niche market network, it's important to share the credit with as many members as you can, even if you are chair or cochair of an event. As I mentioned earlier, what *we* accomplished is much more credible and persuasive than what *I* accomplished.

TACTIC 122   Make the transition to the order.

Avoid waiting for someone in your niche market who belongs to the target network to come to you to place an order. Occasionally, I hear that individuals are waiting for the right opportunity to sell or waiting for someone to ask how to buy. The reality is, you must ask for the sale. Getting involved in your prospects' organizations is important for promotional and access value. Much like an advertising campaign, it creates multiple impressions and great awareness. However, unless you ask for the order at the appropriate time, you are wasting your time and money.

Your job is to maximize opportunities with decision makers. That can only happen if you make the transition from relationship marketing and prospecting to the sale. The decision to buy or investigate your product or service often results from your involvement in your targeted network. The order, however, is most often taken outside or away from the network function. So take your prospect or customer to breakfast or lunch. Meet with them at their offices or call them for a brief meeting. The overall outcome of target networking should be to create a favorable prospect flow so you can make the sale.

Chapter Ten

Strategy: Use Targeted Shows for Concentrated Networking

Objective: To enhance your visibility within your targeted niche market and generate increased prospect flow.

Nearly all business and professional associations as well as recreational or cultural interest groups have vendor or trade shows each year. Typically, these shows are a part of a local, state, or national meeting of individuals within your targeted niche. Trade shows are designed to showcase vendors and their products useful to the niche market group. Exhibiting at these targeted shows provides you with excellent opportunities to gain visibility and access to many normally hard-to-reach prospects. Your prospects are gathered in a very access-favorable, relationship-oriented environment. They are there to associate and communicate with one another and with you. Simply put, you get excellent return for the money and time invested because you have a concentration of highly qualified prospects available to you. The individuals you want to meet are coming into the exhibit area to find out what's new as well as to renew existing relationships.

As a relationship marketing and prospecting tool, targeted shows will build awareness of you, your products, and your services. If you use them properly, they can help you establish and reinforce your position as a vendor who is supporting, supplying, and servicing the niche. They are dynamic platforms on which to demonstrate your interest in the people within your niche and to earn their interest as well. Your involvement indicates to your prospects that you are focused on their industry or organization for the long term, not just the short term. This enhances their sense of confidence and trust in you.

William E. Smith, chairman of Smith, Bucklin & Associates, one of the largest association management companies in the United States, further emphasizes the value of these shows. He told me that for sales professionals and business owners to be effective today, they need to get out of the office and press some flesh. Targeted trade, organizational, club, or cultural shows give you that opportunity. They represent an opportunity to gain not only recognition as a supplier but opportunities to build and strengthen prospecting relationships.

Unfortunately, some sales professionals and business owners use these shows as their sole strategy to access a market. Exhibiting in a targeted show is not a singular, stand-alone strategy. It should be part of your overall mix of activities to interact with your prospects on a favorable basis. Targeted shows pay the greatest dividends when coupled with the other relational strategies and tactics throughout this book. To maximize your targeted shows, employ the following targeted tactics.

TACTIC 123   Be sure the show is aligned with your target group and the attendees can use your products and services.

General shows, such as home shows, county fairs, and so on, attract very broad audiences. They are not effective for reaching specific niche market groups. If you're really targeting and want to maximize your efforts and the money you invest, select a show that is specifically designed for the people in your niche. As I mentioned earlier, these types of targeted shows often accompany local, state, or national conventions and events held for the people in your niche.

TACTIC 124   Call past exhibitors and verify that the people you are targeting will be at the show.

Recently, I was considering a trade show in Atlanta for a specific industry group. My objective was to meet new prospects one-on-one that were potential buyers for my audio albums, custom video products, and speaking/consulting services. The promotional information I received about the show indicated that 42 percent of the people attending were certainly good, solid buyers of the products

and services we are marketing. However, before I made the investment in this show for the first time, I called people from the previous year's list of exhibitors whose judgment I trusted. These were
noncompeting exhibitors who told me that, although 42 percent of
the members of the sponsoring association were listed as buyers,
they weren't the people attending that convention and trade show.
They attended a different meeting designed for the executives in the
industry. I was saved from an expensive marketing mistake by
those calls. Be sure you employ this tactic and check the success of
previous exhibitors before you commit to a show for the first time.
Be certain the prospect you seek is the actual attendee.

TACTIC 125   Choose your booth space early to locate in the best traffic flow.

He or she who waits, loses. Early selection of your booth location
ensures maximum visibility and exposure to your niche market
prospects. When choosing your booth space, start at the entrance to
the exhibit area and stay on the main aisles. An ideal location is two
or three booths away from the main entrance to the hall. If another
major aisle intersects the one to the main entrance, choose one of the
corner spaces where the two aisles intersect. My experience has
shown that the right side of an aisle, when entering from the main
doorway, is better than the left. That may have something to do
with the way North Americans drive—that is, on the right. In countries where they drive on the left, you may want to choose the left
aisle but right side booth. Also, be sure you think about your signage and any support pieces, such as product displays or videos
when choosing your booth location. You want to maximize visibility for these marketing tools. (See Figure 10–1.)

TACTIC 126   Swap booth space for program participation.

If you are asked to sponsor a portion of the program or speak at an
event associated with a trade show, look for ways to leverage your
investment. Often, the convention committee will provide exhibit
space for you in exchange for your efforts. Be sure to ask in a sug-

FIGURE 10–1
Choosing Your Booth Location

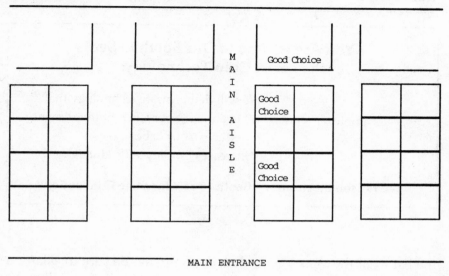

gestive tone rather than a demanding one. That way, you avoid the perception of *quid pro quo*.

TACTIC 127   Rent a booth instead of buying one.

If you only participate in shows occasionally, say once a year, renting will save you money. The key is to buy your own graphics and signs but rent the booth. Your graphics and signs become your trademark, which you can use over and over, even if you purchase a booth eventually. The graphics allow you to build continued familiarity, recognition, and visibility.

TACTIC 128   Acquire a list of attendees from the sponsoring association or organization, and send each person an invitation to visit your booth.

Tie this invitation to the event or the theme of the show. When you pay for your booth space, ask the show management company for the attendee list as part of your booth fee. If that's not possible, buy

FIGURE 10-2
Trade Show Invitation

You Are Invited to Our Booth to See the Latest Chip Technology!

photo
here

We will demonstrate technology that:

- Maximizes Your Current Investment
- Reduces Your Labor Costs
- Increases Employee Productivity

See Wilson Electronics—Booth 10 at Your State Convention.

---

the list from the association, club, or company. Be sure to ask for a discount or package price. A well-thought-out invitation will make a difference in the traffic you get through your booth. Figure 10-2 is a simple illustration of what an invitation can look like.

You can either send the invitation as a self-mailer or in an unusual envelope such as a 6 × 9-inch size or one that is invitation-sized. Obviously, the envelope will get the invitation there in a much more protected fashion. You can even put the word *invitation* on the outside of the envelope to make it look even more personal.

TACTIC 129   Offer a premium for bringing the invitation to your booth.

A couple of years ago, I developed a mailer in advance of a trade show where I was exhibiting. We sent everyone who was registered to attend this conference a poster of a target sprayed with bullet holes and included a spent .38-caliber shell. The poster basically said, "If you're not hitting your target, stop by our booth." I learned something from that mailer because people came by the booth carrying that spent bullet wanting to find the guy who sent it to them.

I should have offered a reward for bringing some part of this invitation to the booth. It was an opportunity to further develop a prospecting relationship—one that I missed. Some valued specialty item or participation in a special drawing would have very effective. There is a lesson here: Always reward behavior you want to encourage.

TACTIC 130   Attract people to your booth by having a drawing for something of value.

Just as door prizes work at meetings, booth prizes work as a trade show draw. Give away something unique. I recognize that competing against some exhibitors may be impossible because they may be giving away expensive items such as big screen TV sets. Be creative in those situations.

A young sales professional who sells to pork producers in the Midwest was faced with a daunting situation while working a local industry show. Although he had a few hundred dollars in the budget for the show, he was told that because his company was small, it had nothing significant to give away. He was advised to do nothing instead of looking foolish by trying to compete with the larger companies and their prizes. Instead, he took the initiative by coming up with the idea to donate a dollar to the state cancer society in the name of every person who came by his booth and filled out a lead card. He thought it would be a good way to demonstrate a positive, caring attitude about others. Over 400 people attended the event; more than 300 attendees gave him a lead card, completely filled out, and most asked him to contact them. He outdrew all the other exhibitors for less than half the money and received more than twice the effect.

To make a favorable impression and control costs, you could give away dinner for two at a restaurant anywhere in the world. Just make it clear that you are not including the airfare! An American Express or Visa Gold gift certificate for dinner would be a great gift for anyone. The size of the booth prize is not as vitally important as the unique benefit or visibility it offers or what positive relational image it conveys.

FIGURE 10–3
Sign 1 (Place on the Left Side of the Booth)

We Specialize in Helping Home Builders

- Save money on materials
- Build to code
- Achieve quality financing
- Landscape to sell

TACTIC 131   Using captivating, descriptive signs and graphics in your booth.

Use wisely the 3.5 seconds you have to make an impression. Two signs will usually suffice in an 8 × 10-foot booth. Make sure the message flows in a logical, left-to-right reading order. Your goal is to inform and arouse interest so prospects want to meet you and do business with you. Be sure sign 1 states that you specialize in the businesses or types of organizations represented at the show. This drives home the message that you know them and can relate to them. Further that message by stating on the same sign the benefits that prospects can obtain from you. Spell it out for your market, whether it is copier dealers, golf enthusiasts, or hospital administrators—what's in it for them?

Sign 2 should spotlight some specific products and services that you offer to them. To put this in visual context, look at the sample signs in Figures 10–3 and 10–4. These are designed for a wholesale home builder supply company.

When you're placing your signs on the back wall, be sure they are visible from the aisle and not blocked by a display of your products. Those displays often fit best in the middle of the back wall between the signs. Use photographs or a video of your products or services if you can't bring them to the show. You can use photographs in other ways as well, providing your booth does not become too busy or cluttered. A photograph of you can tie you visually to your products or services, or a photograph of various satisfied customers in

FIGURE 10–4
Sign 2 (Place on the Right Side of the Booth)

We Offer:

- Same-day service   photo
- Free delivery   here
- Easy terms

---

your particular niche market segment can be very effective in building credibility and interest. In almost every case, less is more, providing less is targeted clearly and portrays high value.

TACTIC 132   Arrange the booth so it encourages prospects and customers to enter.

Booths that are set up in traditional ways get little traffic. I recently spoke at a small-business exposition and noticed that most of the exhibitors were barricaded into their booths. This made it very, very difficult for prospects to get to them. They put tables across the front of the booth. They stacked literature into huge piles on these tables so people had difficulty shaking their hands. They stood behind the tables inside their booths while prospects and customers stood outside on the aisle—not at all relationship friendly. I suggest you do just the opposite. Throw open the booth and arrange it to maximize your contact with the people. The illustration in Figure 10–5 shows you how to design your booth so it encourages the flow of prospect traffic in and out. It's important to get the people off the aisle and into your booth.

TACTIC 133   Throw the chairs out of the booth.

You've been to trade, charitable, and club shows and events where you see sales professionals sitting down. If you're sitting down, average decision makers think, "This person is not really interested

FIGURE 10–5
Arranging Your Booth

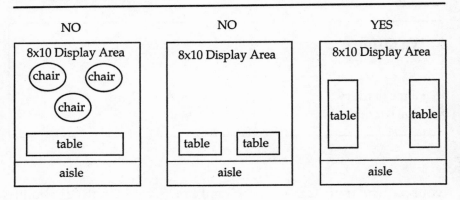

in talking to me." These decision makers simply wave or nod and keep right on moving. The only time you would have chairs is if prospects need to sit at a presentation table or in a theater presentation where seating was necessary. Unfortunately, at most shows, many exhibitors are sitting down, resting, as opposed to standing and arresting prospects and customers in their niche as they come down the aisle.

The worst example I have ever seen was at a fitness show in Orlando. As I walked through the exhibit hall, I saw one exhibitor who was sitting down reading a book, while virtually hundreds of buyers went by. This type of behavior detracts from the image you are seeking and the favorable impression you are attempting to make. Interested, innovative sales professionals and business owners recognize that a trade, club, or organizational show is truly a place to make a lasting impression.

TACTIC 134   Set lead and sales goals for the show.

Success at a show is measured in several ways. Among them are meeting as many people as possible, gaining high positive visibility, strengthening prospecting relationships, and generating good qualified leads from superior prospect flow. One way to plan effectively for immediate return is to use a rule of thumb in determining how many leads you should get from a show. A good sales staff at a show can generate anywhere from 2 to 5 percent of the attendees as leads. As a sales professional or business owner, the 2 to 5 percent level should be well within your reach.

If you want to determine your potential return on a show, take the number of days of the exhibit, times the number of hours a day the exhibit will be open, times the number of people working in the booth, times the number of leads one person can achieve per hour (typically, four to six). For example, if you have a three-day show that was open for five hours a day, that would equal 15 hours. Multiply those hours by the three people working in the booth (yourself with two others) and the four leads per hour each person will generate to get the total of number of projected leads from the show, which would be 180. Then check your closing ratio in the field to determine your return on investment. Figure 10–6 will help you see your potential.

It is important not to base all your decisions about a trade show solely on the number of leads or sales you immediately achieve. There are visibility, positioning, and relationship values that also must be computed into the show and its return for you.

TACTIC 135   Use a preprinted lead card to capture names in the booth.

For a lead card to be effective, it must accomplish three tasks: (1) make gathering vital statistics about your prospect easy, (2) give you an opportunity to write things down that are important to prospects, and (3) encourage additional contact through an action request. The outcome of any show should be increased opportunities to meet with the prospects.

A lead card could use one of several practical layouts: an envelope design for ease in gathering information and a prospect's business card, or a simpler notepad or form design. Regardless, design it for ease of use. Side 1 should contain several qualifying questions for your prospects to help you know them better, such as:

FIGURE 10–6
Calculating Potential Return on a Show

First compute lead goals:

Days × Hours open per day × Number of workers ×
Average leads per person = Projected leads per show

Then compute projected sales:

Projected leads per show ÷ Field closing ratio =
Number of projected sales

---

1. How long have you been in the association [club, group, etc.]?
2. How do you usually decide on a new idea or product?
3. Who is your current supplier?
4. What is the best time of day to call you?
5. If you changed suppliers, what would you want from a new vendor?

Be sure to leave room to write summary answers.

Side 2 could be data such as prospect name, address, company, job title, and telephone number of the person you meet. You can reduce writing time by stapling the prospect's business card onto your lead form or card. Of course, if you're using and envelope-style lead card, simply slip the prospect's business card into it. Be sure to include space on the card to write what prospects want you to do for them (send literature, set up an appointment, etc.). Figure 10–7 is an example of how a lead card or envelope could look.

If more than one person is working the booth, have a space on the card to indicate who took the lead or talked to the person, as shown on the card illustrated in Figure 10–7. Whether you use a lead envelope, card, or simple form, be sure to leave an area for you to write comments. This goes a long way towards helping you recall

FIGURE 10–7
An Example of a Lead Card

Side 1

1. How long have you been in the association [club, group, etc.]? ___
   _____

2. How do you usually decide on a new idea or product? _____

3. Who is your current supplier? _____

4. What is the best time of day to call you? _____

5. If you changed suppliers, what would you want from a new vendor? _____

6. Other comments _____

Side 2

Name _____   Taken by _____

Job title _____   Additional Comments

Company name _____   _____

Address _____   _____

City _____ State or province _____ ZIP code _____

Best telephone number (__) _____   _____

Fax number (__) _____   _____

Response needed:

Send literature _____ Call for an appointment _____

Set up meeting at show _____

My interest is in: Product 1 ____   Product 2 ____   Product 3 ____ each individual and understand his or her needs as you review the cards later.

Also, your lead card can double as an entry form if you are giving away something at your booth. Create several mock-ups of your lead card and role-play with them several times before you go to press. This will help you develop a card that asks the right questions and feels right for your particular application.

TACTIC 136   Qualify the qualified.

Chuck Mascott, president of Commonwealth Financial in Boston, Massachusetts, had a great idea on how to qualify the qualified. He simply had a flip chart in his booth that asked prospects and customers in his niche market to answer a series of qualifying questions. After completing the questions, they were automatically entered in a drawing for a dinner for two with limousine transportation. People answered the questions on a card, prequalified themselves, and registered for the drawing all at one time. This helped Mascott identify his hottest prospects and schedule a personal appointment with them before he saw prospects with less potential.

TACTIC 137   Avoid smoking, lunch, and fraternization.

When you're in your booth but having lunch, smoking, or kidding around with other sales professionals, you really are nonapproachable. Customers simply will not get involved. We've all gone into automobile dealerships where the sales staff were all standing together, cloistered in a corner, snickering, and talking about various things. We typically never go back to that dealership. For the same reason, many people will never come back to that type of booth. Remember, one of your goals is to achieve *positive*, not negative, visibility.

TACTIC 138   Reach out and touch somebody.

At every show, you see sales professionals hanging in the back of the booth, almost hoping nobody will come by and interrupt their daydream. Your goal is just the opposite. You will want to reach out, get high visibility, bring people into your booth, increase their comfort, and reduce their fear, uncertainty, and doubt. Don't wait for people to step toward you—step out and reach out into the aisle and shake people's hands. Catch their eyes and draw yourself to them.

Greet people warmly and exude confidence. Show your interest in getting to know everyone, whether they buy your products or not. At some point, they could become customers. They may be able to introduce you to others and help you deliver more products and services into your niche.

TACTIC 139   Practice your booth greeting and presentation before the event.

Before you go on "stage," role-play your greeting and run through your presentation thoroughly. Practice with a colleague at the show or with another exhibitor if you are alone. Don't hesitate to ask the maid or bellman at the hotel. Focus on being warm and friendly with your greeting. Flex your face, practice smiling, and be sure you know the benefits of your products and services as they relate to your prospects.

TACTIC 140   The goal is to meet prospects and press some flesh. Staff your booth accordingly.

An empty booth can spell trouble. If the trade show has more than 150 attendees, then you may need another person to help you work the show. If the show runs over three consecutive hours, you will probably need relief. If you have no choice but to be alone, use a sign that says, "In the restroom. I'll return in five minutes." Be sure to also ask the exhibitor next to you to let people that come by your booth know that you'll be right back.

One of the worst cases of booth staffing I have seen occurs at a trade show I attend each year. One exhibitor comes in and turns his booth lights on. He leaves a sign, "If you'd like some literature, help yourself." This doesn't help build positive visibility or trusting relationships. Instead, it helps him become well known for all the wrong reasons.

TACTIC 141 Have a relationship-building checklist that you review each day before the show opens.

For example:

- Am I ready to reach out to people?
- Am I feeling warm and friendly?
- Do I have a breath freshener available?
- Are my hands dry?
- Am I in a good mood?
- Have I reviewed my list of customers and prospects so I can quickly recall names?
- Have I practiced greeting people?

TACTIC 142 Have a preshow meeting with yourself and all the others on the booth staff before the doors open.

Here's a checklist you could use to be sure you are focused on the prospect and the process:

- Review your relationship-building checklist with each other.
- What are the benefits of our products as they relate to these prospects in our niche?
- Who is going to handle each product and explain its value?
- How are we going to fill out lead cards? Practice with an actual card.
- Explain any prizes and when they are going to be drawn. Make sure everyone knows and understands the process.
- What is the price of the goods we are selling?
- Set your break times and your lunch schedule so you know who is going to be where at any given moment.
- Have a backup plan in case you get extremely busy and can't stay on schedule. You may also announce an incentive for the best leads or most enthusiastic efforts.

TACTIC 143   Have a press kit in the media room, and invite the press to come by your booth for an interview.

In your press kit, offer an interview to discuss the quality and value of the show. Every good thing you say about how satisfied you are has the potential to be printed in the trade, club, or organizational press. That builds your stature and credibility with the very people you're trying to meet and build relationships with. Stop by the media room, greet people, and press some flesh there as well. Reach out to the media and they will help you gain visibility.

TACTIC 144   Invite the trade, organization, or club press to cover the drawing of your booth prize.

This also encourages publicity. By getting a photograph taken, you will increase your potential for coverage in the local or national publications. This helps reinforce a great message to your niche that you are willing to give versus get. If no press is available, take your own photograph and run an ad congratulating the winner.

TACTIC 145   Give away some item to everyone who comes by the booth.

Make prospects feel welcome and special. Many exhibitors give away things such as pens and hats that are somewhat standard and mundane. Do something different. Give something more usable, such as a set of business cards, laminated luggage tags, or a bag in which to carry everyone else's prizes and materials. If you use a bag, be sure your name is prominently displayed on the outside for maximum visibility.

If your budget doesn't allow for a specialty item, or if you want to do something different from years past, create a sticker or novelty item to put on everyone's name badge. It lets everyone working with you know who has come by your booth. In addition, if the sticker or novelty is interesting enough, people will seek you out to get one. I recently exhibited at an organizational show where we made up stickers that said "Target Marketing Works." We put it on people's badges as they entered our booth. It was very gratifying at the end of those three days to see all the people walking around displaying our stickers. It was even more gratifying that prospects and customers came looking for them.

TACTIC 146   Feed the attendees peanuts, candy kisses, or popcorn.

I realized a long time ago that people like to munch at trade shows. Popcorn is very good at midday, although it's a little messy and can distract people from your message. You don't want to become part of the food vendor group.

I have found that nuts and candy kisses work better. If I'm doing a trade show with a great number of women, I give away Hershey's candy kisses. In my experience, women seem to prefer the original pure, sweet chocolate without any almond inside.

Men, on the other hand, seem to love nuts, particularly mixed nuts. If you're doing a show that has predominantly men in attendance, serve mixed nuts in a bowl. If you're having a good year, put in some extra cashews. The men will stand around and talk to you for hours about their business, and about yours too, while they pick out the cashews.

TACTIC 147   Come early and plan on leaving late.

Just as an empty booth is devastating to your image, so too are sales professionals and business owners who are rushing to leave at closing time. They will be closing up as prospects and customers in your niche are still walking by. What this conveys is, "I'm not interested in talking to you right now. My time is up." Sometimes during the late hours of the show some very powerful centers of influence walk through the exhibit hall. Since they have been tied up in organizational or educational meetings all day long, this is often their only opportunity to come into the show and visit with the vendors.

Frequently, booths are also unstaffed at shows where in the morning the exhibit hall is only open for 45 minutes to an hour to serve the breakfast crowd. The main purpose of this is to give exhibitors more hours with attendees. However, many exhibitors stay in bed during these early exhibit hours—often 7:30 or 8:30A.M.—and don't come until later. Keep in mind, if you're not there when customers want to buy, customers most likely won't be there when you want to sell.

TACTIC 148   Avoid taking literature to a show. Mail it instead.

As I suggested earlier, giving out those plastic bags with your name or logo is good advertising during a show. However, we all know when other exhibitors put their literature in those bags, the literature usually doesn't even make it to the office; it goes to the hotel, club, or convention center dumpster. Get a jump on the competition and demonstrate your responsiveness all in one action. Instead of passing out your own literature, prepare your promotional packets in advance and mail them to your prospects when you get back from the show.

Some sales professionals or business owners will say, "What happens if someone asks 'Do you have any literature?' Do I say no?" Say, "I sure do, but I didn't think you'd want to carry it around with you. Just give me your name and address, and I will sent the literature straight to your office." You can be assured yours will be the few pieces of literature they actually receive and read.

To ensure it is on their desk when they return, fax or hand-carry the list of leads back to your office at the end of each day. Have your assistant send the packets out immediately. You achieve a very positive position with prospects when you show that you have the ability to take care of their needs quickly.

As an added note, professional, trade, and cultural show literature has become such an issue that some sponsoring organizations, such as the National Association of Home Builders, no longer allow vendors to pass it out. In fact, these organizations often provide show attendees with a plastic card that they give to exhibitors when they are interested and want to request literature. The exhibitor then makes an imprint of the card to know who wants the information. The association or organization then gives the exhibitor a set of labels from the imprints. More organizers are going to this system to cut down on attendees carrying around all the literature and to preserve the environment.

TACTIC 149   Have your sales letter written before you go to the show.

By creating a sales letter in advance to accompany the material you will send, you save response time. You will be free to call on your hottest prospects. Include the capability to add a customized line or two to build a sense of rapport and relationship with the individual. In addition to speeding up response time, it cuts down on paperwork after the show.

TACTIC 150   Have your telephone follow-up script written before the show.

This makes you fully prepared to take advantage of every qualified lead you receive. Tie the discovery questions and benefit statements in the script to your booth signage and recreate a similar dialogue. Be sure to refresh your prospect's memory regarding who you are and what your show discussion was about.

TACTIC 151   Cross-sell your products with other exhibitors.

If you have a cooperative arrangement with another company at the show, have a sign in both your booth and theirs. This could be a simple tent card–type sign. The sign could say that their particular product or service is compatible with what you are selling, and vice versa. If your product enhances another product, or if your service provides additional value to something that almost everyone in the marketplace is already using, then say so. A cooperative arrangement with another exhibitor at the show will help you gain additional exposure for the same money and increase your sense of belonging in that niche.

TACTIC 152   Cultivate every name you receive at your booth, whether it be from a drawing or from people that you meet.

Timing is everything. Follow up with everyone, whether they are qualified or casual contacts. Send a letter to those prospects who have shown a casual interest, asking whether they would like more information now that they have seen what's available in the market. Tell them you'd like an opportunity to meet with them and find out more about their needs. Let them know you are willing to earn the right to see them again. You could also offer to demonstrate how your product or service is different. With your hot prospects, follow up with a telephone call. Verify that they received the literature they requested. Be sure to call them as soon as they return from the show—that is, usually within three to five working days. If you wait, your competitors will call them for you. It's important to touch every single person who comes by that booth and cultivate a relationship with them.

TACTIC 153   Focus on the prospects during show hours.

Your goal is not to commiserate with other exhibitors during show hours. You'll have plenty of time to do that during setup, off-hours, and tear-down. Focus, instead, on association and communication with your prospects and clients. Leverage every moment in the show to meet them.

TACTIC 154   Ask for the order.

Sales are typically marginal at shows, mostly because these occasions are looked on as information-gathering opportunities by your prospects and clients. They do want to see what is new and if it can help them. They want to begin or continue the relationship-building process during their time with you. However, many people who already know you and trust you come to the show with the specific intention of spending money now. You want to be able to accommodate them. Be there with your order forms.

TACTIC 155   Do something different. Market yourself outside the exhibit hall.

After exhibiting at a particular show for several years, I felt it necessary to break through the walls and do something different. It occurred to me that if I could broadcast a prerecorded message about our video products and speaking services into every attendee's hotel room, I would have a competitive edge with my targeted audience. I contacted Spectradyne, rented a channel from them, sent them a demonstration videotape, and had them transmit it into every hotel room during the conference.

We encouraged the show participants to watch the dedicated TV channel by putting a letter under their doors. This gave them an opportunity to view my message in the comfort of their own rooms. What is more important, it began building a favorable impression with the target audience before they came to the booth.

Think about how you can do something different to market outside of the show area. For example:

- Attend the educational sessions.
- Sponsor a speaker.
- Sponsor a reception.
- Introduce a speaker.
- Have a hospitality suite.
- Schedule a press conference.
- Present an award.
- Sponsor a secret shopper.

Be creative, not outlandish. Your goal is to increase your visibility, credibility, and relational profile while generating high-quality leads. Work hard to build prospecting relationships to increase a favorable impression. Meet as many people as you can, and promote yourself as someone who is in the marketplace to serve and stay.

IV

ACQUIRING POSITIVE WORD OF MOUTH

"A good name is better than riches."

King Solomon
[the richest man who ever lived]

The power of word of mouth has never been stronger. Prospects are relying on the personal referrals and testimonials of people they know to help them make buying decisions.

The December 1992 issue of *The Public Pulse* indicated that more often than not, Americans say they rely most on their friends for information on a variety of issues. These range from what movies to see to how to choose a new car. Fewer prospects, meanwhile, depend on various editorial and advertising sources for information. What this illustrates is that people rely on word of mouth because it is based on their existing relationships and the credibility of the person passing the word along. It increases their sense of comfort with the decisions they make. In addition, prospects are busier than ever before and have become very time conscious. They are spending less time using broadcast media, TV, and radio as a way to gain information and make a decision, according to the latest Roper polls. This further increases the value of word of mouth recommendations because they save decision makers time.

For these reasons, the recommendations of others are helpful to everyone who is involved in selection and purchasing decisions. These include members of a vendor selection committee at a particular company, an executive who is making or approving the final decision, or the individual prospect on his or her own behalf.

These people want to save time and get the right information by asking people they consider knowledgeable and credible "With whom should I do business?" or "What do you think of this particular product?"

Studies in some industries show that 80 percent of all buying decisions are based on just such a recommendation from others. The simple fact is that a positive mention of your name brings an increased level of confidence and convenience to your prospects, thereby giving you greater access to them.

If you're selling copiers, you will very quickly find out that, if you and your copiers perform, your customers will tell and refer you to others like themselves. Such favorable word of mouth will allow you to work deeper into your niche markets more quickly and effectively.

If you're selling cosmetics for a direct sales company, the reputation that you provide quality products and services to your customers will quickly spread. Word of mouth will communicate that you're the type of person with whom others should be doing business.

If you're selling pharmaceuticals to pharmacies and physicians, the service and thoughtfulness you demonstrate on your customers' behalf is obviously important. Satisfied pharmacists and physicians will tell others like themselves.

Of course, all word of mouth needs to be positive. Any negative word of mouth will do considerable damage to your relationship marketing and prospecting efforts.

Ken Futch, past president of Georgia Speakers Association and a professional speaker, has a wry comment on this whole concept of word of mouth, in both the positive and negative sense. He relates that, "Although a lot of people talk at length about how good they are, their word of mouth is killing them." Regardless of how we may perceive ourselves as sales professionals or business owners, it's the perception of the buyer and the prospect that ultimately determines our success within a market.

Positive word of mouth can come in the form of a referral, a testimonial, or both. To make the distinction, referrals are specific names of people you receive or personal introductions that are made on your behalf. Testimonials are written or verbal communications that convey the confidence people have in you. From a relationship marketing and prospecting perspective, a testimonial in written form is preferable, primarily because it is transportable and can be used repeatedly.

No matter the form, however, testimonials allow customers to say things that you can't say. They can communicate in a positive way the benefits of doing business with you.

Referrals and written testimonials work well together, because the more you can reinforce the referral, the greater the likelihood that the organization or the individual to whom you are referred will give you favorable access. Prospects prefer buying products and services that have already been tried and proven by others. Their decision to see you or do business with you, then, has less risk. Someone else has gone first.

To build a successful sales career and business, acquiring referrals and testimonials should be an important part of the relationship marketing and prospecting efforts you put forth. Such positive word of mouth will help you gain favorable access to your niche market prospects.

From my own experience over the years, three referrals typically result in one nearly immediate sale. More sales will usually result over a period of time. The more referrals and testimonials you get, the easier it is to become well known and build the quality relationships necessary to earn the right to present your products.

Acquiring referrals and testimonials can be as simple and quick as the way door-to-door salespeople used to gain most referrals, which was to go through a target neighborhood knocking on the doors of two houses on either side of their most recent customer and the four across the street from them. This method is still used occasionally and is referred to as "two on either side and four across the street." With the influence these neighbors have on one another and their referent power, an entire neighborhood or subdivision can be prospected. It can be as protracted as waiting until the end of the sales and initial service cycle to ask for the referral. As an illustration, Jim Seymour, a computer consultant who writes for *PC Magazine*, suggests that by giving a tremendous amount of service and by showing a great deal of interest in the customer, you will eventually gain referrals.

First, he goes on all his computer installations because it lets him size up the nature of the customer's business and focus on possible future needs. Then his postsale calls, well after installation, let him make sure that things are still running right and convinces his customers that he wants them to be satisfied with what they bought.

Then, because this customer-focused sales and service process encourages referrals, he simply asks for them. No matter what market you operate in or methods you use, referrals and testimonials should be a part of your normal sales and service activities. As Jim Seymour observes, "Asking must become a habit."

Of course, sales professionals and business owners sometimes say, "Well, I can't get referrals or testimonials." There are many reasons why individuals don't get the positive word of mouth they need to be more successful.

I believe it's important to check the reasons that you may not be getting referrals or testimonial letters by reviewing the following list. Check all those that apply.

1. I had a bad experience.
2. It's not a habit that I have formed.
3. I'm not comfortable with the wording used to ask for referrals.
4. I'm not sure when to ask for referrals.
5. I get caught up in the excitement of a sale and forget.
6. Upon delivery, I feel uncomfortable asking for something else.
7. I don't think the person really wants to push me on friends.
8. It worked so well and I got so busy, I stopped doing it.
9. I'm not sure the customer is that pleased with my work or product, so I don't think I would get a good letter or any referrals.

In the following three chapters are many different tactics that can help you overcome these obstacles. Using them will enable you to systematically acquire the referrals and testimonials you need to reach more hard-to-reach people.

Chapter Eleven

Strategy: Align Yourself with Centers of Influence

Objective: To expand your referral and testimonial base through the centers of influence in your niche markets.

M ost sales professionals and business owners focus on receiving referrals and testimonials only from their current customers and an occasional prospect. To expand the number of referrals you're receiving into your targeted niche, you should also specifically identify, cultivate, and win the confidence of the people who are seen as influential in your niche markets. The quality of your relationship with these centers of influence can represent one of the most powerful and personal ways to gain referrals to and immediate credibility with others.

Their word of mouth promotion, referrals, and testimonials to people they know and people that know them in your niche market are invaluable. They can help position you in your markets by recommending you as someone who is truly different, someone who brings unique value to others. Basing part of your relationship marketing and prospecting approach on these centers of influence allows you to have the most favorable access to many prospects. In short, they can open doors of opportunity to you that are closed to other sales professionals and business owners.

What do we know about these influential people and what makes them centers of influence? The Roper Organization has conducted studies on influential people for the last 47 years. The influential segment of the population is remarkable for its consistency. According to Tom Miller, Roper senior vice president, the key element is activity. They are willingly involved in their communities both socially and politically. This involvement, of course, builds their visibility, credibility, and thus their sphere of influence.

Further, the Roper studies found that the involvement of centers of influence sets them apart and helps establish them as role models. People in a niche market actively seek their advice and trust them. It is important to note that a center of influence is not always necessarily the president or the head individual in the biggest company, organization, or club, but could simply be someone who is a charismatic, well-disciplined, well-respected individual that is constantly moving forward.

Surveys conclude that, in many industries, simply winning the confidence of one of these centers of influence can create at least six loyal customers. With a concerted effort to encourage positive word of mouth and introductions by centers of influence, winning many more loyal customers from a single center of influence is possible.

Contrary to popular perception, Roper studies further show that influential people are not necessarily old or rich. Actually, 54 percent of influentials are between the ages of 30 and 49. In contrast, this age group represents only 41 percent of the general population. How affluent are they? The largest group of influentials (43 percent) make between $30,000 and $50,000 a year in annual income. The most important factor that influentials usually have in common is a college education. Nearly three out of four centers of influence have gone to college. It's clear that North American centers of influence are most likely to be middle-income, college-educated baby boomers who are active in the markets you are trying to reach.

You should focus on meeting and building a quality relationship with the centers of influence in your targeted niche markets because they influence the attitude and acceptance of others. Attitudes of skepticism stem from a lack of knowledge and a lack of trust.

Centers of influence are considered knowledgeable and trustworthy. They are respected for their efforts, their opinions, and their recommendations. Thus, they can help change the skeptical attitudes of your prospects. These influential people deliver, by their support of you, a solid base of trust on which you can build. Furthermore, by positioning yourself and gaining the confidence of the centers of influence in your niche markets, they will refer and introduce you to many of your prospects. They become a valuable added source of referrals and testimonials.

How do you find and approach centers of influence? The following tactics will help you to identify, meet, and build quality relationships with these individuals.

TACTIC 156   Ask questions of individuals in your market.

Start by asking customers, prospects, and other individuals with whom you come in contact who they consider to be the person or persons with the most influence in their company, industry, club, or organization. Create a list of all the people mentioned. Second, ask, "How can I reach and meet these people?" Use the information you gain to frame your approach. Ask the person who gave you the name to introduce you to this person or persons.

TACTIC 157   Review industry, club, and company publications.

Read these publications with a different slant to find the influential people. Review the title pages and look for the names of directors and other officers. Identify those who head committees or seem to be in every picture or behind every event. Look for the names of people who always seem to be receiving special thanks. Read articles for the names of people who are behind the projects. Create a list of people who are frequently mentioned. Then target them as people you want to meet.

TACTIC 158   Review the list of niche market associations, clubs, and organization executives you came in contact with during your information gathering.

These people know who the centers of influence are in your niche market and can introduce you to them. In addition, some of them will be centers of influence in their own right. Call and give them feedback from your research. Let these key people know you have decided to specialize and work with the people their niche market organization supports. This feedback effort may well inspire them to help you further. Tell them you wanted them to be among the first to know because they were willing to share information with you when you were beginning your market research. Ask them out to lunch or breakfast again to "get to know them better" and discuss more ways to get involved. This will help you firm up the relationship. When you meet with them again, ask them to introduce you to other centers of influence in the organization, association, or club.

TACTIC 159   Position your contact with all centers of influence in a positive, win–win way.

When contacting influential people, whether you've met them before or not, make it clear that they are perceived by their peers as being people with valuable insights. Tell them you would like their advice on how best to proceed and become better known to more of their colleagues in a positive way. Emphasize the benefits you can offer to the people they know, rather than just what you can gain.

TACTIC 160   Use the marketing breakfast or lunch.

One of the best ways to meet with a busy influential person is to invite them to breakfast or lunch. Dinner would be a larger commitment than they would be willing to make initially, because it tends to take on a social air. Use a breakfast or lunch to introduce yourself, become known to the person, and begin to build a rapport that will let them become comfortable and confident about you.

TACTIC 161   Be prepared when you meet with centers of influence.

When meeting with centers of influence, it's helpful to have a few questions prepared in advance to help kick off the conversation. Good questions will help you build rapport and will allow the centers of influence to talk more about themselves.

The following are some questions to consider asking them.

- Start always with those that build rapport. What do you do for recreation? How did you start your business? How large is your family? The goal is to find a common ground or area of interest between you.
- Then move forward in a friendly way. How do you pass information along to other people in your group or association?
- What can I do to become more involved in the industry, club, organization, and so on? Centers of influence will often volunteer an idea or two because you have asked. They will frequently get you introduced to the right person, situation, and opportunity to get you involved, thus expanding your reach.
- Be sure to ask who are the individuals they consider influential in their niche market.

It is vitally important that you do not turn this discussion into a sales presentation. Relax and use this opportunity to build rapport and confidence. These people probably do have a need for what you sell. If they express interest, schedule a time to meet again to discuss their need for your products and services.

TACTIC 162 Demonstrate a positive, caring attitude to centers of influence.

The attitude that influential people perceive you to have will be communicated to many other individuals. This is true whether you are enthusiastic and open or negative and presumptuous. Your objective is to establish a mutual relationship with them that clearly demonstrates your positive, caring attitude and trustworthiness. Be positive so the center of influence you cultivate is clearly enthusiastic about your efforts in the marketplace. Remember: Positive, productive people place a priority on producing pleasant perceptions.

TACTIC 163 Be sensitive to time and get invited back.

Roper research has found that time is an influential person's most precious commodity. Be specific about the length of time you will need to meet with them. Be a few minutes early because it shows a level of respect that's important. Don't overstay your welcome, either. Stay within the time frame that you originally set, unless they ask you to stay.

Your goal should be to get invited back for a second meeting, so don't feel compelled to cover every subject your first time out. If you need more time, look for the opportunity to schedule a second meeting, for breakfast or another time, to continue building the relationship.

TACTIC 164   Avoid judging a person's influence.

In today's complex markets, many people are influential. They may be administrative assistants or members of a team recommending the right product to buy. It is unwise to judge someone's influential ability by title or appearance. Orison Swett Marden said, "The influential man is the successful man, whether he is rich or poor." Thomas Edison said, "Opportunity is missed by most people because it's dressed in overalls and looks like work." Avoid judging how much influence a person has in delivering you into your niche market or moving other people to see you. If you've marked them as influential, work to build a rapport with them.

TACTIC 165   Be willing to ask for their help.

There is a wonderful proverb that says, "Before honor comes humility." To capture the interest and support of influential people in your targeted niche, you must get out of your ego and into theirs. State your interest in reaching and selling more people in the market in a positive, confident manner, and then ask for their assistance. Ask how they could help you meet more individuals in the marketplace and build a quality relationship with them. Asking for their assistance is much like asking for the order. If you don't ask for their help, they will probably not offer it. You will be surprised how many influential people respond favorably simply because they are asked in a warm and friendly way.

TACTIC 166   Be certain you stay in touch with a center of influence after the initial contact.

If you become a "hit and run" specialist, you will leave the wrong impression. Develop an ongoing relationship based on mutual respect with centers of influence by staying in contact with them on a regular basis. Make sure they know you're there for the long run. They can help you in many ways if they believe in you and your sense of purpose.

In summary, your goal is to identify centers of influence and build positive, caring, trustworthy relationships with them that will be profitable for you and the individuals in your niche market. Word of mouth about you from these centers of influence will help you become influential yourself.

Chapter Twelve

Strategy: Make It Easy to Acquire Referrals and Testimonials

Objective: To create an endless stream of prospects from your niche markets.

To receive useful word-of-mouth promotion, you must make it easy for your niche market customers, centers of influence, and prospects to give you the referrals and testimonials you need. In addition, you must make it easy for you to ask for them.

As an example, direct sales companies have always focused on making referrals and testimonials easy to acquire, particularly those that use the hostess plan as a way to market their products. The hostess plan centers on satisfied customers who host parties or sales activities of some type, usually in their homes. This could be a dinner party where a cookware sales professional cooks a meal to demonstrate the cookware, much like I used to do. Others may host a cosmetics makeover party or an apparel party where there are six or eight prospects assembled to view and purchase the products. They keep the numbers small deliberately so they can give personalized service. The hostess or host invites friends from work, the neighborhood, church, and so on. Direct sales professionals who are very focused suggest the specific types of people that should attend to ensure that they are qualified and in their niche. At the end of the party or function, the sales professional simply asks two or three people who have just purchased some of the products to host a similar function in each of their homes. This makes asking for referrals easy for the sales professional because it is part of the sales process.

It is also easy for customers to respond because the environment is right. They see the desire to reach and help other people like themselves.

You should follow a similar philosophy of making it easy for referrals and testimonials to be acquired. We know that most people have a sphere of influence. Bob Burn, from Jupiter, Florida, who wrote the book *Endless Referrals, Network Your Everyday Contacts into Sales Success*, suggests that the average individual knows 250 people. Take that a step further and consider that every time you meet someone new in your niche market, that person knows about 250 people.

Of course, not all of them are in your niche. To be effective, you should target your referral requests so that you get referred deeper into your niche markets. If you're selling life insurance to pediatricians, ask for the names of other pediatricians. If you're working with plumbers, then ask for the names of other plumbers in the same union. If you're selling roadside signs to commercial real estate companies, you should ask for names of other individuals in the commercial real estate business with whom you could do business.

This will help you maintain your focus and make it much easier for your prospects and customers to help you. Targeting your referrals will also allow you to develop your own lists of targeted prospects. Tom Stanley, author of *Marketing to the Affluent*, suggests that the best sales professionals develop their own proprietary list of individual prospects. Lists of niche market individuals you develop, through referral gathering and other activities within your various market segments, will give you an added strategic and tactical advantage.

The following tactics will help you to get more of what you deserve—quality referrals and testimonials.

TACTIC 167   Recognize that everyone benefits from referrals.

When customers, centers of influence, and prospects give you referrals, everyone benefits. People often give referrals because it is a way for them to help their friends, colleagues, and others to acquire the quality goods and services that you offer. As an example, there's a young man who has built a successful residential lawn care business in Atlanta. He also services one country club. Asking him how he built this business, he said, "Through word of mouth. I have pride in my work, so people stop and ask my customers who does their lawn. My customers then refer them to me." When I asked him why, he said, "They like to help each other out so they have more time to play golf together."

The same holds true whether you're selling copiers, real estate, ball bearings, roofing, computers, or exercise classes. Referrals and testimonials strengthen relationships between individuals.

TACTIC 168   Let people know why you need referrals.

It's very important for your customers, centers of influence, and prospects to realize that your goal is to reach and work with more people like them. It makes it easier for them to refer you to people they know. Tell them that you want to continue to specialize, that you enjoy working with them, and that their personal referrals will give you an opportunity to serve other people in their industry, social group, occupation, interest group, and so on. This lets them know that your motives are to serve and sell other individuals in your niche in the same professional way that you've serviced and sold them. It will also make it easier for you to ask because you are focused more on them and less on yourself.

TACTIC 169   Avoid asking just for people who are ready to buy.

Your goal should be to use the referral-gathering process to reach all the prospects in your niche market—not just those who are qualified or ready to buy now. Further, by only focusing on those who are in the market for a copier, house, or investment now, you reduce the number of referrals you receive. The average customer, center of influence, or prospect has no idea whether someone is ready or qualified to buy from you right now. Asking them to qualify the people is an extra burden they don't need. To make gathering referrals easy and effective, simply ask for the names of other people in their business, club, or interest group. Then ask if any of them have expressed an interest in your product, service, and so on. Note that information to prioritize contacts. Ultimately, the responsibility to determine whether they are qualified is yours and yours alone.

TACTIC 170   Create a referral talk.

You should have a well-honed referral-gathering presentation for use with every customer, center of influence, and prospect. This will increase your comfort, confidence, and competence. It also makes it easy for your customer, center of influence, or prospect to understand what your needs and motives are. Practice your referral talk with your family, friends, and colleagues. Sharpen your talk so that it sounds natural and comes forth easily.

TACTIC 171   Make referrals part of your compensation in your referral talk.

If you, as sales professionals and business owners, can and want to make referrals part of your compensation, you may wish to follow the advice of William V. Harris, author of *The Encyclopedia of Annuity Selling*. He suggests that you tell prospects and customers in your referral talk that referrals are part of your compensation. In fact, at the beginning of an interview, he suggests that you use this type of phraseology to set up a referral: "Mr. Hones, I receive two types of compensation. First I get paid by the companies that I agree to represent. They pay me a fee for processing their applications, describing how their product works, and for my willingness to be there whenever clients need me. A second form of compensation comes from you. If you feel that I've been helpful and professional, I would like you to tell people that you are my client. This will allow me to help those people just as I helped you."

Of course, you may be uncomfortable or unable to use this compensation approach. If that's the case, certainly the second half of that script works in any referral talk. "If you feel that I've been helpful and professional, I would like you to tell people that you are my client. This will allow me to help those people just as I helped you."

TACTIC 172   Make it easy for referrals to be delivered.

As I've discussed, making it easy is a philosophy you should adopt. At the same time, easy should not be construed as loose. Avoid asking customers, centers of influence, or prospects to jot down the names of individuals on a slip of scrap paper. That may work on the golf course or tennis court under informal conditions. However, I've learned over the years that it's better to have a professional look to the way you gather referrals, as this makes it easy on all parties to process referrals. In addition, it heightens the sense of importance. Here are three proven ideas you can use:

1. Use a referral-gathering form. By giving your customer, center of influence, or prospect a referral form, such as the one in Figure 12–1, and handing it to them at the time that you ask for referrals, you make it easier for them to list the names.

   This could be printed on one side of an 8 1/2 × 11-inch sheet of paper. It could also be printed on a large index card, with spaces for three or four names on one side. What is most important is to use a form or a format that your customer or prospect will find easy to complete.

2. Use a membership list or directory of the people in your targeted niche market. It's not always easy for someone to think up some names of people in your niche without help.

   I found that it's much easier to prompt and stimulate the individual to give you referrals by giving them the names of 10 or 15 people in the market that you are going to be calling on. The way to use this list is simply to show them the list and say, "These are individuals in the industry that I will be calling on. Which ones know you on a first-name basis?" Usually, they will select several names from the list. Then ask, "Who have I left off this list?" This way you will acquire the names of several more people right in your niche.

   By using membership lists from your niche market clubs, associations, special interest groups, and other targeted networks, you are sure to work deeper into your market. If a membership list is not available, you could use prospect lists you compiled from your market research.

FIGURE 12–1
Referral Form

Dear [CLIENT NAME]:

I want to continue to help people like you and companies like yours increase their relationship marketing and prospecting skills. To accomplish this, I would appreciate your referring me to several of your associates in the business you're in. To make this easy for you and to save you time, please simply list the names and telephone numbers below. I will call for their addresses. Thank you for your business, thoughtfulness, and confidence.

Very sincerely yours,

[YOUR NAME]

1. Name _____

   Best telephone number (   ) _____

2. Name _____

   Best telephone number (   ) _____

3. Name _____

   Best telephone number (   ) _____

4. Name _____

   Best telephone number (   ) _____

3. Use postcards to combine referrals and testimonials. Have a brief, benefit-oriented introduction of yourself printed on a prestamped postcard. On the opposite side, leave a place for people to simply write out their comments about you, your product, or your service. Ask your customer, center of influence, or prospect to mail these postcards to five or six people in your niche that they know as a way of introduction to them. Figure 12–2 is an example of such a postcard.

TACTIC 173   When you ask for a referral, also request some personal information about the person being referred.

Any personal information you get will help you begin to position yourself with those people. You'll have a sense of who they are, what they're about, and how they're connected to the person giving you the referral. This will help you know how to approach them and build rapport.

TACTIC 174   Ask for referrals and testimonials consistently and constantly.

There is much confusion on behalf of sales professionals and business owners as to when and how often they should ask for a referral and testimonial. Some presume that you ask once at the beginning of the sale, or perhaps you ask only at the time of delivery. You should ask for referrals and testimonials several times. By asking more than once, you create a cumulative effect and greater results.

Here are several places to ask for referrals and testimonials:

- Ask at the very first appointment, whether it's with a prospect, a previous customer, or a center of influence. People do not have to buy something to refer you or pass on positive word of mouth. They simply need to feel confident about you and your product or service. Ask early and set the stage.
- At the time of the sale. Ask for referrals and a testimonial before you get all the paperwork completed. Otherwise, people are rushed, wanting to move on to the next issue in their lives.

FIGURE 12–2
Referral Postcard

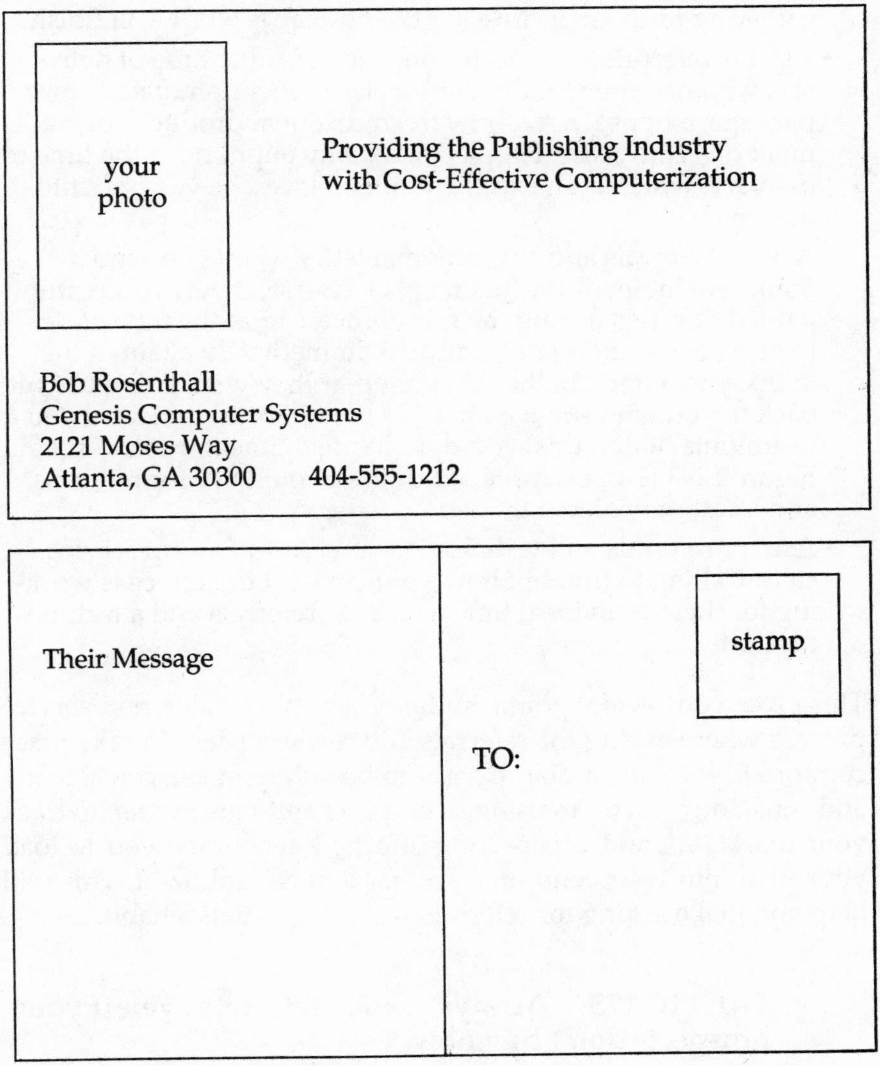

---

your
photo

Providing the Publishing Industry
with Cost-Effective Computerization

Bob Rosenthall
Genesis Computer Systems
2121 Moses Way
Atlanta, GA 30300   404-555-1212

Their Message

stamp

TO:

So, bring forth your referral talk again while you're completing the paperwork. Then the customer can begin selecting from the list of prospects you produce, filling out the referral-gathering form, or addressing the postcards while you finish.

- Ask for referrals and a testimonial letter at the time of delivery, whether your product or service is an automobile, a tour package, a house, new software, nutritional products, or settlement of a court case. People are usually euphoric at the time of delivery, which is an excellent time to leverage yourself into your niche.

- Ask for referrals and a testimonial letter when you send a thank-you note for the business. Of course, if you've already gained referrals during the sales process or at the time of delivery, you wouldn't normally ask immediately again in the thank-you letter. On the other hand, if they were going to "get back to you with some names" or they promised to send you a testimonial letter, this would be an ideal time to remind them. Figure 12–3 is an example of how you could ask for referrals and a testimonial in a thank-you letter.

- Ask for referrals and testimonials in your follow-up service calls. Calling to find out how your product or service is working for them is an ideal time to ask for referrals and a testimonial letter.

This gives you several points in the prospecting, sales, and service process where asking for referrals and testimonials can take place comfortably. Create a plan from it to be sure you ask consistently and constantly. If you're using a computer software system to track your marketing and prospecting efforts, I encourage you to load your plan into your computer, so that you can follow it. This will help you make asking for referrals and testimonials a habit.

TACTIC 175   Always ask for referrals even if your prospects don't buy now.

Sometimes prospects will say, "No, I'm not ready to buy now" but they will be ready to buy later. That being the case, ask for referrals from them even though they haven't bought yet. Let them know that the reason you're asking is to be able to build a quality relationship with more people like them. Use the same tools and tactics

FIGURE 12–3
Thank-You Letter with Referral Request

Dear Sarah,

It was a delight to help you meet your EPA objectives for the new phosphate plant. Thanks for the confidence you placed in me.

You did a great job verbalizing your concerns and needs. Your input was very helpful in helping me formulate my equipment recommendations.

As I mentioned earlier, I would like to meet some of your colleagues in the phosphate industry so that I may offer my services to them. To help me serve them, please list four or five of your friends and business colleagues in the industry on the form I have enclosed.

To make sure they know I can relate to them, please include a short personal letter to me stating how you think my services have been of benefit to you. I may use this to help them feel comfortable meeting with me.

Sarah, it has been a pleasure serving you, and I look forward to the years ahead working with you and North Central American Fertilizers.

Very sincerely yours,

Sam Samuels

P.S. Send your list of industry friends together with your letter in the postage paid envelope I have provided. Thanks.

you would use if they purchased. Usually the only thing that prevents them from giving you a referral even if they didn't buy is the fact that you didn't ask.

TACTIC 176   Ask for testimonial letters when you ask for referrals.

When you ask for the referrals, be sure you ask for a testimonial at the same time. For example, "Would you please write a short letter that expresses your satisfaction in working with me? I am often called on for these letters to help some of your friends and colleagues feel more comfortable in their decisions."

TACTIC 177   To get powerful testimonials, ask clients to verbalize how they feel you helped them.

It's occasionally difficult for customers to put together a testimonial letter because they've never really thought out loud about how you've helped them. An effective way to solve that problem is to ask questions such as:

- How do you feel my services have helped you?
- What impact do you think my products have made on your profitability?
- How do you feel that my products have enhanced the work environment?

Ask open-ended questions germane to your products and services. Be sure to ask in a way that stimulates your customers to think about your value to them. Capture their thoughts on paper as they begin to answer, then simply give them your notes of their comments and ask them to include them in a letter to you.

TACTIC 178   Avoid writing your own testimonial letters.

Some of your customers may simply lack the writing skills or time to put together a letter. They will tell you, "I don't have time to write a testimonial" or "I really wouldn't know what to say." Even though you may have stimulated them to verbalize how they feel you've helped them, some still will ask you to write the testimonial letter yourself. This is the worst thing you could do, because you will say things in your language that do not sound plausible and that could easily be spotted by another prospect. When others decide the letter is not genuine, their trust in you is gone.

TACTIC 179   Provide your customers with guidelines and samples to write a testimonial letter easily.

This makes testimonial writing nearly as easy as filling in the blanks. It gives your customers a path to follow. To begin, give them guidelines like these:

1. Please put the letter on your letterhead so there's an immediate sense of affinity, recognition, and link by others to you.
2. Please address the letter to me. This heightens the credibility of the letter and its worth to those who read it.
3. Use your own words when you describe what I or my product did for you, your profits, and so on.
4. Please reiterate the benefits that you received from my products or services.

Further, give them a sample of three or four letters that you've already received. This will increase their confidence and, most importantly, begin to shape the letter that they're going to write for you. Even if they pick and choose phrases from other letters, they will add their own sense of personality as they frame their letter. You can coach them further by highlighting points from their verbal session with you. This also reassures them that if others have written you a letter, it is okay for them to do it as well.

TACTIC 180   Be sure to get permission to use the letter and their name in your promotions.

You will want to be able to use the testimonial letter in a variety of ways (the subject of our next chapter). Ask their permission to use it to help others feels less skeptical about meeting with you. Also, by letting the customer know that you will want to show it to others, you will often get a letter that is written in a more conversational style. In addition, be sure to ask your customers, centers of influence, and even prospects if you can use their name in promotional efforts.

TACTIC 181   In all cases of referrals and testimonials, you should send a personal thank-you note.

A referral and testimonial is a powerful vote of confidence. It means your relationship is well established with that person. Strengthen it further by sending a personal note of thanks. When you send the thank-you note, a handwritten version is fine. It doesn't have to be typed—unless, of course, your handwriting is less than legible. It could be written on a formal referral card or it could be simply an appropriate note, written on a personal note card. Just be sure that you send one each time you receive referrals. This is far more powerful than a thank-you telephone call or handshake.

TACTIC 182   Give referrals and testimonials to people with whom you already do business.

Make a conscious effort to keep the names of people who have provided you with the right products or services to solve a problem or fill a need you had. Pass along these names to others when they have similar needs. You may also become aware of a prospect for the people in your niche markets. Keep that person's name and pass it on as well.

By giving referrals and testimonials to your friends, customers, centers of influence, and prospects, you gain several benefits. First, you help remove any anxiety that you think others have about giving referrals. You will become more comfortable with the whole referral and testimonial process. Second, you also become energized and more enthusiastic about referrals and testimonials because you see how the process works. You will enjoy the positive feedback from others because of your efforts on their behalf. Third, if you refer a quality prospect to a customer, center of influence, or prospect of yours, they will be even more inclined to provide you with referrals and testimonials to people they know in your niche.

Chapter Thirteen

Strategy: Use Referrals and Testimonials to Differentiate Yourself

Objective: To reach the hard to reach by leveraging the satisfied.

R eferrals and testimonials, when used to leverage your position in the market, can truly differentiate you from the competition. They open the prospect's mind to the idea that you just might have the product or service and commitment to them that they've been seeking. This positive word of mouth, then, creates a unique opportunity for you to begin to build a quality marketing and prospecting relationship with them.

Unfortunately, referrals and testimonials are not used as effectively as they could be by many sales professionals and business owners. Prospects they are referred to never get called. Or, if they're called, they're called so long after the referral was received that the referral loses its effectiveness. That means they miss the momentum that comes from timely follow-up. Further, the tendency after the initial excitement of receiving a testimonial letter is to put it in a drawer without using it. These sales professionals or business owners either don't see the value of using the testimonials for promotion, or the testimonials seem too self-congratulatory for comfort.

To prevent this from occurring in your business or career, think about and answer this question: What can you do to use referrals and testimonials as timely promotional tools to open more closed doors? The following tactics will help you create an answer that will leverage your referrals and testimonials to reach the hard to reach.

TACTIC 183   Ask customers to call the people to whom they referred you.

One of the most powerful things that can happen is for a customer to call a prospect. Once a customer lists the people that he or she knows in your niche market, then ask the next question: "Would you please call these people and introduce me?" Most people will agree to do that. They can then speak one-on-one on your behalf to the individual prospect and answer any questions he or she might have. This works mightily to overcome prospect reluctance and to create a sense of willingness to see you.

Here is an example of the power of such a telephone call. I was attempting to contact several executives at the home office of an insurance company about one of my video learning systems. I was having some difficulty getting their ear. Then I asked the manager of one of their field agencies if he could help me contact them. He said, "I'll do better than that. Let me be sure you have the names of the right individuals and then I'll call them on your behalf."

He then telephoned them to encourage them to take my call, because he felt I had some ideas that they could use. As a result, I not only got favorable access, but some of the executives called me even before I could call all of them. They recognized that my referral to them by someone in their network was certainly a clear sign that my information was something they should review and consider.

TACTIC 184   Call within five working days of receiving the referral.

When you call and contact within five working days, the referral is fresh and the relationship with the person who gave you the referral is still clear in your mind. As a result, quick timing helps you to be more effective. If you let the referrals grow stale, you often lose momentum on the particular account. The sense of linkage becomes fuzzier, and it's more difficult for you to call the referral with a sense of confidence, acceptance, and direction. In addition, it's embarrassing when a prospect asks, "How long ago did you do business with Sally?" and you have to reply, "It's been quite a while."

TACTIC 185   Devise a system to track contact and results.

With technology, it is easy to schedule contact and results. I suggest you create a systematic approach to referrals. By entering them into a calendar system the day you receive them, you avoid losing track of them. By flagging them for contact within five days, you ensure timely follow-through. Keeping track of results enhances your desire to get more referrals and work your market deep. Remember, winners keep and know the score.

TACTIC 186   Call all referrals using a positive telephone presentation.

When you're contacting a referral, be sure you recognize that it is truly a different telephone conversation than a cold call. You are coming from a position of much greater credibility. As a result, you have every reason to be positive, not tentative. Here is a sample telephone script that uses the referral process to its best advantage:

> Hi, is this [*the referral's first and last name*]? My name is [*your first and last name*] and I am with [*your full company name*]. [*Customer's first and last name*] and I spent some time together recently and he [or she] mentioned your name prominently to me and had several nice things to say about you. He [or she] is a customer of mine and told me to call you because he [or she] thought we should meet. He [or she] also said that you [*insert a personal touch—for example, play . . . , belong to . . . , are married to . . . , went to school with . . .*]. How long have you [*played, belonged to, been married to, been out of school*]?

Then develop some rapport by asking more questions and listening more than talking.

> As I said, [*first name of customer*] is a customer of mine and thought we should meet. I would like to hear more about your business [*situation*]. Plus, I could brief you on some of the products and services we offer to people like yourself. It would also give us an opportunity to get to know one another better. I'll be in your area on [*day of week*]. Would morning or afternoon be best for you?"

TACTIC 187   Let your referrers know how things are going.

Update the customer, center of influence, or prospect who referred you. Let them know whether or not you have spoken to the person they referred you to and how the whole relational process is proceeding. Let them know within two weeks of the referral whether you have spoken to their colleague and have a meeting scheduled. Often, they will see this individual again in the near future and will offer to intercede on your behalf. Remember, one of the key reasons people give referrals is so that they can enhance their relationships with the individuals to whom they are referring you. It's to your advantage to keep your sources updated on your progress and to ask them to encourage their colleagues.

TACTIC 188   Send another thank-you note to the referrer after the referral becomes a customer.

This not only helps you continue to work the market deep, it encourages more word-of-mouth promotion by your customers. They'll be encouraged that you're helping people like them and that you are appreciative as well. When they receive this second thank-you note, they will tell others that you are thoughtful. This makes doors fly open. It is also an excellent time to ask them for more referrals.

TACTIC 189   Reproduce testimonial letters in color.

With a little planning, you can add the impact of color to the letterhead of all your copies at no extra printing cost. Many printers offer a free second color on various days of the week. At some printers on Monday red is free, on Tuesday blue is free, on Wednesday green is free, and so on. Use the color that most closely matches the color of the logo used on the original testimonial letter. Using the color nearest the original brings an increased sense of value to the letter.

When these color copies are then sent out to prospects, inserted in sales presentations or used in any other marketing effort, they get much more attention.

TACTIC 190   Omit the dates when reproducing testimonials.

Omitting the dates on a letter focuses the recipient's attention on the message, not the date of the message. A letter that is six months old is still a valid message, providing you're still delivering that level of service. White out the dates on your originals when you file them. You should, however, continually strive for better letters through delivering better sales, service, and results.

TACTIC 191   Stamp "Another Satisfied Client" on the testimonial letters that you're using.

Have a stamp made so you can display these words on the face of the letter. It immediately identifies what the key message is. Here is someone talking about what you have done for them. This helps the reader think, "What can you do for me?"

TACTIC 192   Make it easy for the reader to get to the point of the testimonial.

When using testimonials, whether they are in a letter format or quoted in part, make it simple for the reader to spot the message. If you're sending a letter, highlight the key phrases. People do not want to read the entire letter. They will simply want to look at the key phrases that will reassure them.

If you are quoting a portion of a letter, you can disconnect words and bring them together in a sentence, providing you do not change the message or context. If you are connecting two or three phrases, then certainly let the reader understand by giving them transition punctuation. As an example:

... you have always been responsive to our immediate needs ... In addition, you regularly keep us up-to-date on new product developments that could save us money ... Thank you for making our job easier.

Make sure you don't emphasize how great you are; instead, include and point out what you've done for the client. People want to know, "What's in it for me?"

TACTIC 193   Whenever you use a testimonial, put the person's full name and title with their statement.

Probably nothing looks less credible than a phrase or two that speaks about what you've done for someone but only gives the initials of the individual who said it. No one really knows if that person exists or not. Use full names and titles. You may also want to add the telephone number of the individual with the testimonial. For example: Linda Smith, Vice President of Sales, (703) 555-5555. Be sure you get permission from your customer first when using names and numbers. By inviting people to call, you add credibility to the statement, even if the vast majority of people never call.

TACTIC 194   File your testimonials by market, situation, and industry.

Collect and Store your testimonials by niche market. However you've segmented your market, whether by type of business, recreation, or special interests, organize your testimonials the same way. This system will allow you to locate and deliver those testimonials that match the people you're targeting.

TACTIC 195   Use your testimonials in trade and organizational show booths.

When you're exhibiting at a show, include in your presentation material photographs of five or six individuals who are leaders in the industry. Include a phrase from them testifying about what you have done for them, instead of how great you are. This leverages their credibility in the marketplace on your behalf.

TACTIC 196   Include targeted testimonial letters in all your literature mailings.

When you're sending product, service, or other information to prospects, you should include testimonial letters that are germane to the particular market segment they are in. This brings added credibility to the sales material that you're sending because people in the same market segment or niche are testifying about what the product or service you're offering has done for them.

TACTIC 197   Include testimonials and letters in your sales and marketing presentations.

Be creative with your use of testimonials. Put them on audiotape, on videotape, even in your computer illustrations. There's no reason you couldn't display a testimonial or quotes from testimonial letters on the bottom of a presentation screen. If you're working with a manual system, such as a presentation book or poster, include various testimonials there.

TACTIC 198   Use the testimonial letter as a cultivation piece.

As you receive testimonial letters, include them in mailings sent out to the entire list of prospects in your targeted niche market. Send them a highlighted letter using the same "Another Satisfied Client" stamp discussed earlier. Attach a note or have these words printed at the bottom of the letter: "Dear Colleague, I would certainly enjoy the opportunity of working with you." Send it out as a simple yet powerful way to keep in contact and cultivate an ongoing relationship with your prospects.

TACTIC 199   Use testimonials in your advertisements.

Many companies, including MCI, AT&T, General Motors, Acura, and Lexus, use testimonials in their advertisements. This is a very effective way to communicate a sense of relationship and competitive differential to your niche market prospects. There is nothing more powerful than someone else talking about you. You could publish an ad that simply says, "Do you hear what we hear?" and then list several testimonials. Perhaps your headline could be, "Call today so you can feel this way tomorrow"; then list the testimonials below it. This can be very powerful, particularly in your niche market organization's newsletter, trade, or professional magazine.

You could also run an advertisement that welcomes a particular new customer and then include that customer's testimonial describing what you did for them. Such an ad lets your whole niche know that this person or organization had become a customer. Second, new customers also become centers of influence for you. There are people in your niche who will give you access because the person or company in the ad did.

TACTIC 200   Develop a referral mailer to highlight your testimonials.

Your mailer could be something as simple as a flyer, such as the one in Figure 13–1. This particular flyer clearly states that these individuals are customers of yours.

This approach works best if these individuals are somewhat high-profile people within your targeted niche market. It tells the people who were referred to you that these people are doing business with you, and most importantly, assures your audience that they can feel confident in establishing a relationship with you as well.

TACTIC 201   Be creative with your testimonial use.

There are a variety of other ways that you could highlight your testimonials. You could use testimonial quotes in a preapproach letter

FIGURE 13–1
Referral Flyer

WHAT DO THESE PRINTERS . . .

TONY VALENTI
BILL WILLIAMS
JOHN KEACH
JIM WALKER
ROY LINSTROM
JACKIE McKENNA

. . . HAVE IN COMMON?

They all are saving money and getting same-day service from

JEFF HAYNIE
AM PRINTER SUPPLY
126 Wilson Drive
Carbondale, IL 62901
404–555–1212

Serving Members of the Southern Illinois Print Association

or on a postcard. You could create a pocket-sized brochure that includes testimonials. You could send it to referrals and other prospects prior to your call. Remembering King Solomon's instruction that "a good name is better than riches," use the testimonials at the very beginning of the letter, brochure, or postcard you create. They will capture attention and give you nearly instant credibility. Prospects recognize the testimonials as comments from people they know or have heard about in their industry, professional, interest, or recreational group.

To add the impact of a visual presence, you could also use photographs of the people who gave you the testimonials. Be sure to ask them for permission to use. Let your imagination work for you. Think about ways you can creatively communicate to the prospects in your market that other people believe in you and what you have done for them.

TACTIC 202   Use multiple testimonials.

Testimonials build credibility and confidence. People who receive one testimonial from you think that you're probably pretty good at what you do and that the product you have is pretty good. If they have two testimonials that parallel one another, then you probably have a product that's better than most. Three referrals give them such an extremely high sense of confidence that you can essentially concentrate on developing and enhancing your relationship with this new prospect.

TACTIC 203   Put together a master reference list using the names of key people in your niche.

Be prepared. When somebody says to you, "Do you have any references?" you should immediately produce a strong list of individuals who have given you referrals and testimonials. These people are very pleased with you and your products or services. Whether you keep the list in your desk, your computer, your briefcase, or under the counter, be ready to support yourself. Encourage the prospect to call the people on your list.

The people in my office do that to help reluctant prospects move forward. People will call regarding having me speak at their meeting or to inquire about one of my relationship marketing and prospecting education products. If there's any reluctance at all, they offer to fax a list of satisfied customers right away.

This allows prospects to get on the telephone and call individuals just like themselves. They can get a good third-party perspective about your products and services this way. It's amazing how many skeptics quickly turn into believers when you're so open that you're willing to offer a list of references and telephone numbers. When you encourage them to call these people, you're on the road to building quality relationships founded on trust and confidence. Be sure you create a separate list for each niche market or segment in which you are working.

V

CAPTURING ATTENTION IN THE MAILBOX

"Appreciative words are the most powerful force for good on earth."

George W. Crane

M y wife recently received a letter in the mail that was designed to set the stage for a follow-up telephone call. The envelope was addressed to Mrs. Weylman/or Current Occupant. As if that wasn't bad enough, the letter was addressed to Dear Homeowner. Even worse, it was focused so much on the company that it never did focus on the advantages and benefits she would receive.

The ultimate slap, however, was the phrase, "I will call you shortly to arrange a time that fits our schedule." They never did call. That was a shame, since my wife wanted to ask them why *her* schedule didn't seem to matter. Maybe it's because she is just an occupant.

My wife is not alone in her frustration with what's in the mailbox. The average prospect receives 1,700 pieces of promotional mail each year. It's no wonder, based on this volume, that people are inclined to toss out most promotional mail even before opening it. There is so much received that it has lost its value and, thus, is commonly referred to as junk mail.

Creative approaches are needed, then, to give your promotional mail enough impact so that it gets more than a quick glance—that it actually gets opened and acted on. The primary objective of all your promotional mail should be to strongly convey a sense of link and affinity between you and your targeted niche prospects. By doing so, your prospects will be more receptive. To accomplish this, think of your targeted promotional mailings, whether they are preapproach letters, flyers, offers, or self-mailers, as *niche mail*.

To be sure that the promotional niche mail you send is received, opened, and acted on, several strategies must be employed. The first is to time your mail for maximum impact. *When* you do your promotional niche mail is just as important as *what* you mail. Timing is critical.

Second, design your promotional letters and mailers so that they relate to prospects in your niche market. Clearly indicate that you know and understand them. This relational approach heightens their perception of value. It will certainly increase their response and receptiveness.

Third, because many of your promotional letters and mailers will probably require you to follow up by telephone, you must follow up in such a way as to be complimentary to your niche mail efforts and other relationship-building activities. This calls for an image of professionalism and preparation.

Finally, many sales professionals and business owners alike overpromise in their promotional material and then underdeliver. It is vital to recognize that whether you are promoting yourself or a concept, idea, product, or service, you should focus on the reality of your deliverability. Then strive to overdeliver. Otherwise, you run the risk of destroying the trust and quality relationships you've worked so hard to build.

As you begin to think about your promotional letters and mailing possibilities, recognize that personalized niche mail is simply one strategy to help open closed doors. Promotional niche mail cannot be a substitute for face-to-face contact. It can, however, create additional awareness, increase the desire for your products and services, and position you for further follow-up one-on-one.

Chapter Fourteen

Strategy: Plan Your Promotional Niche Mail to Hit Right on the Money

Objective: To organize and time promotional niche mailings so they can help you open closed doors.

B y now, you're initiating many activities to reach hard-to-reach people on a favorable basis. From time to time you will want to send promotional letters and mailers so that they enhance your one-on-one efforts. Be sure you plan and time your niche mail so that you encompass the following principles.

Principle 1. Promote when you're busy. When you're busy, you have the resources and the right frame of mind to promote more effectively than when you have idle time. By sending promotional niche mail when you're busy, you avoid upcoming low spots and push yourself into a continual growth mode.

As a case in point, I was speaking in Lake Louise, Canada, and a young man approached me prior to my presentation. It was in the spring of the year, and I said, "Are you looking forward to a big summer?" He said, "No, its going to be slow this summer." I said, "Oh, really, why do you say that?" He said, "It's slow every summer." I said, "You could counteract that by promoting now." He said, "Why bother? It's always slow in the summer."

It's slow in the summer because he's doing very little promotion and prospecting in March, April, and May. He's planting no seed. If you sow sparingly, so will you reap sparingly.

There's an old adage that tells us that when you're busy, take on twice as much. You will be surprised at what you can do.

Principle 2. Promote when the people in your market are receptive. Are businesses interested in purchasing certain types of office supplies based on predictable business cycles? If so, promote the right products during those cycles. If you're a CPA, your prospects are probably not interested in getting their tax return taken care of in the middle of the year, but they may be interested in some bookkeeping services that you offer. They might also want your help in applying some strategic principles to plan for the future. Promote these services during the busy tax season. No matter what you sell or in what market, it's important to continually associate and communicate with your prospects and your customers. By doing so, you know when they are receptive and when they have a particular need. You can then plan a promotional preapproach letter or response mailer to match those times and needs.

Principle 3. Consider cumulative effect. One of anything has very little lasting impact on people. Just as attending only one networking meeting or running one ad, one piece of promotional mail has a limited long-term effect. It can take several messages over the course of the year to communicate the opportunities you offer.

Principle 4. Mix your efforts and your offers. Different things motivate different people. Plan to use a variety of ideas and mix your deliverables. This way, you can address the various desires and needs of the individuals in the marketplace. This prevents all your efforts and solutions from looking the same.

These principles are critical to consider as you plan your promotional niche mail efforts. To help you to plan and time your promotional letters and mailers more effectively, here are many different tactics that you can apply.

TACTIC 204   Use promotional letters and mailers after you have visibility in the marketplace.

Plan your mail as an adjunct to personal contact and a way to increase prospecting activity during various and appropriate times. Nothing can take the place of one-on-one contact. Be keenly aware that any promotional campaign should be accompanied by personal visibility in your niche market networks. Be sure you have joined the industry organization, the social club, the cultural group, and any other network of your prospects that exists. Using mail as a substitute for personal contact relegates you back to the Stone Age in prospecting and marketing.

TACTIC 205   Plan your promotional mailings in advance.

The key to planning properly is to remember that the primary reasons for promotional mail are either to elicit a response to a product or service offer or create an opportunity for personal follow-up. Plan with these reasons in mind. To determine when it is best to promote to your prospects and customers, base your decision on market intelligence, not just your own experience. Take the time to sit down and really analyze your targeted niche markets. Understand when your prospects and customers are most receptive and when you will gain the greatest return. Consider, for example:

- When are their trade, cultural, club, and recreational shows?
- When are normal vacation times for the majority of the people?
- What times of the month would be best for them to receive mailers?
- What products or services do you want to promote at various times during the year, based on your understanding of the need for them?
- What holidays do they celebrate?

For planning purposes, a mailer or letter can be sent the same month as an ad runs or that you exhibit in a trade show. Just because you attend monthly meetings does not mean you cannot promote by mail.

TACTIC 206   As you execute and plan, be sensitive to delivering a timely message.

It is vitally important that your promotional letters and mailers match the needs and the mood of your prospects and customers. Avoid developing your material so far in advance that your message is outdated. Your objective is to be so close to your prospects and customers that you can hear their hearts beat. The next chapter will give you tactics to help you keep track of your ideas as they occur so you can use them on a timely basis.

TACTIC 207   Create a calendar of deadlines for each promotional piece.

I suggest that you color-code a calendar in your office so that you can easily reference your niche mail schedule. Start with the days you want the niche mail to be received, then work your way back through the calendar. You should identify, at the very minimum (1) when the strategic concept will be finalized, (2) when the copy will be prepared, (3) when it will be proofed, (4) when it will be produced or printed, (5) when it will be mailed, and (6) most importantly, what day it will be received. Remember, the day you want it to be received determines all other schedules. Also, if you are going to test a piece, be sure you include that in your schedule.

TACTIC 208   Test your letters and mailers.

Sales professionals and business owners often rave about how well a promotional mailer or letter has done. Yet, the true effectiveness of an approach can best be measured by mailing two different versions to two small groups of prospects.

Even if you're mailing to a group as small as 50 people, test your pieces by dividing your niche market segment into two separate groups.

Testing allows you to find out what phrases, colors, and formats are working. A particular letter may work—but with a different phrase, it might produce a much better reception or response. Code your call list or your response cards with a color dot to help you track them. From the results, you can quickly determine which one is working better than the others.

This will help you plan and create more effective pieces for further mailings.

TACTIC 209   Decide how you're going to respond to calls in advance.

When you're sending out a promotional letter or mailer that calls for a response by the prospect in your targeted niche, you should determine in advance how you will track and service the inquiries. Be sure you know how those calls will be served. Your staff should know about all promotional efforts you make. Even if you only have a secretary or a receptionist, inform him or her about what has been sent out. This information helps them be more professional and sensitive to any incoming call, fax, or mail.

In our office, we have a bulletin board where we post all of the various promotional letters and mailers we have sent out. The bulletin board keeps the staff up-to-date on what's occurring and how to respond. You can also address these at staff meetings, as we do. This also allows for input from them and an opportunity for you to explain why you're doing what you're doing.

TACTIC 210   If you're going to use the telephone to follow up, your call volume should dictate your mail volume.

Perhaps one of the most frequent promotional errors made today is to send out promotional niche mail to a large number of prospects that indicates you'll be calling shortly. Not only is it very unlikely you will ever get to call all of them, even if you do, a long period of time will have elapsed. The people often have no idea of what you're talking about by the time you call, for too much time has gone by. This can create a negative impression.

Avoid this situation. If you are going to follow up your niche mail with a telephone call, decide how many people per week you are willing to call *before you send out the mailing.* Are you willing to call and talk to 5 new people a week, or perhaps only 3, or as many as

9, 10, or 20? Plan for and send out only that number of mailers. Let your call volume dictate mail volume, as opposed to the other way around. This will allow you to call these prospects and keep your word to them. Otherwise, by promising to call shortly and not doing so, you damage the trust and confidence you have already built through other relational activities.

TACTIC 211   Plan your mail so it is received on the lowest volume days.

To determine which day of the week is your lowest volume day, survey your own individual area. For the next month, determine how much promotional mail you get at the office each day of the week. Through this process, we have discovered that we are receiving less mail on Tuesday and Wednesday at the office. Also test mail to yourself. See how long it takes for a piece of mail to arrive at your office. This will help you set your plan. Our surveys indicate two-day delivery locally.

If you're mailing to residences, track and test your residential mail. We've discovered that we receive less mail on Monday and Tuesday at home. This is probably because we receive Saturday delivery at home and not at the office. So in our area, we drop first-class mail to residences on Saturday to ensure Monday or Tuesday delivery. We drop first-class mail to offices on Monday to arrive Wednesday. Be certain to test by mailing to yourself. Results vary widely.

Once you have an idea of the lowest mail volume for the week and how long mail takes to get delivered, determine which weeks of the month are best. You'll typically find that mail received at the beginning of the month is caught up with the bills and all the other activities that are going on. Conversely, all the mail that is received at the end of the month may not be read by business owners or individuals you're trying to reach because they are pushing to close out the month profitably. To avoid these cluttered times, I suggest you plan to send mail to arrive on the lowest volume mail days of the second or third week of the month. There will normally be less mail volume to compete with your message.

TACTIC 212   Schedule and prepare in advance the information that you will use as a response piece.

Lack of responsiveness can destroy prospects' confidence quickly. For example, a good friend of mine builds his own fishing lures. He was very interested in getting a new annual catalog on the various materials used to make these lures. He called the company that sells these materials to request a catalog. After some period of time, he had not received it, so he called again. The person who answered said it would be sent right out. Two weeks went by and my friend still hadn't received the catalog. He called again and the person he talked to said, "Our mistake, we'll send it right out." Another two weeks went by and he still hadn't received it. He called again and asked to speak to a supervisor. She said, "Oh, we're a little short, but we'll get you one right away." So she sent him a catalog. Unfortunately, she sent the previous year's, so he still hadn't received the current year's book after several weeks of waiting. Although the company had offered the new one, it still hadn't sent it. Obviously, this company was totally unprepared for the response, although my friend did better than some people. Recent surveys indicate 23 percent of requests for product literature are never fulfilled.

If you promise information on request, have a systematic approach in place before you send the mailer. Letters that will accompany brochures should be drafted in such a fashion that they can be fully customized and quickly sent. Brochure packets or samples should already be organized and preassembled so that they can be sent out the day the request is received. By demonstrating your prospecting responsiveness, you indicate that you will also be responsive throughout the sales and service cycle.

TACTIC 213   Organize your mail by ZIP code to save money when you're mailing in large quantities.

The US Postal Service rewards you for organizing your promotional mail and making it easier to sort. Prebundling mail is most helpful if you're mailing out several hundred pieces to your niche market. Bundling them by ZIP code provides significant savings on postage. I believe that in the near future, post offices may require that even very small mailings be organized in ZIP code order. This will add to your mail preparation time. If it happens, plan accordingly.

TACTIC 214   Be aware of variable mailing costs for various types of letters and mailers.

Using a mix of envelope sizes is desirable. However, it's important for the budgeting and planning process to know that any odd-sized mail will cost you additional postage. The US Postal Service, as do postal services in some other countries, levies additional charges for mail considered to be oversized, such as 9 x 12-inch envelopes or larger than standard postcards. If your piece requires a larger size, remember to include the extra cost in your budget.

TACTIC 215   Use post office sources for savings and procedures.

The US Postal Service produces a wide number of publications to inform you how to use the system of delivery more effectively. One publication I've found particularly helpful is *Memo to Mailers*, a monthly bulletin of the US Postal Service. Write to National Customer Service Support Center, 6060 Primacy Parkway, Suite 101, Memphis, TN 38188. For those outside the United States, check with your local postmaster.

TACTIC 216   Plan a series of mailers to promote short-lived offers.

There are times you will want to speed an important message to your prospects and/or customers. You may wish to present an offer in a very tight window of time or to seize a fleeting opportunity in the marketplace. Consider, then, sending a series of mailers. These are usually referred to as wave mailers. They are typically a minimum of three different pieces sent to the same group of people over a period of several weeks. Wave mailers could consist of fly-ers, letters, brochures, notes, self-mailers, testimonial letters, post-cards, and so on. They may ask for a response or be followed with a telephone call.

A dramatic example of the power of wave mailers appeared in the August 13, 1992, issue of *USA Today*. The article indicated that someone was mailing magazine and newspaper articles critical of then Secretary of State James Baker to the State Department press corps. Thomas L. Friedman of the *New York Times* said that he had received several of them. "I'm definitely on somebody's mailing list, but I get so much mail and so much odd mail that it didn't re-ally jump out at me until about the third one."

Well, I'm not surprised. The cumulative effect of a series of mail-ers in a short space of time creates a sense of awareness. Target prospects realize they are receiving a variety of pieces from you, and their curiosity is aroused.

Moe Targosz, with Manufacturers Life in Kitchener, Ontario, demonstrated this effect. He initially had a difficult time reaching very affluent corporate executives in his niche market. He put to-gether a networking effort and combined that with a very-low-vol-ume wave-mailing strategy. Moe's wave mailing included a note that said he would be calling shortly to schedule a time to meet one-on-one.

The surprise came when one of the corporate executives to whom he mailed called him even before Moe had a chance to call. This in-dividual said, "I throw all mail away from insurance agents. How-ever, your marketing tactics are so different, I decided to call you. I want you to come by and tell me how you're marketing yourself and perhaps you and I can do business."

What this illustrates is that you can capture people's atten-tion short term using creative ways. The mailers should all be different in format, yet shorter in content. Time them so that they are received on the lowest mail day of the week for at least three consecutive weeks. Three should give you recognition. Avoid doing more than five weeks, as they lose their punch. If your message is that you will call them, then call two or three days after the last mailer is received, if they don't call you first! Make sure that each mailer builds on the one before it, and if you promise to call—call.

TACTIC 217   Use outside services when appropriate.

If you're producing and mailing a small number of promotional letters or mailers to your niche market segment, in most cases you can do those in-house. However, if you're mailing to several hundred people in your niche, you may want to use a mailing service of some type, many of which can be found in the Yellow Pages of your local telephone book. You want someone who can give you timely turnaround and a price commensurate with the job.

Most require you to pay a small setup fee and then pay on a per piece basis. Be sure the service provides you with the names of three to four customers they're currently serving, so you can call them for references. Not all mail houses are created equal.

TACTIC 218   Plan on using recycled paper.

Although you may find that recycled paper is a bit pricey, particularly when you use a more finished stock, remember—the environment is an important issue in our society today. Most customers and prospects appreciate your efforts. Even though they may not be using it, they feel like you're contributing to the environment for them.

Interestingly enough, in Canada there is a much higher sensitivity, at this particular time, relating to environmental issues. A current survey by *Canada Post* tells us that 44 percent of the Canadians interviewed expressed an environmental concern about the volume and type of paper used in mailings.

TACTIC 219   Analyze your results to know what worked and what didn't.

Analyzing your niche letters and mailers helps you plan better in the future. Ask yourself: What was the desired response? What was the actual response? What type of access and sales did you get? What adjustments would you make in the future to a similar mailer or letter, so that you have a better result?

Recently, I was on a flight sitting next to a physician who had started his own business called Kelly Docs. We spoke briefly, and I discovered he has several hundred employees and provides temporary help to the hospital industry. What most impressed me, however, was a procedure he was working through. He was evaluating a recent project, and he was listing all the mistakes that were made. Then he began to list all the things that they could do differently on the next project.

This is good strategic planning, whether you are a sales professional or a business owner. In all your promotional efforts, you must determine how you can improve.

TACTIC 220   Keep on file all promotional letters and mailers.

When you plan next year, next month, or next quarter, you can go back and see what you've done in the past.

In addition, you can see what worked and what didn't, so you will be able to make a much better decision about your upcoming schedule. Capture the information on a form to help you to track what you're doing and how it worked for you. Figure 14–1 is an example.

TACTIC 221   Get yourself on the mailing lists of all the companies that are mailing to your niche.

This is an outstanding way to be able to track other promotional mail into your niche. To get on these lists, call various suppliers who advertise in your niche market newsletters and magazines and request to be on their mailing list for promotional offers, brochures, and catalogs.

Also, be sure you've joined your niche market associations, clubs, or interest or industry groups so you automatically will get all mailers to them. This gives you an opportunity to see what your peers, colleagues, and perhaps your competitors are doing. Having this information allows you to create a better promotional mail approach and strategic plan.

This will also help you in the creative process and prevent you from positioning yourself similarly to someone else or duplicating an illustration or headline. Be sure to track when other businesses

FIGURE 14–1
Promotional Mail Tracking Form

Promotional Letters and Mailers

Name of letter or mailer:_____

Date mailed:_____

Mailed to:_____

Number mailed:_____

Postage: First class_____Bulk, metered_____

Date concept set:_____

Art created by:_____ Date_____Cost_____

Art proofed by:_____ Date_____Cost_____

Printed by:_____ Date_____Cost_____

Mailed by:_____ Date_____Cost_____

                              Total postage_____

                              Grand total_____
Date our sample received _____

Response _____%

Number of success calls_____

and sales professionals are sending their mailers, so that you have an opportunity to either get there first or make sure that you don't get there at the same time with a similar offer. That would dull your competitive edge.

Chapter Fifteen

Strategy: Create Promotional Niche Mail That Gets Read— Not Trashed

Objective: To deliver so much value into the mailbox that you increase response and reception.

According to Don Kanter, direct mail expert, most marketing and sales material currently written and being used in the marketplace is really not worth the paper it's printed on. There is a tremendous amount of money, time, and effort spent producing all types of marketing and sales documents that, unfortunately, do very little to help a prospect make a decision about seeing you or buying from you.

Dr. Jeffrey Lant, a noted author writing in *Mail Profits* magazine, suggests that if you pick up any 10 sales documents, you'll find that fully 8 of them focus more on the company selling the product or service than on the person buying it. That's right, four out of five promotional documents portray the fatal flow of talking about themselves rather than focusing on the needs, aspirations, and anxieties of the prospect.

To ensure that your promotional letter or mailer is read, you must first answer prospects' questions regarding why they should see you or respond to you. Defining the benefits to them creates interest and adds a sense of value to the mail piece.

Prospects barely spend a scant two to three seconds holding your promotional letter or mailer before they make a decision whether they read it or trash it. By quickly helping them focus on benefits, they will then read on. Further, it helps them shape their thinking about you, your product, or your service, and how it can make a difference for them when purchased through you.

In addition, with a battle going on every day in the marketplace for the prospect's mind, it is essential that your promotional niche mail be easy to read and to act on. Prospects need a clear understanding of what the offer is, what it can do for them, and how to respond. If you want them to call you or send a reply to you, make it clear. If you are going to call them, be sure to tell them to expect your call. People are pushed for time, so ease of reading takes precedence sometimes over laws and principles of design.

Finally, regardless of desired outcome, personalize your niche mail by writing to prospects and customers, not *at* them. You increase your credibility and acceptance by using their language and frames of reference. In addition, personalizing your letter or mail piece increases their readership.

Perhaps the company that has recently demonstrated just how personalized niche mail can be with today's technology is the Nutra-Sweet Company in Deerfield, Illinois. In a recent promotional mailer, it was marketing a new frozen dairy dessert. It sent out a personalized piece that went far beyond putting the prospect's first and last names in the address.

It was so personalized that it included the first name of the prospect throughout the promotional piece. A cartoon figure on the outside had the typical dialogue balloon floating over its head. Inside was the prospect's first name—"Paula, have I got a scoop for you"—and then inside the mailer was a full story in cartoon style with the recipient's first name mentioned throughout. Most importantly, it was done so that it looked as though the prospect's name was originally part of the cartoon, not added in or on as simply an overprint or afterthought. What a brilliant way to get close to prospects!

In summary, as a business owner or sales professional, you should focus on your prospects as you write your promotional letters and mailers. Kanter says, "Copywriters [that's what you are when you are writing a letter or the content of a mailer] often think their job is to write copy. That's the equivalent of a salesperson saying their job is to talk." In a literal blizzard of marketing messages, only by sending clearly written, personalized niche mail, full of relevant benefits, can you ensure your mail will be read.

The following tactics will be useful when designing your promotional letters and mailers to ensure high readership and market access.

TACTIC 222   Be certain whatever you are creating is clear to you.

If you start off a promotional letter or mailer with, "The purpose of this letter or correspondence is . . . ," I can assure you it is headed to the trash can. If it's that unclear, don't send it. What is the purpose? Is it to position you for a follow-up call? Is it to have prospects respond to you with an order or inquiry? Be sure that your purpose is clear and singular; then write or create with that single purpose in mind. State your case clearly throughout so that recipients know what actions they need to take or expect.

TACTIC 223   If it occurs to you, keep it.

You will continually see needs that will stimulate a variety of promotional ideas to help you reach your targeted niche market. I encourage you to write them down so when the time comes for you to write a letter or create a mailer, you can reference those needs and ideas again. By capturing them, your promotional items will look both fresh and timely.

TACTIC 224   Have the resources available to create the right letter, flyer, or other type of mailer.

Avoid creating your mailers on the fly. To be effective, have resource materials available to use during the creative process. For example, books such as *Words that Sell*, by Richard Bayan, prompt you and give you marketing and prospecting words that are persuasive.

Niche market magazines and newsletters help you know what the current buzzwords are in your niche market so you can use the language of your market when putting together a letter or mailer. It's also helpful for you to review your market information prior to your design time. It may provide you with that unique slant you're looking for.

TACTIC 225   Be sure your first promotional piece to prospects declares you as a specialist in their niche.

People want to see that you specialize in their type of business, profession, or recreational or interest group, so tell them so. Don't let them guess. Avoid falling into the trap of assuming that your prospects know that you specialize in working with people like them. Just because you've been to association, group, or club meetings or because you've put together your network of people doesn't mean your focus is clear to prospects. It's very important that you state it; otherwise, you risk the possibility that they won't tie the promotional mail piece to your other relationship-building activities.

TACTIC 226   Focus on who will be receiving the promotional mail that you're sending, and do the research necessary to promote properly.

The wrong products or services can be, and often are, promoted to a niche market. It usually happens because the average sales professional or business owner does not take the time to match prospect needs with appropriate products or services. This understanding is essential, however, to gain favor with prospects and earn the right to see them.

Find out what motivates your buyers, what their particular needs are, what the things are that agitate or irritate them currently, and design your letter or mailer to incorporate and meet those needs. Use your market knowledge to make sure people have a desire to meet with you or respond to you because they see that you can solve their problems.

TACTIC 227   Leave plenty of white space.

If you're creating a promotional flyer, make sure you leave lots of white space so that it will be easier to read. Include a broad left border because people read right to left. The larger left border says "this is easy to read." Use visuals if you can, as they will save yards of text.

TACTIC 228   Keep letters brief and to the point.

Any letter that you're sending to position a request for an appointment should be no more than six or seven sentences in length. Let your prospects know you specialize in their niche. Capture their attention by promising at least two important benefits that you can deliver. Then quickly expand into two or three product or service features that can support the benefits you mentioned. This way, readers can better understand what you're trying to meet with them about. Then ask for the appointment.

To capture this idea fully, read the letter in Figure 15–1. You'll clearly see how the first two sentences position the sales professional and give the reader two benefits. Then you will see how they are followed with a couple of supporting features about the product and a call for the prospect to act.

TACTIC 229   Turn cover letters into sales letters.

Current thinking tends to be that because a promotional brochure costs so much more money than a cover letter, the brochure must be far more important. Nothing could be further from the truth. The letter is far more important, for it builds that sense of personalized contact with the people in your niche market.

The letter you send out with a promotional brochure or sample should be a strong sales piece that motivates prospects and peaks their interest. Be specific about what you can do for them, and point out the fact that you have included a brochure simply to give them

FIGURE 15-1
A Letter to Position an Appointment

Dear _____,

As an individual who specializes in helping steel manufacturers promote their specialty products, I can help you reach more buyers and save you money at the same time. Our new and powerful advertising program for manufacturing companies in the steel industry is designed just for companies like yours.

I have enclosed a brochure outlining many of the features of this program, including the exclusivity guaranty for your specialty steel products and our easy dollar-stretching payment plan.

Many of your colleagues in the industry have discovered that this new program is the right answer for their own specialty steel promotion needs. I look forward to meeting with you. Please alert your assistant that I will be calling shortly.

Very sincerely yours,

---

some additional relevant information. The letter is what will capture their attention and stir their interest to read further into the brochure, not the other way around.

TACTIC 230   Give the benefit to prospects in the headline or first two sentences of your letter.

Readership surveys show that 75 percent of the American population now will read only the headline of a promotional piece or up to the second sentence of a letter. If it doesn't address the question, "What's in it for me?" you should rest uneasy because it will be discarded. Make sure you give prospects the benefit of what you can do for them early in the piece.

Lead off with a benefit-oriented headline in a mailer. If you are writing a letter, explain the benefits in the first two sentences. Later on, you can mention product or service features and things about you. First, you have to capture their attention and let them know you know them. Make a list of benefits before you begin to write or create so that you can be sure to include them.

TACTIC 231   Use high-impact words to enhance their desire to see you.

It's important to convey your ideas in a way that captures the reader's attention. Some of the most persuasive words in the English language are the following: *you, money, save, new, result, easy, health, safety, love, discover, power,* and *guarantee.* To further enhance readership, use lively verbs. The following list of lively verbs will add spark to your message.

Prepare	Structure	Select	Set
Increase	Foster	Make	Change
Identify	Build	Master	Improve
Define	Conduct	Write	Monitor
Create	Play	Overcome	Transfer
Interface	Demonstrate	Handle	Get
Develop	Explore	See	Find
List	Draft	View	Sketch
Distinguish	Use	Pinpoint	Apply
Perform	Describe	Focus	Organize
Match	Determine	Divide	Examine
Design	Train	Avoid	Start up

Of course, there are other words and phrases that are so powerful that you should consciously include them in your promotional niche mail whenever possible. According to René Gnam, a direct mail expert, the single most powerful word in the English language is *you*. The two most powerful words are *thank you*. The three most powerful words are *would you please?* The four most powerful words are *what do you think?* The five most powerful words are *I am proud of you*.[3]

Use this type of phraseology to capture readers' attention, to increase their interest, and to build the relationship so that you have an opportunity to reach them.

TACTIC 232   Strive for clarity.

Ruthlessly edit your words, and be certain that you strive for clarity. Keep the language simple so that it is easy for the prospect to grab the concept or idea and move ahead. Omit anything that doesn't clearly communicate what you want to accomplish. That means you may have to plan, refine, and fine-tune this promotional letter or mailer to hone it down to as few words as possible. In doubt as to what to cut or leave? Always leave in the value of and need for you and the prospect to do business together.

TACTIC 233   Use a stimulator to capture the attention of your prospects.

Sometimes it's difficult to reach those hard-to-reach individuals unless you do or use something really different. For example, a sales professional I heard about in the financial services industry mails out 20 letters a week with a dollar in each letter. He begins, "Here's your first tax-free dollar. I'll be calling you shortly to talk about how together we can help you get some more of these."

A company that's done an outstanding job of using a stimulator is CIT Group, a New Jersey–based corporate finance company. It was having trouble reaching senior executives in its tightly focused niche markets. It decided to spend a significant amount of money to gain the attention of the executives in a unique way. By sending Stan Musial–autographed baseballs and, in some cases, Willy Mays– autographed balls, it has really differentiated itself and stimulated its prospects. Most importantly, 93 percent of the 350 executives it contacted agreed to see the CIT sales representative. This has allowed CIT to write a great deal of business because it has gained access through a unique promotion that says, "We value the opportunity to meet with you and we're willing to earn the right."

Stimulators typically work when they are either expensive or unique. They must capture attention, not appear to be a gimmick. Test any stimulator before you think about wide-spread use.

TACTIC 234   Use a catchy opening sentence or phrase.

René Gnam, the direct mail expert I mentioned earlier (see page 198), suggests that you may want to start a business letter with this catchy opening sentence; "This may be the most important letter you read today." You might say that sounds awfully bold; however, if you follow up immediately with a reason why that letter is so important—that is, give a benefit—you can capture the interest of the individual.

Catchy phrases also work. As a case in point, I was staying at the Bridgeport, Connecticut, Hilton prior to a speaking engagement, and a flyer was slipped under the door. The flyer started off with, "Prime rib and steaks are king at the Bridgeport Hilton. We put our money where your mouth is." Normally, you'd get a flyer that would tell you the customer is king and ask you to buy a steak. It was a catchy way of conveying a message we've heard over and over again. Yes, the steak was great!

TACTIC 235   Whenever you write to someone, make sure you address him or her personally.

I received a note from a PacTel cellular sales representative when I was shopping for cellular telephones. The note that she sent to me was a very nice card, well made and on high-quality paper. It had "Hello" preprinted on the front, and inside she addressed me by my company name—that is, "Dear Achievement Group." Admittedly, Weylman is hard to spell and harder to know how to pronounce ("Whilemen"). Yet, just because she couldn't spell it, she shouldn't have ignored it (although this was better than Dear Occupant).

She went on to write that she was a sales representative and that she would give me a free $40 toward the purchase of cellular equipment or air time. I thought thanks, but I wasn't asking for a discount, only information, very little of which was enclosed. I didn't take advantage of her offer. I bought from Bell South Mobility, which had a more personal approach—its representative called me by my own name. If you don't know the name of the individual, pick up the telephone, call the person's office, get the name, and make sure that you address him or her personally in the salutation and on the envelope.

TACTIC 236   Avoid setting "appointments." Tell readers you'll be calling them for a briefing.

If you are writing to individuals with the intention of calling them on the telephone to schedule an appointment, rephrase and use the word *briefing* instead. Since the Persian Gulf war, *briefing* has come into vogue. People today are so pressed for time that an appointment has many negative images. It works far better to simply schedule a briefing.

An example is: "I'd like to come by and brief you on some of the services we offer and that others in the industry are using." Another is: "I'd like to brief you on how I could solve some of the office equipment efficiency problems you indicated you had the last time we met."

When you schedule these briefings, schedule them at 10 minutes before the hour and 20 minutes after the hour, for two reasons. One, it appears that the time needed is going to be brief, the second, the odd time encourages prospects to mark it in their calendars. Experience indicates that people are much more likely to be on time for your particular meeting if you have identified an unusual starting time in advance.

Think about those occasions when you fly on an airplane. If your flight is at 8 o'clock in the morning, once you check your ticket, you never check it again. But if that flight is at 8:07 AM, you check that ticket a half dozen times to make sure you're not going to be late. It works the same way when you schedule meetings or briefings at odd times. Prospects and customers constantly check to be sure they're on time. A word of caution—be sure *you* are. The key to this tactic is by getting in for 10 minutes, you should be able to get yourself back for another meeting.

TACTIC 237   Use a mix of letterheads in your promotional efforts.

There's a variety of different stationery that you should have to send the right promotional message at the right time. In addition to your regular letterhead, you should have a more formal version, such as monarch size, for upper-level business correspondence. Monarch size is usually engraved or has a different type of letterhead than regular stationery. I use it for personal letters and personal business correspondence. Use only the front of these. If you need additional space, use blank sheets.

You should also have a quantity of correspondence cards. These are typically an 8 1/2 × 11-inch card stock divided into thirds. You could have your picture on it and have it printed with your full name and address. Use these to write out informal thank-yous and short notes. Of course, use only the front of the card.

Finally, avoid using 20-pound copier paper in promotional efforts. It hurts your image in the marketplace because it is perceived as having little value, which can translate to a prospective customer's perception of you. As an example, years ago I had designed a unique goal-setting plan anyone could follow. I had reproduced it on 20-pound copier paper before I knew any better. I met a very well-known TV personality and gave one to him. He looked startled, thanked me, and slipped it into his pocket.

Several years later, we were guest hosting a television program together in Canada. He told me then about the negative impression he had when he received that 20-pound bond goal-setting plan. Once he saw what it was printed on, the plan and my status dropped in his eyes. Learn from my mistake. Use paper that has a watermark in it, either a linen stock or paper that is no less than 25 percent rag content. You can ask your local stationery shop or quick printer to show you a wide variety of samples. Be sure that you're using paper that promotes the image of quality and credibility.

TACTIC 238   Use their language to personalize your mail.

Speak the prospect's language in every promotional letter and mailer that you create. This develops a sense in recipients' minds that you know them, you understand them, you can truly identify with them. Use words that grab prospects' attention because the words are in their vocabulary and they are used on a day-to-day basis.

As an example, when you're writing to farmers, you could talk about how your product or service could help them to *grow* or to *harvest*. When writing to florists, *bloom* and *flower* are important words. Teachers relate to words such as *curriculum, lesson plans,* and even *recess*. Doctors relate to the use of the word *practice*, not *small business*. Ad agency heads want creative ideas. Attorneys would respond to words such as *precedent* and *antecedent*.

In addition, small-business owners would prefer you don't write to them as "small-business owner." Use the specific business name to which they relate. If you're writing to people who own a print shop, talk to them as print shop owners. If you're writing to people that own electrical supply houses, let them know you know they're in that business.

Using their words also demonstrates respect for who they are, and they, in turn, will respect you more.

TACTIC 239   Restate to create a strong PS that will capture their attention.

As a sales professional or business owner, you've heard over and over again that the postscript (PS) is very important. However, it's often difficult to figure out how to write a strong one. Even it it's catchy, it can sound trite or take the prospect away from the purpose of your letter. To create a strong PS, simply have it restate your most important point, or add a testimonial from someone that your prospects in that niche would know.

If your strong point is such that it is so obvious, give your reader a reason to act now. Simply tell them in your postscript, "Please call me at your earliest convenience so we can schedule the best time to meet," or "I'll be calling you shortly. Please notify your secretary that I'll be calling." A strong PS that restates your important point, that builds your credibility, or that calls them to action makes each promotional letter you write more effective.

TACTIC 240   Check with your staff before you finalize any copy.

Often, your staff is very close to customers because of frequent interfaces with them. Your staff can give you many good ideas as to what the prospect's particular needs are now, what people are talking about, or what particular buzzwords are being used. As you design your approach and your copy, be sure you include your staff's input.

TACTIC 241   Be sure your promotional pieces say "sale" differently.

When sales professionals or business owners write to customers and prospects in their niche market to tell them of a discount they're merchandising or a special promotion available to them, the word *sale* creeps into their vocabulary. This teaches people to wait and buy on sale. As an example, if there's anything you hear murmured throughout the shopping malls in your area, it is "let's wait until this goes on sale." You want to rephrase your offer to ensure this doesn't catch on in your niche. We can learn from retailers that have come up with new and different ways to offer sales without saying so. They basically use a form of wordplay to make it happen.

Lands' End never has a sale, but they do have price rollbacks. Price cuts are available from some retailers because they don't want to use the word *sale*.

I recently purchased a car, and I admired the way Eric Konicksburg, the sales professional, handled my offer. He said, "We are unable to merchandise a deep discount on this vehicle." Well said! I raised my offer.

To reduce your price, create a favored customer offer, which tells them they're extra special; perhaps a seasonal offer, which can mean they're getting special treatment; a two-for-one or premium offer that says they're receiving extra value; or a half-price offer that says they're getting special savings. Avoid the word *sale*. Present the reason to act now as a value-added focus on them. Otherwise, you teach your prospects and customers that the only time to be in touch with you, contact you, or meet with you is when something's on sale.

TACTIC 242   Use effective color. Color means power.

Color is a powerful communicator and is no longer a luxury; it is truly a necessity because it creates a sense of emotion and mood. It is important, however, to recognize that various colors communicate distinctive images. White means purity; yellow indicates sunny or happy; black equals mysterious or erotic; green denotes money, the outdoors, and fun; and orange reminds us of food. Blue, to men, means quality; to women, it means professional but stuffy. Red, to women, means warmth; to men, it means exciting but dangerous. When you create your promotional niche mail, stay tuned in to what your color choices are and what they mean. Be particularly sensitive to the way a color will be received by the people in your niche.

When selecting paper color, use white paper if you're using photographs in your promotional piece. If photographs are not being used, an appropriate paper color could be ivory, which is a very popular because it connotes a sense of professionalism. However, be sure it goes well with your ink color. Yellow on ivory is usually a disaster. Papers that are gray or similar washed-out color tones typically convey a less distinct image and probably should be avoided unless your market is fairly gray.

TACTIC 243   Use clip art visuals to convey a benefit.

People today are very visually oriented. You may want to use clip art from your computer to convey an idea or concept. Be flexible enough to use a humorous visual as well. It can be very effective in the proper context. Visuals help prospects in our very visual society see the benefit more clearly.

TACTIC 244   Fun can be effective.

Hogback Fashions, in Sapphire, North Carolina, bills itself as a "fun place to shop for New York ladies' fashions at the foot of the beautiful Hogback Mountain." It specializes in dresses, jewelry, sportswear, and shoes. My wife and I are on their mailing list because of occasional visits to that part of the country. Two or three times a year they will send a flyer to ask my wife and me to come back and shop there again.

Their flyers are always funny and almost funky. The last one we received had photocopied photographs of each of the three women that work there. A handwritten note was on the face of the flyer. It has scribbles, little designs, and little cartoon-type characters printed all over the piece. I noticed several effective techniques the flyer incorporated. First, it was very personal. Second, it was geared to a specific time of year, Mother's Day, to encourage customers to come.

Third, the benefit offered to us was very straightforward. The flyer stated that all the jewelry was at half price only for very special customers. No sale, just an opportunity for special customers. They closed by indicating who to contact for more information or to order by mail. Your niche mailer can be funny. However, it must first and foremost be personal, deliver a benefit, and tell your customers they are special and how to respond.

TACTIC 245   If you want people to order, use customer-friendly order forms.

Order forms are usually treated as though they're just something that goes in the package and are not anything that needs much attention.

In reality, busy people may only scan your letter. They may simply move to the order form because your product or offer interests them. The order form should sell them. It should include a benefit-oriented headline so that it continues to move the selling process along. Use the appropriate Visa, MasterCard, Discover, and American Express logos to make the form look more professional. The form should call people to action, be easy to understand, and be simple to use. Use arrows and/or numbers to direct customers in a logical completion sequence. Encourage people to act in a clear and concise way. If you process faxed orders, put your fax number in large print so customers can find it.

If you're shipping products, make sure that you ask for the right address on the form. As an example, ask for the street address if you have to ship something to customers via UPS or other personal delivery service. The easier the form is to use, the more people will use it.

TACTIC 246   To get your mail opened, avoid labels, window envelopes, or dot-matrix printing.

If you use envelopes with a window or with a label, it is almost always defined as junk mail. Further, research has shown that handwriting should be used only for sending mail to a residence or sending a very personal note to a prospect or customer. However, in all cases, a typed or laser-printed envelope is much more likely to be opened when it lands on the desk or kitchen counter.

There has been some argument recently that using clear laser labels on business envelopes can take the place of having them individually typed. However, the clear label is not yet indistinguishable. It's still perceived as a label. These should be avoided on envelopes as well, at least until technology catches up.

Of course, mail such as postcards, self mailers, or oversized 9 1/2 × 12 1/2-inch shipping envelopes could take a label without any image cost. For these pieces, you may want to use the clear mailing label so that it doesn't look so promotionally oriented. For oversized envelopes, a shipping label works well. Otherwise, avoid them to get your mail opened.

TACTIC 247   Avoid putting "Personal and Confidential" on the envelope.

Usually, this phrase is used to get past a secretary or assistant who is screening the mail. Stamping envelopes "Personal and Confidential" is overused and has a large pitfall. It detracts from your credibility if you use these words and the reader determines that the contents of the envelope are neither personal nor confidential.

If you're trying to get mail on the prospect's desk, stamp "Private Please" on the face of the envelope. It will have the same effect; however, it will not erode your credibility or your integrity.

TACTIC 248   Use attractive seals or stickers on the outside of your envelopes to make your mailer look personal and unique.

Foil seals or paper stickers can do an effective job of differentiating your promotional letter or mailer and capturing the interest of the prospect. There are many different seals available from specialty advertising firms. They can range from notifying prospects how long you've been in business—5, 10, 15 years and so on—to a response sticker that says "You asked for it—information you requested." The seal or sticker makes your mail look personal and unique, both of which encourage people to open the envelope.

TACTIC 249   Use a mixture of envelopes.

When promoting, think about testing envelopes in several sizes. The number 10 envelope, of course, is often viewed as business advertising mail. You would be well served to use a 6 × 9 or a 9 × 12 occasionally or other envelope sizes that are available. These should be tested to see which ones work best for you, keeping in mind that odd-sized envelopes carry a higher postage cost. The extra cost may be worth it if more prospects are opening the niche mail you send.

A low-cost way to test various envelope sizes is to ask your quick printer to notify you when they have an overrun on a job that required odd-sized envelopes. These are usually difficult for the printer to sell, which often means you can buy them at or below cost to test their effectiveness.

TACTIC 250   Use commemorative stamps.

If you observe the administrative people in your offices, you will notice that they usually put stamped mail on the top of their mail stacks because it looks more personal. Furthermore, commemorative stamps on an envelope create the perception that this piece of mail is very personal. For that reason, they usually end up on the very top of your prospect's incoming mail. Using commemorative stamps increases the likelihood your prospect will see, open, and read your promotional mail.

TACTIC 251   Process bulk promotional mail by using meters instead of preprinted indicia.

The post office will encourage you to use a preprinted indicia (the preprinted bulk mail permit information within a box on the upper right-hand side of an envelope). However, it immediately looks like promotional junk mail and is perceived to have no value.

I would encourage you not to use the preprinted indicia. If you're sending out more than 200 pieces to prospects in your niche market via bulk mail, use a mailing service. Have them process your bulk mail with a postage meter. They can meter the amount of the bulk rate on the envelope so it appears less generic or promotional.

In addition, the post office now has available bulk mail stamps you can apply to your niche mail in-house. Although they're not commemorative, they do help make the mail look more personalized and remove that negative indicia image.

TACTIC 252   Write "Hand Deliver" on the face of your envelope.

To get special treatment of your mail, write "Hand Deliver" in red on the left-hand front corner of the envelope. Of course, all mail is hand delivered. However, our experience has proven time and time again that your niche mail will get special treatment. I even know of cases where interoffice mail so marked gets delivered separately from all the rest.

TACTIC 253   Fuel your mind with ideas, concepts, and information.

To continue to inspire your promotional letters and mailers, you must have a steady flow of new thoughts. To accomplish this, you will need to begin to gather information.

Start tearing ads that appeal to you from customer magazines. Save your junk mail and look for new ideas and approaches. Review trade, club, and cultural magazines that serve your niche. Watch and listen for the words that seem to be prevalent in various marketing and national promotional campaigns, including those outside your niche markets.

Ask your prospects and customers to what ideas would they respond. Find out what words best describe their needs and how they would describe their desired solutions. Then use these ideas and concepts to generate your own niche mailers. Continue to grow by reading books on mail and mail design. Keep the information going in and you will have great ideas coming out.

Chapter Sixteen

Strategy: Use the Telephone to Leverage Your Efforts

Objective: To melt chilly receptions by warming up your telephoning techniques.

The telephone is one of the most powerful marketing and prospecting tools in use today. The challenge is how to use it to build relationships with people in target markets and not be judged as just another nuisance call.

The average prospect is bombarded with telephone calls from people trying to sell them something. Virtually all day long, calls now come into businesses from sales professionals no one has ever heard of or from companies with whom no one is familiar. These are quickly being relegated to the same category as junk mail. They have no value and are seen as junk calls. There has even been a court judgment against a nationally known investment firm that kept making unwanted sales phone calls to Alan J. Schlesinger, a Boston attorney. He not only won the case, the court levied fines against the investment firm while barring any of its employees from calling him again.

The barrage of telephone calls is being felt in the home as well. Prospects are now receiving calls at their residences far past what is usually considered an appropriate time—no later than 9:00 PM. Now, calls are coming at 9:30, 10:00, and even as late as 10:15 PM. Early morning calls are made on Saturday morning, awakening most of the household, including prospects who are generally less than enthusiastic.

This indicates two things: (1) the telephone is recognized by many as a very effective tool to reach prospects, and (2) it also indicates the tremendous frustration sales professionals and business owners have gaining access to buyers.

To thwart unwanted incoming calls and to help manage time better, people are now using a wide variety of devices and methods to screen them. In the business community, these range from voice mailboxes to assistants who field all calls. In households, calls are screened by just hanging up if there is no perception of immediate value or by using various mechanical and electronic devices such as answering machines.

These efforts and devices should not discourage you nor give you a negative outlook about using the telephone as a marketing and prospecting tool. It's an important means of contact, and it's second in effectiveness only to one-on-one prospecting activities. Using the telephone effectively can create a favorable impression with prospects because it can convey your enthusiasm and interest in them.

Through the telephone you can contact a great number of people in your niche in one day and, therefore, achieve more effective use of your time. With new technology arriving daily, such things as video telephones and PC video cards will actually make it possible to see the individual to whom you are speaking. This will further heighten the power and impact of telephoning and telecommunications as a relationship marketing and prospecting tool.

In spite of the benefits, some sales professionals and business owners say they're uncomfortable using the telephone. The reasons given range from the fear of personal rejection to a fear of failure. Some fear that by saying the wrong thing over the telephone, they will never gain access to the prospect.

The challenge, then, is how to overcome the barrier and anxiety issues that surround the use of the telephone.

By warming up your telephone techniques, you can melt that chilly reception and reduce those anxiety chills. Here are the tactics you can use.

TACTIC 254   Make warm calls versus cold calls.

Cold calls into a niche market make very little sense in a day and age where relationships and affinities are the key. They do very little to build visibility. In fact, cold calls often build a sense of animosity. You're better off calling people with whom you already have some visibility and name recognition. Call prospects you have been introduced to through a networking activity or through a highly focused and personalized niche mailer. These prospects will know who you are, that you specialize in working with people like them, and that you speak their language and can communicate with them effectively on a one-on-one basis.

TACTIC 255   Make a favorable impression when using the telephone.

Remember, the telephone is an interruption to most prospects, so it is vitally important to start off on the right foot and make a favorable impression. Smile and be friendly. Project that positive, caring attitude I've talked so much about.

Set the tone of the call by speaking softly with enthusiasm and slightly faster than prospects. They will perceive you as being intelligent and interesting. Also, sound expectant in your tone, as though you would be surprised if they were not willing to meet with you or respond favorably to you.

Use their names, because that establishes a feeling of relationship with you and connection to them. It also lets them know that you know them, and it makes them much more comfortable. Be careful you don't use nicknames or, in some cases, even first names until such time as you've met with them one-on-one or they give you permission. Being too familiar at the outset can make them uncomfortable and put them further out of reach.

In addition, prospects like to be heard and understood. Demonstrate that you care to hear their point of view. Be prepared to listen and show patience in your listening. Tell them you are listening by saying softly, "I see," "I can appreciate that," and so on as they explain their point of view. A favorable first impression here will open the door to hard-to-reach people.

TACTIC 256   When you call, have the purpose of the call clear in your mind.

Sales professionals and business owners frequently get on the telephone simply because they think that it's time to make calls. Identify and know every time you pick up the telephone what the purpose of that call is. Your objective could be to follow up on a response that they have made or to call someone to schedule a time to meet with them. No matter what the reason, be sure you call on purpose, not just to make calls.

TACTIC 257   Make using the telephone fun.

Some sales professional and business owners see using the telephone as drudgery. Yet, from my experience, you can make it fun and improve your success rate.

Have some friendly competition with someone else in your office or in another office. Compete to see who gets the highest number of appointments or orders that particular day. To make it fun, hang a bell and ring it every time someone makes an appointment or a sale. This allows you to adjust and set your attitude so there's a sense of anticipation as opposed to a sense of frustration or trepidation. Focus on the positive results you will achieve. List your goals and work your way towards them. If you're taking things too seriously, as we say in our office, "Lighten up!"

TACTIC 258   Have your presentation clearly defined.

Just as making a favorable impression on the telephone is vital, so is knowing what to say. There are four parts to a presentation that you should consider as you script or outline your call.

The first part is the way you greet the prospect. To focus on listening and building rapport, write out your greeting. Be sure it is friendly and interactive.

The second part is the questions that you will ask to establish need and desire to meet or to respond to an offer. The questions should be open ended, and they should generate a sense of dialogue, not a sense of monologue. Who, what, why, where, and when still work. Write them out to help you maximize the discovery process.

Third, keep the call focused on the prospect. To accomplish this, you should write out the benefits the individual will gain by meeting with you or buying from you. Answer the question What's in it for them? Be specific and use words that paint pictures of value. Individuals need to have a clear sense of the positive results they will receive.

Fourth, be sure to give prospects a variety of choices for the day or the time you want to meet with them. People want to feel as though they have some control of their lives and the process. If you are responding to their inquiry, give them congruent choices regarding the products or services they can buy. Give them a choice such as, "Would you like two, or would three be better?" If you're asking them for a meeting time, give them choices that are similar and related such as morning or afternoon. If you say tomorrow morning or sometime Wednesday, it is harder for them to choose. In addition, to avoid sounding as though you are desperate to meet (a common mistake, "Oh, we could meet anytime"), preface your first choice by saying "Knowing we are both busy." Then finish by giving them a clear choice such as "Would Tuesday or Wednesday be best?"

These guidelines will help you develop and know in advance what you're going to say, allowing you to concentrate on what the prospect is saying. Most successful sales professionals and business owners use scripts or outlines when they make calls. Why? A prepared professional telephone presentation has been proven to reduce anxiety and overcome barriers to access. It allows you to focus on the prospect and the relational aspects of the call.

TACTIC 259   Use confident words and phrases to produce positive results.

Think about your image on the telephone. You want to use words that instill confidence and create comfort. Words that are weak create confusion, reduce interaction, increase the marketing and sales cycle, and decrease the effectiveness of your message. These are commonly referred to as weasel words and phrases. For example, instead of using words and phrases such as *I think, I might, maybe,* and *possibly,* use confident words and phrases such as *I will, I can, I know,* and *definitely.*

To further instill confidence and to create comfort in your prospects and customers, speak the language of your niche market. Use words to which prospects and customers can relate. Couple them with some of the high-impact words discussed in Chapter 15. This will help you to make your presentation more pleasing to everyone and productive for you. Confident words delivered persuasively in the language of the prospect distinguish you from all other calls and help open closed doors.

TACTIC 260   Have your leads well organized and your call times planned.

The night before you make outbound calls, determine who and when you're going to call. Organize each group of targeted leads geographically so you can schedule appointments in the same area. If you are calling places of business, call early before prospects get into their meetings. Recent surveys show 47 percent of all executives are in the office by 7:30 AM, 78 percent by 8:00 AM, and 97 percent by 8:30 AM. Your goal is to *reach* them, not to just make calls.

To reach your hard-to-reach prospects, call company receptionists; tell them you will be calling the company after hours and ask for the night number. Call that number before the switchboard opens. You will usually find your prospect will answer the telephone. The same holds true at the end of a busy day. Decision makers come in early, stay late, and don't like a ringing telephone.

If you're calling residences, know enough about your niche market to call when they are the most receptive. Avoid traditional dinnertime, and make your last call by 9:00 PM.

TACTIC 261   Schedule briefings versus appointments.

As I mentioned in Chapter 15, prospects are busy. To gain access, ask for 10 minutes to brief them on some of the things you can do for them. Focus on the benefits to them. This will help you to get in for 10 minutes. Once you're in, you can easily get yourself invited back.

TACTIC 262   Handle voice mail, answering machines, and services effectively.

The telephone call, by its very nature, typically has no cumulative effect. Calling and leaving a message for someone once a week or once a day on any message system has very little impact. People have so many telephone messages that they find it difficult to get back to most callers. As a result, busy prospects will respond first to those calls they feel are urgent. Usually, this is determined by the number of repeat calls they receive from an individual. Therein lies an opportunity.

Call your prospect several times in a day to create a sense of cumulative effect. My experience has shown that if you call a prospect the first thing in the morning and learn that he or she is not available, you should then leave a positive message for them. If they have not returned your call by lunch, call again right after lunch. If you fail to reach them, leave a second positive message. If the individual has still not called you by the close of the business day, then call and leave a third positive message.

Make each message a little different and make sure it is benefit laden. Be sure that you demonstrate empathy for their schedule and ask the individual to call you instead of demanding that he or she call you. My experience has been that over half of the people for whom you leave a warm, friendly, benefit-driven message using this multiple call method will call you by 10:00 AM the next day. I believe it's because the old adage "the squeaky wheel gets the grease" certainly applies to this process.

Here's an example of the type of message you could leave: "Mr. Smith, this is Marge Jackson. I'd like to discuss a piece of real estate with you that has an excellent investment record and more potential for increased cash flow. I don't want you to miss this opportunity to hear about it. Then, you will be able to judge for yourself. Please call me at your earliest convenience." Leave several telephone numbers where you can be reached to further increase urgency.

This will not work if you just say, "Call me." You have to give them solid benefits so they have a reason to return your telephone calls.

TACTIC 263   Work with receptionists, secretaries, and assistants to gain access.

For years, sales professionals and business owners have been taught that receptionists, secretaries, and assistants are adversaries, and the only way to beat them is literally to beat on them. However, in today's more participative management organizations, secretaries, assistants, and even receptionists have a great deal of influence. Your customer or prospect will ask them, "How is this person on the telephone with you?" These support people now feel empowered to complain about a potential supplier who's being rude.

Take a positive approach with these individuals. By better understanding their job description, you can gain an opportunity to work through them. To overcome what is commonly called secretarial barriers you should:

- Be enthusiastic about what you're doing and be interested in what he or she is doing.
- Speak in less formal tones so that a sense of relationship can be built. Don't become so informal, however, that you appear to be taking their goodwill for granted.
- Continue to build a relationship with them by knowing who they are and saying their name. Find out something about them. It's amazing what a birthday card or an anniversary card or a small gift can do to build a positive influence.
- Ask them, "Would you please help me?" Most people will react positively to this request. It makes them feel important. You could also ask: "Could you please arrange an appointment for me with . . . ?" "When would be the best time to call . . . ?"

Staff personnel of all types will be more willing to help you speak with your niche market prospect when you make them feel good about speaking with you.

Of course, occasionally you'll run into a situation where you simply are not going to be able to build a relationship with them. In this case, you can still be positive with them. If you've sent correspondence in the past, and they ask what this is in reference to, say, "He [or she] will know, we've been corresponding, and he [or she] is expecting my call. Is he [or she] in?" If you've met the prospect at a networking activity or through a center of influence, you could say "We've met before at a club [industry, company, etc.] function. Is he [or she] in?" This is a way for you to be able to let the secretary know that you're not a cold call but someone with whom the prospect is familiar. By asking "Is he [or she] in?" you take positive control of the call and move forward with your agenda in a positive way.

Occasionally, a secretary will recognize your name and simply screen you out. In this case, have your staff person call the prospect for you and request a meeting on your behalf.

TACTIC 264   When calling a residence, avoid alienating a spouse, a child, or a single.

In this day and age, more and more people are buying things from their home. As a result, your prospects are receiving more telephone calls at home from sales professionals and business owners attempting to sell them something. To be effective when you call their home, consider these guidelines.

When you talk to spouses, treat them as equals. You certainly don't want to damage your image or the quality of your relationship by making a spouse feel as though he or she is a secondary citizen. You can make a good impression by being friendly and taking a moment to ask questions that generate interest and build rapport. Be sure that the time is convenient by asking if it is.

To avoid alienating children, be sure that they're comfortable with you before you attempt to leave a message. Many are instructed to tell people their parents aren't available for safety reasons. Avoid pushing them or they'll become flustered. Make sure the message is simple and shaped around the benefit to Mom or Dad. No matter what, avoid getting irritated with someone's children. That will destroy your opportunity to build a relationship with the parent or parents.

Some organizations make a habit of alienating people. One example is an organization that calls residences to get donations of used clothing or furniture. If a man answers, they ask for his wife. The assumption that only a wife can donate clothes or furniture can make a bad impression. Another example is people selling investments. They usually do the opposite and make a bad impression on females. If you're unsure, ask discovery questions such as, "Are you the person I should talk to about donating clothes?"

Be tuned in when you call a residence. Housekeepers and housesitters have influence, too. Treat them well.

TACTIC 265   Be positive when everything you've tried doesn't work.

Sometimes, you simply can't reach the prospect. You've talked with the prospect at a meeting. You have worked hard to build a quality relationship based on respect and mutuality. You've sent the information that was requested. You've tried to build a positive relationship with the secretary. Yet the prospect simply won't take your call. Nothing seems to be working. What I would suggest you do, then, is use these ideas to help you move forward and to reach this hard-to-reach prospect:

- Send a note similar to one that speaker Dave Yoho suggested some years ago, which says, "I can take a no as easily as a yes, providing we talk. Please call me at your earliest convenience. Thank you." Another I often use is, "Please don't mistake my enthusiasm for pressure. I simply want to have an opportunity to brief you on some of the things that I've done with colleagues of yours so you can judge for yourself if this would be useful to you. Please call me at your earliest convenience. Thank you."

- Change your request. Instead of a face-to-face meeting, schedule a telephone appointment through the secretary. Call the secretary and ask if he or she controls the prospect's calendar. If so, schedule a time to speak with the prospect on the telephone.

- Take the secretary or assistant to lunch. Find out what makes this prospect tick. How does this individual interact with suppliers? How does he or she select people with whom to do business? What would be the best way to schedule a time with the prospect?

- Create additional awareness of yourself. Many individuals won't meet with you or take your call because they simply don't know or remember who you are. They may not remember getting a piece of mail from you. To build greater awareness, mail to them again. Then follow up. For those you've met, send them a personal note telling them you enjoyed meeting them to remind them of when they met you. People who meet many people often have a hard time remembering everybody. Reestablish contact and awareness of who you are and what you can do for them. Then ask for the appointment again.

TACTIC 266 Use a precall checklist to ensure that your calls are successful.

There is no substitute for good preparation prior to making your telephone calls. Whether you're following up on a personalized letter or responding to prospects or customers who have responded to you, preparation will allow you to relate to the people in your targeted niche. Use the precall checklist shown in Figure 16–1 as a place to start. Add to the list the things that will improve your telephone skills.

FIGURE 16–1
Precall Checklist

Precall Checklist

1. I have my target leads organized   _____
   geographically.
2. I know the purpose of my call.   _____
3. I have my presentation outline in front   _____
   of me.
4. I have reviewed the benefits of why I am   _____
   calling.
5. I've warmed up my voice and practiced my _____
   greeting.
6. I will project enthusiasm.   _____
7. I am prepared to listen and respond.   _____
8. I have read my presentation out loud today _____
   at least twice.
9. I am prepared to track my efforts and   _____
   results.

   My results are: Today's date is   _____

                        I am starting at   _____

                        I have ended at   _____

                        Number of contacts   _____
                        made

                        Number of appts. or   _____
                        briefings scheduled

                        Number of sales made   _____

VI

HOW TO KEEP YOUR NAME ON THE MINDS OF THE PEOPLE

"He who wishes to be rich in a day will be hanged in a year."

Leonardo da Vinci

The skepticism and cynicism prevalent within the minds of the prospects in the marketplace have made them ever more cautious. When people are cautious, they delay their decisions about which person to see and what product or service best solves their problem or fills their need. Thus, the sales process for most products and services continues to lengthen, as does the number of contacts necessary to reach the prospects and create the opportunity for a sale.

Focusing on targeted niches and building quality relationships from the first point of awareness or contact will help you overcome much of this cautious behavior. As your relational efforts gain momentum, the amount of time it takes to reach new prospects and greater sales will shorten. However, there will always be some prospects who will not see you or buy from you immediately.

Often, it is a matter of timing. They don't need or can't buy a copier, a PR campaign, a new home, or an insurance policy right now. Further, they may have had such a negative experience in the past that in order to reduce their risk, they want to see you only after several others they know and respect have done so. Regardless, they are prospects for the future.

Unfortunately, too many sales professionals and business owners discard prospects who don't buy immediately. They continue to focus on instant results in a cautious marketplace. Further, they lose business by not staying in touch with customers who have purchased in the past. Nothing is quite as devastating to their own return on effort and resources invested than this short-term thinking.

As I've discussed at length, the key to reaching people and increased sales and customer loyalty in the marketplace is by building solid marketing and prospecting relationships. However, these relationships cannot only be for the short term. Customers and prospects alike should, and need to, be cultivated on an ongoing basis.

Cultivation is a process of consciously deciding to stay in touch with the people in your niche markets. They need to be cultivated so they know you and know that you will be there when they want to buy—not just when you want to sell.

Often, sales professionals and business owners think just having a competitively priced product will motivate prospects to do business with them. They may believe that because they provided excellent, prompt service in the past, that's enough to keep existing customers loyal. However, the best way to get people to continue to pay attention to you is to continue to pay attention to them.

Jay Leno clearly demonstrated this on his way to becoming the permanent host of "The Tonight Show." When he was touring the country with his comedy act, he visited every NBC affiliate and began an ongoing relationship with station owners and managers. The effort came back to him in the form of tremendous support by the affiliates when he was being considered for Johnny Carson's job. Later, during the time when there was some concern that NBC was going to dump him for David Letterman, the affiliates again rose to the occasion and lobbied hard with the NBC senior management team to be sure that Leno stayed on the job. By starting a relationship with the affiliates in the beginning before he had the job, and then staying in touch, he won their long-term loyalty.

Cultivation is effective because first, it conditions people to buy the first time and then helps them to continue to buy. You increase their confidence and your identity. They translate your continued interest in them into a perception that they're working with a real human being versus a nameless, faceless organization trying to sell them something. Second, it continues to establish you in your targeted niche market so prospects and customers have a clearer idea of what you can do for them. They see you as a resource and a solution provider through the products and services that you sell. Third, it lowers their resistance to your ideas, your products, and your services. Simply put, their comfort level increases and their skepticism decreases.

To cultivate effectively, you must keep your name in front of clients and prospects frequently. How can you cultivate and continue to position yourself in your targeted niche markets with prospects and customers alike? Practice the "I" principle: Not "Here I am" but these three *I*s of cultivation:

- *Inform* your prospects and customers from time to time with information that they can use in their careers, businesses, recreational pursuits, or other special interests.
- *Inspire* them to give you access and motivate them to do business with you by doing the little things that make a difference.
- *Integrate* niche advertising and PR into your ongoing efforts so your name stays on their minds.

The following chapters will provide you with the strategies and tactics to implement the three *I*s of cultivation and keep your name on the minds of your prospects and customers.

Chapter Seventeen

Strategy: Inform and Inspire the People in Your Niche Markets

Objective: To continuously educate and motivate your prospects and customers to give you access through a continual sense of relationship.

W hen you enter a Home Depot store, ask any employee about a particular item or service and he or she will take you directly to its location in the store. If you are unsure about how to do something, the individual working in that department is well versed in both concept and technique to help you solve your particular problem. This, of course, has come about because the Home Depot employee is well trained. Bernie Marcus, who is the CEO of the organization, understands the benefit of having employees so well trained that they can educate the consumer. His philosophy is that if you take the time to inform and educate your prospects and customers, you will condition them to want to buy from you. Furthermore, they will tell their friends to shop at Home Depot.

In the same way, providing your prospects and customers with information they can use positions you as a sales professional or business owner who is bringing added value to the relationship. Educating them helps separate you from the competition.

However, to simply deliver information and educate people is not enough. As in the case of Home Depot, the people inspire you to buy there because they convey a sense of personal interest in you. They don't simply point you in the right direction. They take you to the right location in the right department. Small effort—large difference. You can achieve this same result in your business or career.

By informing and showing personal interest in your niche market prospects and customers, you help them define their interest in you. As a result, like Marcus, you can be in the enviable position of being sought out by your buyers.

There are many ways to inform and inspire your prospects and customers. However, in order to reach them on a regular basis, you must maintain an accurate list of information about them. Today's computer technology makes it easy to load all your targeted prospects and customers into a database. Enter each person's name with a market code to identify his or her market segment, record the date when each name is entered along with any special dates, such as birthdays, purchase dates, and business anniversaries. You can also include the mail you've sent or telephone calls you've made to them in their individual data records.

Having this information in a database makes it easy for you to stay close to your niche market prospects and customers. You can communicate with them through the ways they associate and communicate with one another. You can gain access faster by timing your information message and tailoring your personal touch to match your market segments.

To move forward, ask yourself, "How can I inform and inspire the prospects and customers in my targeted niche markets?"

The following tactics are designed to help you answer that question.

TACTIC 267   Send articles of interest to your prospects and customers.

Look for articles of interest in various magazines, newspapers, and general-interest periodicals. Clip these articles out, obtain permission to reproduce them, and send them to your niche market prospects and customers on an ongoing basis. There are really three criteria for success with this tactic:

1. The article should inform your readers about something of interest to them. It could be about their industry, interests, or recreational activities.
2. It should be accompanied by a simple note card that says, "I thought this would be of interest to you." You could also use a Post-it-type note to make it appear even more personalized.

3. Mail or fax it with "Private Please" stamped on the outside of the envelope or the fax cover sheet. This helps communicate the special nature of the contents when it arrives on the desk or in the home of the prospect or customer.

Sending articles not only informs, it shows your interest in prospects and customers. In turn, this stimulates their interest in you. You may even get a thank-you call, note, or fax from them.

TACTIC 268   Hire a clipping service to keep a constant flow of informative articles and ideas.

Throughout the country, there are businesses that specialize in clipping items of interest for you from newspapers and periodicals. They will send you clippings you specify on a regular basis for a prearranged fee. They are organized in such a way that you simply give them the key words or key topics that you would like them to locate. They will scan and read for those particular key words or key topics. These words could be the name of your niche markets, such as automobile dealers or registered nurses in a particular area. Topics could be specific issues of interest to the people in your niche markets such as the luxury tax or cancer research.

This gives you an increased supply of articles and information that you can fax to your prospects and customers to keep them informed. Again, be sure to ask permission from the publication before you copy the material. A telephone call or faxed request usually will do.

TACTIC 269   Set up a hotline number for your prospects and customers to call with questions.

One of the most effective ways you can educate your prospects and customers is to be available when they feel they need information. Letting them know they can call on you for the information they need adds another dimension of quality to your marketing and prospecting relationship. The hotline could simply be your telephone number published in the local club or cultural newsletter or professional or trade magazine. You can position yourself as the place where they can call to get an answer to any relevant question.

General Electric has taken this to a whole new level with their prospects and customers by setting up the GE Answer Center. It has certainly been a tremendous boon for their business. It has not only built customer loyalty, but it has also encouraged prospects who are thinking about buying from GE to get answers to their questions leading up to a purchase.

TACTIC 270   Create and send a newsletter on tape, by mail, or by fax.

Newsletters that are sent two, three, or four times per year are an ideal way to stay in touch with your prospects and customers. The content should not just sell your products and services. You can achieve a higher level of professional respect among readers by producing a newsletter that is educational in tone. It should contain usable information that is of interest to the people in your target market. You can offer free solutions, new ideas, and fresh insights into the value of your new products and services. There should be a good balance between the appearance, the format, and the general layout of the newsletter. A newsletter is usually formal, which is what many people prefer. If it's overdesigned, however, it sometimes is underread. Newsletters generate incoming calls, repeat business, new business, and even referrals. They bring added value to your relationships. Be sure you send newsletters to all your niche market customers and prospects.

TACTIC 271   Send a personal message on audiotape.

A creative way to inform and educate is to produce a personal audiotape once or twice a year. People who receive your tape not only hear about ideas and issues of use and importance to them, they also hear your voice. This allows you to convey your personality into the message so that prospects have a better idea of who you are. It also allows you to use humor in a positive way.

As in a newsletter, include topics that inform prospects and customers about issues of interest to them and new products that are in development. Include ideas they can use to increase their business or enhance their lifestyle. Be sure to speak their language and you'll achieve a stronger relationship with your prospects and customers. Refer to a similar tactic in Chapter 9 for ideas on how to get your tape produced and duplicated inexpensively.

TACTIC 272 Be sure your voice mail message informs and inspires.

Be sure that your greeting is not just a dry, cumbersome "leave a message at the sound of the tone." Instead, use your greeting as an informative message about your business that, at the same time, encourages the individual that has called you. For example, "I'm so glad you called. I look forward to making a difference in your data management results. Please leave your name and number at the sound of the tone, and I will return your call either later today or first thing in the morning."

Change your message occasionally so that repeat callers don't hear the same words over and over again. Of course, make sure you give callers accurate information on when you will be able to call back or how they can reach you. Specific information helps callers feel that you are available and that you are giving them service even when you're not there.

One final point here is to use plain English. Voice mail systems will often instruct the caller to "hit the pound key." There are many people who are not familiar with that expression, so you should request the caller to "press the number sign."

TACTIC 273 List some things that make you unique, and inform the prospects in your market about this important point of difference.

Send this to your prospects as a cultivation piece with an informative tone. Avoid being egocentric and self-serving. Focus on the most unique benefits and features you or your product can offer to them. One of the best examples I've ever seen of this was a cookware sales professional who sent a note to all of his prospect, who were still unsure. It simply said, "One of the things you get with my cookware is my personal guaranty. What that means to you is I'm part of every set. You will always have someone you can call for answers. Please call me when you're ready to let me be there for you." Mail it or fax it to them. There is no need to follow up. The point is made.

TACTIC 274   Create a list of 20 ways to make your prospect's life or business better.

Send this list to the prospects and customers in your niche. A marketing, sales, distribution, display, or printing idea that furthers their sales or profits is always welcome. In recreational market segments, golf tips or tennis tips would be helpful, as would school safety ideas, or fundraising or meeting ideas for special-interest segments.

Look for ways to identify your prospects' and customers' needs. Be observant so you can spot ideas you can use.

TACTIC 275   Ask your prospects and customers what they'd like to stay informed about.

A single survey asking them to rank important issues faxed to them can capture this information for you. By asking their opinion of what's important to them, you receive permission to continue future contacts. In addition, by asking and then honoring their wishes, you increase their level of respect for you. At the same time, they begin to look at you as an integral part of their business, even before you're a supplier. Seeking their opinion will differentiate you from the competition, give you favorable access, tear down the wall of skepticism, and put you in a most favorable light.

TACTIC 276   Inspire prospects and send them a thank-you note for saying no.

When individuals don't buy from you now, that doesn't necessarily mean they won't buy sometime in the future. Let them know that you're always open to work with them, irrespective of present circumstances.

A thank-you note for saying no could be something as simple as, "Disappointed we're unable to do business now. Look forward to working with you in the future. Always feel welcome to call." This places you in a position of taking the higher ground and it allows the prospect to save face. A thank you for saying no helps open closed doors in the future.

I've also discovered this tactic helpful when I've been told I lost a sale to someone else. After sending a note, I've called back in 30 days and asked how things are proceeding. More than once, prospects have said they're still uncommitted. As a result, the door of opportunity reopened. The prospect had been reluctant to call back for fear of losing face.

TACTIC 277   Send a thank-you note after the sale to inspire future business.

Frequently after a sale, sales professionals and business owners will simply say "thank you," shake hands, walk out the door, and move on to the next sale. Remember, a thank-you note is remembered long after a handshake is forgotten. A personalized thank-you note sent to the decision maker helps continue your relationship and ensures future access and sales.

In addition, send a thank-you note to the secretary or assistant for helping you to set the appointment. Send a note, as well, to other individuals on the decision-making team who influenced the decision. This will help you build goodwill and loyalty with them for future purposes. Further, as the organization continues to grow, the junior people that you thanked may at some point become the final decision makers. Your thank-you note will give you a leg up on the competition both now and after they reach their new level of prominence.

TACTIC 278   Always express thanks to a prospect who hears you out.

A show of appreciation early can encourage even the most reluctant prospects. As a sales professional or business owner, it is vital that you encourage them. After you meet with them to discuss their needs and your solutions, drop them a short note and thank them for hearing you out. Let them know you are interested in them and will follow up with them as promised.

TACTIC 279   Inspire them with your responsiveness.

People go where they are invited; they stay where they are appreciated. Every prospect and customer expects and deserves a return call from you the same day they call. The only exceptions are when they call so late in the day they know you cannot reach them until the first thing the next morning. However, even in that case, you have an opportunity to really demonstrate your responsiveness. Go ahead and make the call even if it is late. A positive voice mail message after hours will exceed their expectations. Your responsiveness inspires them to give you access as it creates a feeling of confidence and trust. Slow response usually results in just the opposite.

TACTIC 280   Treat people fairly and ethically and inspire them to open the door.

There's not much substitute in today's business society for treating people on a fair and ethical basis. Although I've talked about ethics at various times through the course of this book, it's important to reiterate here that prospects will be inspired and more loyal if you have a reputation as a fair and ethical individual. You will be able to reach them because you represent what they are looking for in a sales professional or business owner. A key to opening the door is to continually demonstrate that you are fair and ethical. In all cases, actions speak louder than words.

TACTIC 281   Do something helpful for the people in your market.

Many years ago, when Chuck Reaves, a fellow speaker, worked for AT&T, he had difficulty getting access to a large telemarketing response company. During a severe snowstorm, this company was shorthanded, trying to handle 800-number calls from all over the country. Many of its operators were trapped in the snow. Chuck discovered this and decided he would drive over to this company and help out. He manned the telephones there for many, many hours. That was the action that gave him most favored access to the decision maker and the opportunity to deliver one of the largest sales in the history of AT&T at that time. Do something helpful for your niche market. Review the networking section of this book. Find something that you can support on its behalf, which will inspire niche members to give you access and a sale.

TACTIC 282   Inform and inspire by sending special notes on special days.

Continue to build a solid relationship with your prospects and customers in a highly valued way by sending a card or note that is different. Send a Labor Day card or an Independence Day card. To small-business owners, you could send a "Happy Anniversary for Another Successful Year in Business" card. You can find out the month that they went into business from the chamber of commerce, the Better Business Bureau, or by simply calling the receptionist of that business. Load the date into your database. For your customers, you could send them a Happy Anniversary card for "Another Successful Year Doing Business Together." You would send this on the anniversary date of whichever month they placed their first order.

People often ask, "Should I send Christmas cards?" Being a fan of Christmas, I would like to encourage you to send them. However, experience has shown that they get lost in the shuffle. Consider sending a Thanksgiving Day card or a New Year's card so that you have the opportunity to stand out from the crowd. Sending that special card or note on special days makes a powerful impression on people and helps you earn the right to see them.

TACTIC 283   Send a postcard from anywhere.

A customer and friend of mine who is a vice president for Jazzercise stays in touch with her friends and many of her franchisees when she goes on trips by sending them a thoughtful postcard. The next time you go away, whether for a weekend or a business trip, use this idea to your advantage. Send 20 of your prospects and customers a postcard. If you're at a business meeting, tell them you've picked up a couple of ideas they would be interested in. Tell them you'll call when you get back.

TACTIC 284   Send a Thanksgiving or Special Event letter that informs and inspires.

Over the years, I've had the privilege of becoming friends with Fess Parker of Davy Crockett fame. Several years ago, he started Parker Vineyards in Los Olivos, California.

One of the things that Fess does to cultivate an ongoing relationship with prospects, customers, and friends alike is to send out a Thanksgiving letter. He typically writes a two-page letter that tells you about his family and some things going on with the vineyard such as plans for the future and new ideas he has. He doesn't mention products nor does he ask you to buy anything.

He writes in a personal style that makes his prospects and customers feel as if they know him personally. He writes about his children's latest triumphs and his grandchildren's latest accomplishments. At the end of the letter, he often says something that is inspirational such as, "Marcy and I are truly blessed to have friends like you." This encourages and inspires many people. You could do something similar.

TACTIC 285   Develop a slogan for yourself or your business.

This informs and inspires people and becomes another way for you to communicate value. By developing a slogan or tagline, you communicate so clearly the value of your products and services that the benefit of doing business with you is absolutely obvious. Use a slogan or tagline on your business cards, stationery, advertising, fax cover sheets, envelopes, and so on.

To be effective, a tagline or slogan should be no more than seven words, so that it's easy for individuals to understand. Here are some examples:

Josephine Smith, Helping Physicians Heal Their Finances.
Samuel Jones, Saving Dry Cleaners Time and Money.
Donna Davis, Serving Those Who Serve Others.

You see the point. Developing a tagline gives you an opportunity to really convey a sense of value to your prospects. It helps to inform them of what you do, and at the same time inspires them to see you because you specialize in people like them. You should have a different tagline or slogan for each of your niche markets so the message always relates.

TACTIC 286   Send a personal note to inspire.

Each day, send a warm and friendly note to 5 to 10 of your prospects and customers. Omit any sales literature; just send a personal card to let them know you're there.

A good note has a personal tone that cultivates, informs, and inspires. It should be no longer than three sentences or it becomes a letter that requires an opening, a middle, and a close. Mention something interesting, or simply give them a word of encouragement. It will demonstrate that you value their business in a personal way.

TACTIC 287   Initiate a contact to visit, not just to sell.

You don't want to be accused of only being interested in selling all the time. Sometimes a friendly contact goes a lot further than a formal sales call. If you're in the neighborhood, visit your prospect or customer. If you have an opportunity to pick up the telephone, call someone for just a few moments and don't always make it business.

This helps people feel that you have their best interest at heart and they can have contact with you without having to always feel like you're selling them. As an example, when Hurricane Andrew devastated South Florida, my staff and I called as many prospects and customers as we could reach to simply encourage them. Those we couldn't reach, we wrote to. Prospects and customers alike want to have a sense that sometimes you're simply investing in them because of who they are, not how much money they can spend. The great irony is that this relational contact will inspire them to want to do business with you.

TACTIC 288   Pay attention to the little things.

Because value today is determined by the buyer and not the seller, it's the little things that make a difference, particularly in relation to how you build a mutually rewarding, long-term relationship with them. It's not just how well a brochure or mailer is designed or how professional it looks. Sometimes it's just the fact that you've taken the minute to write someone that counts.

It's the cup of coffee that you buy, it's the chocolate or cashews that you bring to the secretary, it's the thank-you notes you send, it's asking about the children, it's finding out about how the wife or husband is doing, it's telling someone you're going to pray for them and then letting them know you have; it's all these little things that make a difference. All these things help people in your niche markets know you in a special way. We know that people are less brand-loyal than ever before—they have become people-loyal instead. It's the people-loyalty that we must concentrate on if we want to open closed doors.

Chapter Eighteen

Strategy: Integrate Niche Advertising and PR into Your Ongoing Relationship-Building Efforts

Objective: To keep your name on the minds of your prospects so when the door of opportunity opens, you are the first one in line.

I n addition to informing and inspiring individuals, it's vitally important to integrate advertising and public relations–type activities into your ongoing relationship-building efforts.

All advertising and PR campaigns are part of the cultivation process. Even if an ad is designed to create immediate response when seen by the individuals in your niche markets, it is perceived as additional contact from you. Further, when they see something in print from a public relations effort, they call you to their remembrance. Of course, some will argue that advertising and PR activities such as press releases are far too broad-based to be effective in a specific niche market segment. They are if your niche market is local and you choose to run ads and releases only in national or regional publications and local newspapers. However, advertising and public relations efforts aimed at local niche market media that you know your prospects and customers read can add to your presence in the market. These can range from special trade, professional, and industry magazines and publications to local club or interest group newsletters and newspapers.

Advertising and PR efforts that are niche market centered will not only help you to build stronger, more prominent relationships before and after personal contact, they will also help you to sell yourself and your products and services. To be sure they reinforce all your other relationship marketing and prospecting approaches, focus on your customers and prospects. Clearly state in all niche advertisements and press releases how they can benefit. Boldly tell them what you and your products can do or have done for them.

Here are several tactics designed to help you use your advertising and public relations efforts to open more doors, cultivate ongoing relationships, and create more sales.

TACTIC 289   Build awareness and cultivate relationships with specialty advertising items.

There are many different organizations throughout the country that create specialty advertising products. All types of items can be used to promote your name with a specialized message. These can be sent or given to your prospects and customers to build awareness and a desire to see you.

For example, I received a specialty item that was essentially a magnetized business card. The sales professional put a note with it that said, "Richard, I thought you'd like this because this is a mailing piece that sticks. Call me so I can help your promotional mail stick." You could do something similar. Put a cultivation message on a magnetic background, such as, "One thing you can be sure about, I'm here to stay." Include a note and ask recipients to call when they need you.

For something with greater usefulness, try promotional pieces such as calendars and posters. Carpenter Reserve Printing Company in Cleveland sends poster-type calendars four times a year. Each quarter, they change their marketing message and tie their identity to that particular poster. These calendars are anticipated by their customers and prospects each quarter and many collect them. According to Lynn Brewerton, the Sales Manager at Carpenter Reserve Printing, "It's been a great tool for us." The company uses the calendars to keep their name in front of current customers and to cultivate prospects so they can earn the right to see them on a favorable basis. Check with your local specialty advertising supply house and visit its showroom for a multitude of ideas.

TACTIC 290   Place press releases in niche market publications.

Whenever an article or release about you appears in a niche market publication, it brings a higher degree of credibility than any advertising that you could buy. If prospects and customers see you as newsworthy, then you are, in fact, truly noteworthy in their mind. Articles and releases about you help build that highly desirable top-of-the-mind awareness you need. Often, people will call you in response to seeing your name in print.

Press releases have been touted throughout the years as something that everyone should be sending to local newspapers and to various national publications. However, to maximize the effectiveness and the likelihood of press releases being used, you should target them specifically to niche market publications.

In what instances should you use a press release? You could use a press release when you introduce a new product or service, when your business is building a new manufacturing plant or office, when you move to a new location, or when you're replacing an old product or service with a new one. You may want to use a press release to announce a promotion or an award that you've received or to let people know about a new brochure or newsletter that's available from you. Or you can simply let them know that you specialize in their industry or interest group and use that as a positioning statement.

Press releases, when written and submitted correctly, will work for you. Unfortunately, 9 out of 10 press releases are pitched into the round file because they are not written in a way that is truly newsworthy. You can't pass off an ad as news. You want your releases to be of interest to the editors of the niche publications. Be certain you send them newsworthy items such as those mentioned above versus an advertisement rewritten as a press release. That is not to say your press release cannot sell. It can—it just can't advertise.

To write an effective press release, you can follow several different formats. You are well advised, however, to take the advice of

Tana Fletcher, coauthor of *Getting Publicity, a Do-It-Yourself Guide for Small Businesses and Non-Profit Groups*. She suggests that there are several rules for writing press releases:[4]

1. Type your statements, double spaced, on business stationery, with the words PRESS RELEASE just below your letterhead, followed by RELEASE DATE (fill in the earliest date the announcement may be published or broadcast) and CONTACT (fill in the name and telephone number of the person the media may call for further information. You can put yourself if you wish). Include both day and evening telephone numbers with area codes.

2. Skip a line and type a short headline to let the recipient know the subject of your announcement.

3. Write in journalistic style, so your press release can be used as is by the media. State who, what, where, and when in the first paragraph. Always refer to yourself in the third person—as "he" or "she"—and stick to the facts. Avoid superlatives, flowery language, and hype such as "This is the most wonderful idea to come down the primrose path in a long time."

4. If your press release runs more than one page, type "—more—" at the bottom of each page. Type "—end—" at the bottom of the last page.

5. Send your press release to the appropriate niche media, including neighborhood and association newsletters, club bulletins, alumni publications, corporate publications, and trade journals.

In addition to Tana's suggestions, avoid technical language and be certain that you check for typing and grammar errors. To see a sample of how a news release could look, see Figure 18–1.

TACTIC 291   Use *Bacon's Publicity Checker* to know exactly where to place your press release.

Bacon's Publicity Checker lists trade and professional publications and newspapers by specialty. It gives you a wide range of publications from which to choose within your targeted niche. *Bacon's Publicity Checker* is available at virtually all public relations firms and most public libraries. Some college libraries and advertising agencies will have a copy as well.

FIGURE 18–1
Targeted Press Release

PRESS RELEASE
FOR IMMEDIATE RELEASE

Contact: John Doe
Telephone: (444) 777-1111 Days
                   (444) 111-7777 Evenings
Anytown, IA

Supplier Gets Service Award

John Doe was awarded the Centurion Medal for Meritorious Service to the Automobile Industry by his peers last Thursday in Anytown. Said Mr. Doe, "It has been a privilege to serve this industry."

The gala evening was held at the Berkley Forest Club where the President of Anytown's Auto Dealers Association, Darlene Smith, presented the award. Said Mrs. Smith, "This award allows us to recognize John Doe for his service to the industry."

Doe has been with Achievers Finance Institute for the past five years and an active associate member of Anytown's Auto Dealers Association since it was founded. He has written articles about tax strategies for member dealers and has conducted several local seminars on investment strategies.

—end—

TACTIC 292   Use the *New York Publicity Outlet Guide.*

This is a handy guide to industry magazines and new publications. It points you to a variety of different areas in which you can get publicity within your niche market. You can get it from the Public Relations Plus, Inc., Washington Depot, Connecticut 06794; telephone 203-868-0200.

TACTIC 293 Contact your local IABC chapter or Public Relations Society for help with a press release.

If you're not confident about putting together a press release, I would encourage you to call your local chapter of the International Association of Business Communicators or Public Relations Society for help. You can find them in your local Yellow Pages. They can point you to a qualified free-lance PR person. If there is no chapter in your area, contact someone who teaches PR at the local university or secretarial school. Ask them to work with you on a free-lance basis.

TACTIC 294 Make news to achieve positive press.

Budget a portion of your time, money, and energy to develop newsworthy stories about yourself and your company. I would suggest that you pursue awards whenever possible so that you have an opportunity to gain recognition and to have reporters write about you and what you're doing. These could range from awards in the industry in which you sell to awards for community service.

In addition, you can receive radio and television exposure by letting people in the local media know you are available to appear as an expert in your product or service area. You may get called to do things such as appear on local radio or cable television stations to discuss your particular area of expertise. Your chances of success are good if your topics are informational, entertaining, or of interest to a large number of people in the audience. For example, if you sell office equipment, you could appear as an expert on office automation. Or, if you sell commercial real estate, you could discuss cycles in the market and market trends. These types of activities and exposure add to your credibility. They help you to keep your name in front of your prospects on a favorable basis.

TACTIC 295 Use the power of niche advertising.

Sales professionals and business owners often ask whether they should advertise regularly. The following prose, the author of which is unknown, sets the record straight:

Why is it—a man wakes up in the morning after sleeping under an advertised blanket on an advertised mattress and pulls off advertised pajamas. Takes a bath in an advertised tub, shaves with an advertised razor, washes with an advertised soap, puts on advertised clothes, sits down to breakfast of advertised coffee, rides to his office in an advertised car, writes with an advertised pencil. Then, he refuses to advertise, says advertising doesn't pay, and if business isn't good enough to advertise . . . he advertises it for sale.

If you believe in your business and want to build it . . . Advertise.

However, to effectively advertise in today's fragmented marketplace, you should choose only to advertise in your niche market publications.

Niche advertising can accomplish things that national and broadbased ads can't. First, niche market publications most likely have shorter deadlines, which means you can be more responsive to the needs of your niche markets. Second, usually you can advertise more frequently because costs are lower. Third, your ads make a clear-cut statement that you are a part of the niche you are trying to reach. The power of regular niche market advertising,then, is undeniable.

If your niche is recreation- or special-interest-oriented, place your advertisement in neighborhood and local weekly newspapers, as well as club, PTA, or cultural newsletters. For business or professional niche markets, select the local trade magazine or newsletter to run your ad. Niche market ads put you closer to the people you want to reach. Run your ad every month if you can. If you can't afford every month, schedule it every other month. Be sure to run an ad no less than three times to be sure it is seen and recognized.

As a sales professional or business owner, you should set money aside for niche advertising activities.

TACTIC 296   Make your niche advertisements stand out.

What makes an advertisement stand out? Recent surveys by Cahners Research analyzed 996 top-scoring ads over several years to determine what made readers notice and read them. The ads were selected from business publications covering a cross section of industries. Here are some of the findings.

A benefit-driven grabber headline specific to your niche market audience is very important to capture their attention. The headline should never be a statement about who you are or what you do. A photograph or illustration was found to be a key element in stopping power—98 percent of the ads contained a photo or illustration. In two-thirds of the top-scoring ads, the photograph or illustration covered between one-third and two-thirds of the ad. In addition, the descriptive copy primarily stressed more of the benefits the products or services would provide for the readers in carrying out their jobs. It clearly articulated how it could help them. Their summary is, your ad must grab readers' attention and invite them to read the message. In addition, to be sure it cultivates and positions you, state clearly that you specialize in serving or supplying people just like them. Be specific; name their type of business, profession, recreational activity, or area of interest. Keep your ad clear and simple. Avoid overdesigning it so that it is out of character with the publication. If you ask the reader to respond, make it clear how to proceed—by telephone, fax, or mail.

As a case in point, a sales professional in Rochester, New York, ran an ad using the guidelines above in a local meatpackers newsletter. Standing in line at a grocery store the week after the first ad appeared, he was surprised by a woman in front of him who turned around and said, "I know you. You're the guy who had the ad in the newsletter." Shocked, he said, "Yes, that's right." The woman proceeded to say that she and her husband were in the meatpacking business and needed someone just like him to help them in their business expansion plans. That never would have happened if he had not advertised in a targeted publication and included his photograph.

TACTIC 297   If the niche publication that you're working with doesn't offer creative assistance, work with a local printer or design shop to create your ads.

To get started, use the information from the previous tactic as a guideline. In addition, you should have ads you've torn out of various magazines that have caught your eye. Ask yourself what makes them work. Use these to communicate your own ideas to your designer. First, have your ads sketched out. Then take them to four or five niche market prospects and customers and ask them to which ones would they respond. Be sure you go with their first impression, not their opinion crafted after a long review. When people in your niche see your ad in print, their first impression is the only one that prevents them from turning the page. Ask them why they like the ads they choose. Also ask them what they would change to make the ad even more effective. Use the input from your prospects and customers to create your final ads.

TACTIC 298   To help control costs, place a one-third- or two-thirds-page ad.

Most publications will not place another advertisement on a page containing a two-thirds-page ad. Take advantage of this practice and save the cost of a full-page ad. You will still control the space and capture the attention of the reader.

If you want to achieve cumulative effect in the same issue, split your ad placement in two. Run two one-third-page ads on two different pages in the publication. Ask for a two-thirds-page rate, as it is normally less expensive. To ensure that you get maximum visibility and results from all your ads, always request your ads be on a right-hand page. Further, one-third-page ads or smaller should be on the upper right-hand corner of that right-hand page. In the case of the two one-third-page ads in the same issue, ask for them to run on sequential right-hand pages.

TACTIC 299   Use classifieds to your advantage.

If you are on a very limited budget, take a hard look at a classified ad as an option. If there's a clearly-marked category that fits your products and services, you can get a good bargain by advertising in the classified section. A well-written classified ad with a catchy benefit headline can drive response and help you gain continuous visibility.

TACTIC 300   Mail all niche ads to your prospects and customers to cultivate your relationship with them.

When you run an ad, ask the advertising department for tear sheets. This is simply an additional copy of the ad printed on a single sheet of paper. Ask for enough that you can mail one to each of your niche market prospects and customers. By sending this as a cultivation piece, you give them another opportunity to see the ad. If response is what you're looking for, this also may stimulate them to respond. In every case, it will help you cultivate your prospects and customers through additional contact with them.

TACTIC 301   Do annual surveys of your prospects and customers.

Perhaps the greatest sources of PR and advertising ideas are your customers and prospects. Survey them annually and ask questions such as:

- What problems do they want to solve, or what needs do they have this year?
- How do they currently prefer to get information about products or services from you?
- Do they usually read the advertisements in the local convention or special event programs?
- What words would they use to describe market conditions right now?
- What type of advertising do they like—response-oriented or information-oriented?
- What publications do they currently read the most?
- How often do they read the advertising in them?
- What has a greater impact—the articles they read or the advertisements?

As a case in point, I recently conducted a survey of a niche market for a customer to determine what its particular promotional preferences were. By adjusting PR and advertising activities to reflect the results of the survey, I was able to focus the company's approach so that it is parallel to the way the people in that market like to receive information.

Second, I used words and phrases that they gave us; by simply paraphrasing them, I was able to convey that the company and its people understand current market conditions. Third, and perhaps most important, these prospects now know the company is really interested in who they are. As a consequence, they are more open to learning how that company's sales professionals can help solve many of their challenges and fill their needs.

EPILOGUE

"In all hard work there is profit, and mere talk brings only poverty."

Proverbs 14:23

The lines between marketing, prospecting, and even selling are blurring. As a sales professional or business owner, you are involved in each of these activities now more than ever before. As an integral part of the distribution system, you are increasingly responsible for making things happen in your marketplace. To ensure your future in this environment, you need a personal plan of action. There are many analogies from which to draw. As an example, a pilot has a flight plan. The pilot knows in what direction the plane and passengers are going, from whence they're leaving, and, more importantly, the path they're going to follow to arrive at their destination safely.

A coach has a game plan for a particular day and has a sense of how the team is going to play the game. The coach knows the things that he or she is going to do to use the players effectively, to thwart the competition and, in the end, come out on top. In the same way, an interior designer has a floor plan. The designer has a very clear picture of what the finished building will look like. With this vision in mind, a plan is created to pull all the pieces together.

Your own plan of action should be designed the same way, with the end result in mind. Your plan should fit your specific niche markets and the people in them. It should be dynamic because the needs and expectations of the people in your markets are constantly changing. Plus, unexpected opportunities for visibility and access will occur frequently. Thus, the ability to change, to be entrepreneurial, is vital for your long-term success.

Develop a plan that will implement the relationship marketing and prospecting strategies, tactics, and ideas presented in this book. Focus on groups of people who associate and communicate with one another. Build strong, ethical, quality relationships with the people in your niche markets from the very first point of awareness or contact. For in the words of my good friend Terry Sullivan, "Unless you build on people, you build on nothing."

ENDNOTES

1. Robert E. Linneman and John L. Stanton, Jr., *Making Niche Marketing Work* (New York: McGraw-Hill, 1991).

2. Reprinted with permission from *Daily Guideposts*, 1993. Copyright ©1992 by Guideposts Associates, Inc., Carmel, New York 10512.

3. René Gnam, *René Gnam's Direct Mail Workshop* (Englewood Cliffs, N.J.: Prentice Hall), 1989.

4. Tana Fletcher, "Promote Yourself with Press Releases," *Speakout*, May 1992, p. 10.

Index

C. Richard Weylman is president of the Achievement Group, Inc., an educational firm specializing in the development of prospecting, marketing, recruiting, and personal achievement skills.

As a Certified Speaking Professional (CSP), seminar leader, and marketing consultant, he provides a wide range of resources for businesses and individuals including:

Fully Customized On-Site Presentations, i.e.,
 Keynote Presentations
 Seminar and Workshop Programs
Strategic and Tactical Marketing and Prospecting Consulting
A Variety of Audio and Video Programs on
 Prospecting
 Marketing
 Recruiting
 Personal Achievement
Corporate Television Programming
Company and Industry Specific Video and Audio Productions

For more information and to schedule live appearances, please call, write, or fax:

The Achievement Group, Inc.
P.O. Box 95331
Atlanta, Georgia 30347
770-662-8798
770-416-0881 FAX

For information on the wide range of resources available from Richard Weylman, call (404) 662-8798 or drop this card in the mail.

Please send information on:

❑ Richard's On-Site Custom Keynotes and Seminars
❑ Audio and Video Products
❑ Consulting Services
❑ Corporate TV and Video Presentations
❑ Annual Marketing Conferences
❑ Newsletters

(PLEASE PRINT)

Name_____

Company_____

Address_____

City_____ State/Pro. _____ Zip/PC_____

Phone (_____)_____Fax (_____)_____

BUSINESS REPLY MAIL
FIRST CLASS   PERMIT NO. 17925   ATLANTA, GA

POSTAGE WILL BE PAID BY ADDRESSEE

The Achievement Group, P.O. Box 436,
Boca Grande, FL 33921